Praise for

Looking Up

"Linda Pressman paints a vivid portrait of her Holocaust survivor parents' assimilation into American culture, while raising their seven daughters in Skokie, Illinois. *Looking Up: A Memoir of Sisters, Survivors and Skokie* is horrifying, tender and irreverent. A skillful and engaging writer, Pressman allows the richness of her European ancestry to shine in spite of bearing the weight of her parents' trauma. This book about a family of nine figuring out life's complexities is like no other memoir I've read on the Holocaust."

- Sandra Hurtes, Author of *On My Way To Someplace Else* and *RESCUE: A Memoir*

"Linda Pressman gives us a glimpse into a world that no longer exists as a child of survivors who attempts to navigate both the old and new world. With grace and honesty, she taps into the hearts of her family and into her own heart, and gives us stories that will pierce the heart of the reader."

- Janet R. Kirchheimer, Teaching Fellow at the National Jewish Center for Learning and Leadership and the author of *How To Spot One Of Us*.

Written by a child of two Holocaust Survivors, *Looking Up: A Memoir of Sisters, Survivors and Skokie* tells what it's like to grow up with parents who have survived the unsurvivable, who land in an idyllic northern suburb of Chicago - Skokie - where they're suddenly free to live their lives, yet find the past has arrived with them. In a book that's both funny and somber, and a story universal in its scope, Linda Pressman creates an unforgettable portrait of adolescent angst, traumatized parents and a search for faith among the ashes, ultimately finding that her parents' stories are her own.

LOOKING UP

A Memoir of

Sisters, Survivors & Skokie

Linda Pressman

Printed in the United States of America
Charleston SC

ISBN: 145647068X
ISBN-13: 978-1-4564-7068-5

Library of Congress Catalog Card Number: 2011903815

Cover photograph courtesy of the author
Cover design by the author

http://barmitzvahzilla.blogspot.com
http://lindapressman.blogspot.com

lookingupamemoir@hotmail.com

For book club and general ordering, please see Amazon.com

Looking Up is a work of nonfiction. It is a story of growing up told from the author's perspective as a child; it may not reflect that of other family members or other participants in the events in the book. In various places in the book humor has been used and, in those places, the narrative should be considered humorous rather than literal. Names have been changed and some composite characteristics may have been utilized to protect the privacy of the individuals involved.

Contents

In Honor of my mother, Helene Burt

In Memory of my father, Harry Burt

Looking Up

Opening
Breaking Bread

My mother always starts with the pig's head. Whenever she tries to cajole me into eating, she drags out her two most miserable food stories from the Holocaust, when she lived in the forest, starving and running from the Nazis. The first one is about the pig's head.

One day during her two years in the forest, the Partisans slaughtered a pig and gave her family the head to eat. They were thrilled.

"A pig's head? To eat?" I look at her like she's joking. If someone handed me a pig's head I'd have nightmares about it for the rest of my life.

She nods. "It was delicious. I'll never forget it."

I still don't believe her. Because I'm ten and my job is to doubt everything she says, I give her a skeptical look and say,

"Weren't you kosher?" Like I have to remind her that her family was kosher so maybe she can come up with a more believable story to get me to eat.

"Not during the war we weren't!"

She's a little jubilant at this point in the conversation since she's conveying one of her core truths to me: that food is anything that doesn't eat you first, a truth she learned at eleven that stayed with her always. But there's also a little criticism here, of the idea that being kosher matters at all, and astonishment towards my grandparents for becoming kosher again after the war. Like once you eat a pig's head, there's no going back.

I try to imagine my mother, my uncle, and my aunt - all children at the time - and my grandparents, carrying around the decapitated head of a pig; and not just as food but as precious, coveted food. Not surprisingly, this image doesn't make me hungry. It has the opposite effect. I feel ill, like maybe I'll never eat again.

The other story my mother tells me about food is told every time she sees me trim the crusts off slices of bread. As I slice them off she looks on in horror at the horrible waste.

And then I get to hear the Crust Of Bread Story.

She says, "In the forest, one time I had to survive a whole week on a crust of bread, just like that one. A whole week I nibbled at it slowly, crumb by crumb, sitting in my pocket. It got cold and hard and tinier every day, yet still I was so happy to have that tiny crust of bread. And there you are, just throwing it away!"

She is incredulous. What's more, each time she sees me do it she's incredulous again like she never saw me do it before. Sometimes she grabs the crusts before I can throw them out, saving them to eat later.

I don't know what to say to this. I never have an adequate response because no matter how much she had starved and no matter how long she had nibbled on that crust of bread in the forest, I still don't want to eat the crust. Born in the United States, a second-generation child of Holocaust survivors, I cut off those crusts anyway.

One

Vertical Shtetl

It's late 1959, September. I'm not born yet. My Dad's family is living in a brownstone apartment building on Sawyer Avenue in Chicago, one stacked on top of the other; a vertical Jewish shtetl. My Dad, Mom, and my five older sisters who are born already live in a two-bedroom apartment on the second floor; my grandparents live a floor down. My Dad's two newlywed brothers and their pregnant wives are scattered elsewhere in the apartment building, and later one of Dad's sisters moves in, the whole family connected by an umbilical cord running from their individual apartments to that of their parents. Where there aren't family members, there are Jews.

My aunts and my mother are in and out of each other's apartments all day and all night - talking, gossiping, fighting, making up. They inspect each other's apartments for many things

- how clean they are, how kosher, whether dinner is on the table.

Before I'm born, my mom has managed to pop out these five older sisters of mine – Francine, Lauren, Brenda, and the twins, Denise and Sherry. After me she'll have one more, Mindy. With just two or three girls she would perhaps have been the object of pity among the other Jewish mothers, but with five girls, then six girls, and eventually seven, she becomes the stuff of legend.

At this particular time, in late 1959, my Mom and my aunts Rose and Ida are big, bigger and biggest, all pregnant at the exact same time. My soon-to-be cousins and I are swimming around in their bellies, sucking up all their energy and their oxygen, swelling up their feet, and popping out varicose veins and stretch marks.

Aunt Ida is the biggest. She gives birth to my cousin Barry in October 1959, resulting in my Uncle Sid announcing, "It's a boy!" glowing with pride and, I imagine, my Dad gnashing his teeth in frustration. After all, Mom is pregnant with his sixth child - me - and he already has five daughters. Does he glare at the belly?

Aunt Rose is the second biggest and the next to go. She gives birth to my cousin Aaron in December 1959, resulting in my Uncle Meyer's exultation, and a second announcement of, "It's a boy!" most likely rankling my father. Both of his younger brothers having boys for their first children, and my Dad sitting there like a *shlimazel* with five daughters already! But maybe he started thinking they were all going to have boys; that there was something magical about this time out.

He waits and waits until March 1960 rolls around since Mom was due the last of them all. And then I am born, the one who will be a boy for sure. I show up headfirst so it's looking good, both boys and girls have heads. My shoulders emerge and, again, I could be a boy. My belly appears and they still can't tell. Then my bottom half pops into view and it's unmistakable. I am Not A Boy. Again.

Uncle Meyer and Aunt Rose go on to have three boys. Uncle Sid and Aunt Ida end up with three boys and a girl. Dad has seven daughters.

Later that day the baby me is lying in the newborn nursery at Edgewater Hospital in Chicago. My father shows up at the hospital, my mother tells me, coming over after he closed our laundry on Division Street that day, to see me. He is standing at the nursery window, noticeable for his Polish round head, short-sleeved button down shirt, baggy khaki pants and a skinny black belt.

If I wasn't just a baby, I'd be very worried right now. Mom is sitting in her hospital room chewing on the end of a pencil with my Hospital Birth Certificate in her hand, the one with my footprints on it, her head tilted to one side. Having made her decision, she ponders the name she's already chosen for me, "Jane," which is already recorded on my Cook County birth certificate, and then pencils in above and in front of it, "Linda." She does this because her brother, my Uncle Herbie, has already come to the hospital to meet his new niece. He saw me and held me in his arms, marveling at the thick black hair sticking up on my head.

Then he said to my mother, "What did you name her?"

"Jane," she said, and he almost dropped me.

"Jane? Jane? This is no plain Jane! How could you name

her Jane?" And he renamed me Linda, with my Mom penciling in the change.

That's how I got my first name.

Another reason I should be worried is that when my Dad comes to the hospital and stands in the Newborn Nursery, he's looking for a bassinet with the last name "Burstein" on it but his last name is "Burt." Just who is this guy anyway?

But he is my father. He's just changed our last name already.

Dad had name problems for a long time. He had too many names, for one thing. Being Jewish and Eastern European, he had been born with a Hebrew name, Tzvie ben Gershon; then he had the name his parents had given him in Yiddish, Herschel. The name Herschel had always sat heavily on him as being too Jewish. In the Displaced Persons camp in Germany after the war he got another name, Hersz, the German equivalent of Herschel. Then, when he arrived in the U.S. in 1951, he translated his name into English, choosing the American sounding Harry, which took care of his first name.

Our last name also had its spelling permutations. In the old country our last name was Bursztyn; in the U.S. Dad spells it Burstein, but his brothers spell it Burstyn. No matter how it's spelled, it's a problem for Dad; it's just too Jewish for someone who's uncomfortable with everyone knowing he's Jewish. Dad will do the deciding about when and if to tell people he's Jewish; he doesn't want his name to do it for him. Of course, he won't tell anyone at all, so he doesn't want his name announcing it.

On top of that, it has to be spelled all the time. Anyone who hears our name thinks it's "Bernstein," so that spelling our name becomes the bane of Dad's existence, translating Polish sounds and letters - his first language - into English sounds and letters, which is more than he wants to do day in and day out.

In 1956, in between sister number three, Brenda, and the twins, sisters number four and five, Sherry and Denise, he changes our name. First he gives it a lot of thought. It should sound a little like our original name - so should it be "Burst" or "Stein?" He pretty much decides on "Burst," telling Mom that we're going to be the Burst Family. She hits the roof and says that if he knew anything about English, he'd know that "burst" means to pop, like an explosion.

"It's not a name you pick on purpose," she tells him. "It would be very bad for the girls to have a name like that."

"Oh." Dad is deflated. He doesn't want to jeopardize marrying us off.

So he ponders it again, now down to "Bur" or "Stein." He doesn't want Stein because what's the use of getting another Jewish name when he could slap some bland, American name on our family and let us pass for Christian?

While he's thinking about this, Mom says, "What about 'Burt?'"

No sooner does Dad hear this than his mind is made up. My Dad always leaps before he looks, he always has to *chop and clop*; he never has any patience. He's a man of action, impetuous action, so he lops off half of our name, sending those extra letters packing, off wherever someone can appreciate an extra syllable. And so we become the Burt Family, which he ends up spelling every day anyway, all the days of his life. *No, not Birt. No, not Bert. No, not Byrt. B like in boy. U like in umbrella. R like in Robert. T like in Tom. Burt.*

Then Dad had another problem. The three oldest girls were born "Burstein" but now our name was "Burt." So he decided to have the rest of us born under the name "Burstein" as well, just to keep everything consistent, or inconsistent, whichever.

I'm born Jane Burstein, but within minutes of my birth she no longer exists. I leave the hospital Linda Burt.

The final thing I'd be worried about if I wasn't just an oblivious baby is that my birth certificate says my mother was born in 1930 in "Krzywieze, Poland" and my father was born in 1926 in "Wyshkow, Poland," and they're both Jews.

This is not good. After all, there was a war that occurred in the villages where my parents were born, almost in their front yards, in between then and now, a war in which ninety percent of the Polish Jews were killed, as I'll later find out. There was a war in which the Nazis marched on Eastern Europe, right to the places my parents lived, and killed as many Jews as they could. There was this war that my parents survived physically but not altogether mentally or emotionally, if it's ever possible to survive a war like that mentally and emotionally, and I'll get to relive it with them every day of my little life.

A lot has happened in my family before I'm even born. There are sheaves of photos in which my face doesn't appear. There is a whole place they used to live, the mythical apartment on Sawyer in Chicago, that I don't remember since I'm six months old when we move to Skokie, a northern suburb. In these photographs there is a two-toned 1954 Oldsmobile sedan parked in front of the apartment building on Sawyer, the apartment that's filled with my little girl sisters, who are smaller than I'd ever seen them, smaller than I was even then. They're beaming - happy, somehow, even before I'm alive. There are other things: first days of school and kosher meals and the fluent Yiddish they spoke as an immigrant family, until my sisters' teachers crushed that right out of them when each of them started kindergarten and then, mysteriously, they could no longer speak it, only understand. There was our move out to Skokie, the sudden luxury of a three-bedroom house, the play potential of a swing set.

My oldest sisters are the Yiddish-speaking, apartment dwelling, kosher children of immigrant parents. I end up being the suburban dwelling, English speaking, non-Kosher child of parents who appear to be American – on the surface anyway.

They tell me about life in the apartment on Sawyer. Two bedrooms filled with little girls. My crib in the dining room, the twins playing beneath it, me sleeping through all the noise, watched with anxiety by my grandmothers, both certain I was deaf.

"How can she sleep through such *tsoris*?" My mother's mother laments, wringing her hands. She yells in my ear to check if I'm deaf and wakes me up.

The reason for my parents having so many of us was a topic of great conjecture. Was my mother trying to repopulate the Jewish world after the Holocaust? Or maybe it was Dad who was goading her on, was he trying for that elusive boy? Or was it the faulty birth control methods of the time, the diaphragms, the rhythm method, the primitive version of the birth control pill? Maybe Mom didn't understand the instructions for using her diaphragm since English wasn't her first, or even her fourth, language? Would there have been less of us if the instructions had been written in Yiddish?

For ease, the seven of us are given numbers, with the twins smack in the center of the family, taking numbers four and five. I'm number six, down at the forgotten end of the family, the evil number six, where, if we were Christian, I'd have had to worry about the Mark of the Demon, the triple six. But I don't; six is nothing in Judaism. None of my relatives look at me in terror, expecting me to burst out speaking in tongues; no one ever examines my scalp searching for the other two sixes. I'm just the next single birth below the more notable twins, the one who isn't the youngest, the middle child of the bottom set.

Being number six is a very low number in this family. It seems capricious, like if Mom had managed to get some reliable birth control, I wouldn't be around. So being of precarious existence, I guard my spot jealously. After all, I want to move up, to push the other sisters out of the way. In a family where everyone wears their sister number proudly I fidget under the weight of mine. I hide the ugly part of me, the part that wants life and the world and all our existences to begin with me, with March 7th, 1960, with Skokie, with the house on Drake Street, with English, with three bedrooms, with the station wagon - just one-toned, blue - and nothing else.

Two
Overcrowding

It's normal to me that there are nine of us living in our three-bedroom house in Skokie. In 1963 the youngest sister, Mindy, is born and then we're complete: there are seven girls and our two traumatized, atheist, Holocaust survivor parents. We move in when I am six months old, in September 1960, my birth convincing Mom and Dad that maybe, just maybe, their two-bedroom apartment on Sawyer wasn't large enough for all of us. Maybe they need just one more bedroom - that should be enough.

Since my parents came from the Old Country, a place where, according to them, a family of ten would be content to share one room, they see no problem with all nine of us sharing three bedrooms. This seems very spacious to them. Based on this bedroom split, our family ends up with a natural dividing line among us girls, the oldest three are one mini sibling set and the youngest four are another, and that's how we sleep, piled up in those two remaining two bedrooms, an assortment of trundle beds, bunk beds, fold out sofas and single beds smashed into the rooms. The largest bedroom in the house goes to the people who seem to need it the least. Our parents.

Closets, windows and doorways cause no difficulties for Mom, she just puts the furniture where she wants it and if we need to open the window or get clothes out of the blocked closet, we just have to figure out a way to do it. Really, how much of a problem is it for me to crawl over my little sister's inert form on the bottom bunk of the bunk bed, slide open the closet door, and stand inside the closet itself to pick out my clothes for school each day?

Our bedroom contains trundle beds for the twins and a bunk bed - the one that blocks the closet - for Mindy and me, and I have the coveted spot on the top bunk. I sleep there before there are safety rails, so two quick rolls and I'm off, flipping through the air like a gymnast, hitting the floor in front of Mindy's horrified eyes. After a few times of doing this, I don't even wake up.

The older sisters don't have it any better. Francine and Brenda, sisters one and three, have single beds on either side of the room and in between them is a worn, spring green, fraying, single-bedded fold out couch, and that is Lauren's bed for her entire life. Springs, cushions, bumps, lumps. Her bed has to be folded and unfolded, turned back into a couch in the daytime because, of course, Mom can't stand an unmade bed. They are squeezed into their room with a shoehorn - pried in, bunched in, locked in, kicking and screaming, snarling and spitting. They customize their areas, delineate their spaces, hang batik tapestries and bedspreads. They tape off the floor, marking out footprints to each girl's section, Do Not Trespass signs marking the edges.

Our bedroom has no such problems because my younger sister, Mindy, and I are the fetch-and-carry slaves for the twins, Sherry and Denise. When the twins become pre-teens and turn our room into a swinging teenage pad, they kick the two of us out to live in the basement on the fold-out couch in the family room. In our new room, a line of half-broken TV sets that Dad has accepted in trade at his laundry are lined up along one wall. On Saturday mornings, desperate to watch cartoons, Mindy and I move from TV to TV, all the way down the line, trying to find one that works. But most of the time we just sleep across from these unblinking glass eyes, watching our lives unfold in the reflective glass of their screens.

Besides the bedrooms, our house contains an assorted mash of other rooms. We have our public rooms, Mom's showcase rooms. We have grayish beige sculptured carpeting that extends in a big L through the living room and into the dining room. Making a smaller L was Mom's silk damask couch with French turned legs and purple flowers. It has three pieces, the two on the ends are straight and the one that fits between them is curved so that it becomes the Great Wall of China Couch in that room, depending on how she sets it up. Mom pulls it apart from time to time, rearrange the pieces, sometimes into a regular couch with a matching curvy loveseat, sometimes all facing each other, like a railroad car.

The tables are marble, one with a heavy pedestal base and one with a diamond cut out wooden base. The lamps on them have gigantic barrel-shades with bulbous lamp bases, and over the dining room table hangs a crystal teardrop chandelier so big that it needs extra ceiling supports in order to be installed. But nearby, ruining the whole damask, crystal and marble thing, ruining the whole Jewish Mausoleum look Mom's going for, is our laminate wood HI FI blasting out Monkees songs.

We have a linoleum-tiled downstairs family room with a big shag rug and a built-in bar for Dad's collection of ornamental Canadian Club whiskey bottles. There's Mom's kitchen with its Harvest Gold appliances, dark wood cabinets, and floral wet-look wallpaper. There are bathrooms - a full, a half, and a three-quarter. There's a foyer that starts out as a small square by the front door when we bought the house, but through Mom's creative use of tile it ends up taking over a swathe of the main floor, undulating its way past the up and down staircases all the way to the kitchen, millions of pieces of marble-looking tiles forming intertwined flowers. The front door never changes. It's oversized, made of blonde wood, with one skewed window in it and a doorknob in the vast expanse of wood. There's a laundry room with a laundry chute; there are hallways and stairs.

The laundry room is the one room in the house that Mom allows us to mess up but, even there, nothing can stay out overnight. If we spend a whole day building a Barbie doll mansion out of books and scraps of carpeting and wallpaper, the whole precarious thing held together by leaning and folding, still, at the end of the day, down it all comes. Even though the room has a linoleum floor with a drain in the center and maroon sponge-painted walls, even though the only furniture in there is a large metal folding table and Mom's antique singer sewing machine in a beige moderne cabinet. Even though there is an enormous coal-burning furnace, an overflowing laundry basket under a laundry chute with clothes forever falling, and a hand drawn chart on the wall showing our heights and the years all seven of us hit them. Even though the décor is minimalist, to say the least, it too has to be cleaned up, everything shoved away, come nightfall.

Though she tries to keep everything neat and tidy, my mom can't control the middle of the night. There's the tucking in, the lights out, the house settled, and yet during the night a bunch of us sleep walk. There are the sisters who sleep in the real bedrooms and then there's Mindy and I, who eventually sleep downstairs in the family room, and we pass each other on one of the two staircases, sleepwalking like ghosts, not seeing each other, or having imaginary conversations with whomever else is in our dreams, walking beside us.

Lauren and I are the worst, planted at opposite ends of the family, she the second from the oldest and me the second from the youngest. She gets out of bed in her room, walks into the twin's bedroom, climbs up on their high dresser and begins to hold court, like an imaginary Miss America, regaling her audience with all the things she's going to do when she wins the crown. In the middle of her speech, the one about how she'd bring about World Peace, she falls into a deep slumber, swaying on the top of the dresser, her long slick hair falling over her face, her skinny teenage shoulders slumping down to her flat stomach. Sherry and Denise, who've been enjoying the show from their trundle bed, run to grab her before she falls.

There's nothing as exciting as this about my sleepwalking. I walk up the two staircases in a mundane way, like I'm awake, and then I sit at the foot of one of the twins' trundle beds, whichever one is still awake. I have normal conversations about a variety of mundane topics, no Miss America performance, and then, without warning, my head tilts forward, my brown hair falls into my face, my shoulders slump into my flat stomach, and I sleep.

Mom is not shocked by sleep disturbances. She's prepared for nightmares, for recurrent dreams; she's ready for night terrors, for bedwetting. She's up in an instant, ready to grab anything near at hand to handle the emergency and get the house back to bed.

For wet beds she spreads a towel on top of the wet sheet, over our ruined mattresses, and pats us back to sleep. For nightmares it's a bed improvised on the floor next to her own, the comfort of Dad's snoring and her wheezing, and the disconcerting feeling that there just might be something staring back at me from under their bed. For imagined noises, she cruises the house and charges fearlessly into pitch black rooms, scoffing at our fears.

"After all," she says, "Is it the forest?"

Anything that's not the forest isn't scary. She snaps off the black and white TV sets; she tells my older sisters to get to bed. She talks calmly to Lauren and me when we're sleepwalking so she doesn't distress us and get us caught forever in the pretend world we're in, and then she tucks all seven of us away and makes her way back to Dad.

Our house has a few other features that makes it unique in Skokie. For one thing, unlike all the other houses on the street, we have a garage. This isn't a backyard garage facing the alley, but a garage that has a door into the house. Second, although it looks like a ranch home from the outside, our house has an upstairs and a downstairs, each just seven or eight steps in either direction. This means no nosebleed second story for us, and no sinkhole basement either. Our downstairs has real windows that are above the ground outside, so that they look like they're planted and growing out of our backyard garden. All these features, I think, make our home qualify as that elusive thing, a tri-level.

The inside is unique too in one special way - it's always decorated up to date. It's inconceivable to us that some of our neighbors move in their homes, decorate them once, and then forget about them. Mom is always monitoring our decor; she always has her finger on the pulse of the newest styles, the newest colors. There's the stuff she does every day, moving pictures and vases, flower arrangements and rugs, and then there's the major stuff.

Every couple of years, Mom snapped out of her half-somnolent, gossipy doze on the phone, hung it up, turned off the sewing machine and ran around the house frantically examining the larger items up close. Everything, it appeared, had grown out of style while she'd been talking. She needed to retile, recarpet, repaint, rewallpaper; she needed new fixtures, new appliances, she needed to sew new curtains.

Then there were the fights with Dad, his, "What do you think, I'm made out of money?" And her persistence, agreeing to trade, to reduce the cleaning lady's frequency, to cut back on piano lessons. And then the constant stream of contractors would arrive at our house day after day while the youngest of us sat watching them. That's how we end up with three different colors of wall-to-wall carpeting installed over our wood floors. That's how Mom gets her Harvest Gold kitchen, that's how we end up with four chandeliers.

If there's no money in the budget for purchases, Mom just picks up all the furniture in a room and flings it all back down again, like dice, to see how it looks this way or that way. She rearranges things so that we bump around; we can never get through a room in the dark, the furniture is never in the same place. And since she never thinks a decorating scheme through ahead of time, just tries it out right away, she leaves us stumbling through rooms at night, never sure where the couch is, just sure of the permanent things, the things she can't move, like light switches and staircases.

It's also of critical importance to Mom that the house is clean, at least on its surface. She always has a problem with the chaos seven girls can produce. She has to shove all the junk out of sight; even rubber bands are looped around doorknobs like they're steel ponytails. In Mom's eternal quest to have a perfect house, one that goes to bed clean and wakes up clean, she was heading for the next plane, the nirvana of clean, one in which the house scrubs itself down when a smudge appears, where shoes left out are gulped up by a closet.

She attempts to exert some control by neatening everything up at nighttime. This means that our family doesn't just go to bed, our shoes go to bed, our clothes, any toys left out need to be put to bed too. Anything we've worked on all day, a painstaking Monopoly game, an elaborate Arabian tent constructed out of all the sheets in the house, all that has to be put to bed for the night too.

In the small details too, our house is just like us; it looks good on the surface but there are problems lurking beneath. It's an ill-equipped Holocaust house. With just a cursory look around, it's apparent that our parents don't do things the way regular Americans do and that maybe they're being done in this particular haphazard manner because of what my parents had learned in the forest and in Siberia.

Every pen or pencil in our house is broken or in need of

sharpening, but that's okay because Mom writes notes in lipstick, a viable writing implement for her. The one pair of scissors we own is hidden away in her sewing box, like it's made of gold. We have no can opener, instead using a bottle opener to make triangular holes in cans until they're all connected, then prying the lid off. Just like Mom did in the forest.

My life is spent searching for things, like an archeologist. Everything is hard. Leaving the house is hard when my shoes are kept in one huge box with my six sisters' shoes because Mom can't pair them up and put them out of sight, she has to move fast, throwing them all in a box to mingle.

If it's urgent that we find what we're looking for, we can always look in one of the many junk drawers we have in our kitchen. These are the drawers filled with the small stuff Mom has no patience to sort. There are the long-lost items like shoelaces and glue, essentials like bottle openers and screwdrivers; inconsequential things like old tokens to the public swimming pool, and old library cards left on the counter, all swept into these junk drawers by Mom.

"Your mother has quite a job cut out for her!" I hear these words over and over again from neighbors, relatives, strangers, and teachers – anyone Mom happens to come across. All she has to say is one little phrase, mention one little thing – that she has seven daughters – and she has them in the palm of her hand.

To help her with the daunting task of running the house, feeding us, feeding Dad – who needs to be fed separately from us – keeping the house clean, and sewing her own clothes and curtains, there's our cleaning lady, Velma. To my mother, having a cleaning lady isn't a matter of status; she has no interest in acting superior to Velma. In fact, she acts subservient to Velma, cleaning the house before Velma arrives and making her large, elaborate lunches filled with the foods Velma prefers but that we've never heard of, like chitlins and grits.

Mom has a system, which involves the three of us like a miniature convoy. First Mom swirls in and out of each room ahead of Velma straightening up so Velma won't find the rooms too messy to clean. Then Velma, apparently unaware of this and finding our house plenty messy enough, gets to each room and cleans whatever Mom's left her. And finally, there's me, the caboose, following along behind Velma with my own broom and dustpan, chattering nonstop and wondering why I could have a broom yet no maid uniform like hers?

Three

Seven Sisters

We are quite the novelty, the seven sisters. I grow up believing that we are famous like the Seven Sisters Constellation, like Snow White's Seven Dwarfs, like the movie *Seven Brides for Seven Brothers.* I think that maybe soon there will be tour buses driving up and down our street in Skokie, idling in front of our house, diesel fumes filling the air, the tour guide's voice gushing out of the megaphone that *this* is the home of the Seven Sisters.

We are trotted out like show ponies any time our mother has the relatives over, on Passover, Yom Kippur Break the Fast, Rosh Hashanah. People love to look at this strange phenomenon, "Seven girls in one family, with no boys! *Kenehora*!" They're almost expecting to see septuplets, I think, and are a little disappointed when we're so dissimilar, so disordered, so unalike. We're obedient; we stand there for the inspection, then we kiss the aunts watching us, or anyone else our parents ask us to kiss, people they swear are relatives, all from unpronounceable Eastern European countries, from lineage tied up in knots, criss-crossed through cousins marrying cousins, so that we're doubly related to everyone.

We aren't just seven sisters; I grow up believing that we have something mysterious and karmic going on. When the seven of us share a couch, we lie down like a litter of cats, in a pile with a scramble of legs upon legs, heads resting on bellies like pillows, and all those heads skewed and scrunched towards the TV set. Even our fights are dramatic, tragic, legendary. Hockey pucks aimed at someone's head, lamps thrown across a room, or maybe just a rolling ball of girls, biting and snapping and clawing, making its way like a boulder through the hallways until we land at Mom's feet, her head clutching a telephone, the telephone cord the lasso with which she ropes the boulder, breaks us apart, and resumes her conversation.

When we were little we lined up in a formation that pleased the eye. The oldest sister was always the tallest and the youngest was the smallest. But as we get older, we become uneven, jagged; some of the younger ones grow taller than some of the middle sisters; some of the middle sisters grow wider than those at the top. The hand-me-downs that Mom makes us squeeze into don't look cute any longer; the huge fabric bows our neighbor makes in her basement and ties onto combs no longer look darling perched crooked on the tops of our heads. People don't want to see this. They want to see a line of seven girls, from oldest to youngest, from biggest to littlest, with no deviations.

The worst inspections are by our aunts, and the worst of these from our Aunt Etta, my father's sister.

First the aunts discuss us in detail; comparing us to each other, which of us is the prettiest, the thinnest, the fattest? What are our respective marriage prospects? Kind of like they're betting on horses. When they're done picking us apart, they change the topic and move on. But not my Aunt Etta.

"Oy, this one's the prettiest! And so skinny!" she says with a wistful sigh, touching my sister Lauren's face while the rest of us look on. My mother stands nearby and starts reciting an exaggerated litany of our hidden qualities that may not be discernable to Etta, things not as apparent as Lauren's beauty. There's the speed typing by one sister, artistic talent with crayons by another, the ability to haul laundry bags alongside our dad by another. But Aunt Etta is done with her compliments. She is only interested in Lauren, fascinated by her perfection. She shifts into Yiddish for the criticisms, commenting on the least pretty and the most fat among us. Of course we understand her completely. Illiterate in Yiddish for everyday use, we are, nonetheless, fully fluent in Yiddish for insults.

What are we but a circus sideshow anyway? We aren't of vast super-human intelligence, or at least we aren't burning up the curriculum in our schools, setting records or zooming off to spelling bees all over the country. We aren't great athletes. We're pretty enough but not the world's greatest beauties, not hauled off by Mom to modeling auditions. And, of course, we aren't even boys. No, we're only the seven sisters so we better just stand still and be admired for that one inadvertent accomplishment.

I'm told a few things about my early years. Amazed that my mother can even remember the details of specific births when she had seven of us, I'll take any memories she's got.

She tells me I'm the stuff of legend at Edgewater Hospital,

where I'm born, apparently because I'm born with some kind of Dark Shadows-ish newborn long black hair sticking out of my head. This is always followed by the next statement, "Of course, that fell out right away and you grew this color," indicating the color growing from my head by then, blah brown. But for just a few days there, she says, I'm so beautiful that nurses from all over the hospital come flocking to see me in her arms.

Later on I'm a suicidal toddler, learning to run only straight towards the street, dashing off from the grown-ups, lured by the whir of cars driving by our house in Skokie. Most of the pictures of me are those of a typical immigrant family. I play outside in my underwear, no shorts and no top. After all, did they have shorts and tops in the Old Country? I am probably potty trained under a tree.

I also know that when my little sister Mindy is born and I lose my place as the youngest in the family, I turn from suicide to homicide, turning into one of those crazy little girl older sisters who have to be watched to make sure they don't murder the baby. I rock her bassinet too hard trying to make her fall out; I spend a lot of mental energy wondering why she can't just go back where she came from. Later still, I'm the worst sister ever, a totalitarian dictator of a sister, at least until the day she pounds me flat.

But because of her my babyhood goes to age three and a half. Mom's ominous growing belly counts down my days as the baby of the family.

My sister Brenda points this fact out to me with a little thrill. "Soon there'll be a new baby and you won't be so special anymore!"

And when it happens, as I know it will, I'll be relegated to the blob of middle children - five of us stuck in the middle - there to live out our lives in obscurity, our recitals unattended, our report cards unsigned. Number six.

Later I move on from bothering the baby to bothering my older sisters. After school each day I stalk them mainly because I'm eight and sneaky by nature, and also I'm setting up the template for my life and I have five older sisters to pick from. Whose life should I emulate?

I establish my stalking precedent with Francine, the oldest sister. I have a lot of choices after school every day of things to do. I can watch the endless array of 1960s TV shows, from *I Dream of Jeannie* to *Gilligan's Island.* I can jump rope endlessly in the driveway. I can have a heart attack playing cops and robbers through the alleys with the neighborhood boys. Or I can stalk Francine and wait for her current boyfriend to kiss her.

And Francine has plenty of boyfriends. This is mainly because she's the kind of girl boys marry. She's the last of a dying breed, the last of an ending era in 1968. While other teenage girls are burning their bras, protesting the draft, turning on and dropping out, my sister has the glamour of a Vietnam-era Sweet 16, the anachronism of a hippie-era Sweet 16, of being somewhat different than her fellow teens. She's sparkling, virginal, shiny-faced and innocent; a nice girl among girls who are going bad, doing drugs, running away. Francine's a throw back to an earlier era.

This changing world doesn't touch Francine somehow, and not due to any child rearing philosophies of our parents. Because of the Holocaust, their child rearing philosophy is, "Keep the children alive." Nothing fancy about it.

Francine's had already gone through her neighborhood

teenage rock band phase, playing tambourine in a Monkees/Beatles imitation band that practiced in each other's basements and performed in the public parks on bookmobile days. We'd already had these band mates of hers, prospective suitors, guys with guitars and drum sticks, wandering through our house, stricken with love for her, all pretending to care about the music but just trying to get her alone to propose.

She'd already been through the teen club scene at The Pump Room in Evanston, made her way there in Mom's Chevy Nova on Teen Nights to drink ginger ale and smile at the boys. She's Sandra Dee, Annette Funicello and Gidget all wrapped into one package; the bikini clad, tambourine-wielding teenage temptress, who is expected to marry early and marry well. But even though she knew she had to marry sooner rather than later, she didn't fall in love with any of those Skokie boys.

Although we attend Evanston schools, all the Jewish boys who live across the Skokie school district line discover my sister and then camp on our doorstep just to ask her out on dates. These are the boys who attend Niles North, where the classrooms are filled with stretched out Bar Mitzvah boys, where a boy can be cool and be named Ira. I watch all of this going on around me and find it much more interesting than my favorite TV shows, so I stalk Francine and her various boyfriends throughout my childhood, watching them through windows, waiting breathlessly for a kiss.

My stalking of Lauren, sister number two, doesn't go as well. Of course, she's already been anointed the prettiest girl in the family by our aunts. She's the perfect height at 5'4 and thin, and she's just about tanned herself into a different racial group, a lovely even brown, which matches her sleek hair and gigantic eyes.

I'm proud of having a sister as pretty as Lauren. I believe that she's destined for amazing things because of her looks. Her later teenage modeling career only helps to prove this; her dashing boyfriends prove this too.

Unlike Francine, Lauren isn't quite as amused by my stalking. She sees me peeking out of the kitchen window when she and her boyfriend Marty are in the backyard. It's impossible for me to resist, especially because I have my own crush on Marty, with his black hair, tan skin and a ready, gleaming white smile, who looks like a movie star. So she sees the curtain move and my bulging eyes as I watch them hold hands.

When I did this to Francine, whose boyfriends weren't nearly as cute as Marty, Francine would call me out of the house to entertain them like I was their own personal monkey, to say inane things to them that only a child of eight could say, like, "Are you going to kiss now? Can I watch?" And they'd laugh. But that's not what happened the day Lauren motioned for me to come outside.

Perhaps she fumed over me spying behind those fluttering curtains. I emerge exultantly, ready to entertain, but when I get out there Lauren slaps me in front of Marty, yelling at me not to watch them.

But Marty doesn't just sit there frozen. Once I run in the house crying, he breaks up with her, which, of course, she blames on me.

Around the time that she turned sixteen, in 1970, Lauren decided that there had been some horrible mistake – she could not be related to our parents – those immigrants. She could not be descended from that Jewish peasant stock. So she decided she wasn't part of our family anymore. She was either going to be our neighbor Sylvia Simon's long lost daughter, since there were no other daughters in that family, or just toss it all away and declare herself Catholic instead, and an only child. She didn't study Catholicism or convert; she already knew all she needed to know about it, that it was Not Jewish.

Now that Lauren was a Catholic only child, when she went out on dates, her boyfriend pulled up in front of our house in his blue Jeep and Lauren waited for him outside, jumping up from the doorstep, stepping out of her life and into his car. She'd been born without any telltale signs of her background, nothing the Nazis would have drawn as stereotypical Jewish features, and, like all of us, she'd had no Jewish education so she knew nothing about Judaism that could pop out of her mouth by accident. Well, she knew about murder and death and paranoia but that was all somehow just as well suited to Catholicism as Judaism, so there was no danger of contradiction.

Lauren seemed to have a plan and, as far as I could tell, her plan was to leave us all behind as soon as she could manage it. Her first step was this change of religions and removing herself from our family and background. She also got a job at Nina's in Evanston, an upscale clothing store, and began modeling part time, her photos appearing on the back of the local Evanston paper.

Lauren was inching towards what appeared to be her ultimate ambition – marriage to a rich guy. Or even anyone who appeared to be rich, acted rich, pretended to be rich, or anyone who was named Rich. She started with this particular Jeep-driving boyfriend since he was Not Jewish and drove that dangerous Jeep that had canvas windows and doorways with no doors, almost as dangerous as the ultimate Not Jewish vehicle: a motorcycle.

Lauren had good reason to believe she was perhaps adopted. She was a talented artist. Soon after she graduated from high school she could be found carrying around a wooden artist's suitcase stocked with toothpaste-like tubes filled with paint and Craypas. She was also a great critic, and I knew this because she had always narrowed the beam of her criticism on me, had always told me just what she thought of my childish sketches, the drawings I made of designer Barbie dresses, or of our house in Skokie, the window shades pulled down like sleepy eyelids.

But one day Lauren came home from Art College, took her wooden artist's suitcase and threw it in the garbage, the whole thing, the latch latched, each tube and craypa inside locked in its prearranged spot. No one was to go near the suitcase; nothing was to be touched. It was a vertical wooden tombstone to Lauren's talent, standing upright in our dented steel garbage can in the alley waiting for the garbage men for days.

We were never to say the word "art" around Lauren again nor any two word groupings where "art" was one of the words, like "art college," or "art project," "art supplies," not even "Art Carney" or "Art Linkletter." That era was dead and gone in Lauren's life. And we weren't even allowed to ask what happened.

After that she looks at my loopy drawings with more interest, as if she hadn't ever drawn before in her life, like she doesn't know much about it but would be happy to try and venture an opinion but she wasn't quite sure. And so she looks down from her greater height than me, looks down at my sketchbooks filled with the pictures I'd drawn, the careful outlines, the shaded in centers. She looks down at my drawing of the front of our house, the diamond-shaped wooden design in our single garage door, the wrought iron balustrade by our front door, and she turns it, around and around and around, until she's looking at it upside down and then she says, "Nice refrigerator."

My dad has a certain casual disregard for all of his daughters to some degree - we are only daughters, after all. As he tells us many a time, he would trade all of us to an Arab sheik to be his harem for just one sturdy little boy if he could. But he has a certain amount of respect for Brenda, sister number three. This is mainly because my dad respects a hard worker.

He says, "This is good - it's good to be strong, Bubbola, because you're built for hard work, like a horse pulling a plow in the old country. Not like your skinny sister Lauren who would fall over in a strong wind." Brenda glares at Lauren.

And Brenda is a hard worker. While I busy myself doing nothing every day, or sit endlessly smashing caps with rocks on the sidewalk, she works. She works early on in her teen years, and then is dragged off to our family laundry later, there to handle the real hard labor of the laundry machines.

I don't spend any time stalking Brenda mainly because there is no boyfriend activity going on. She's popular but in a different way. Brenda has a lot of friends both at school and in the neighborhood. More than anyone else, her friends' homes zigzagged our home; she doesn't have to leave our block to find someone to hang out with. Our house ends up filled with her friends, a huge gang of girlish boys and boyish girls who all have nicknames like Boomer, Mush and Dodi, and then some who have normal names, like Patti, Marla and Missy.

When this crowd of kids hits adolescence, they all begin pairing off but Brenda's still considered to be everyone's friend, not considered competition by the girls or girlfriend material by the boys. She's always the girl that the boys talk to about the girls they like, somehow forgetting that Brenda is a girl too. This is because Brenda is out of the running in the romance game. She's overweight, and this gives her permanent friend status.

In June 1966 I'm sitting at a round kids' table at my Uncle Herbie's wedding. I'm six years old, wearing a red polka dot poplin dress, my dark brown hair cut in a severe Beatles' haircut. At the same table is my sister Sherry who is the exact same size as me, wearing an identical dress, her hair in an identical haircut. We're dressed as twins, we look like twins, but we aren't twins. We're my Mom's fake twins.

Of course, there are real twins in the family, Sherry is one of them, but I am not the other. Elsewhere at this children's table at Herbie's wedding is the other one, Denise, wearing yellow chiffon, who Mom had decided just didn't look enough like a twin to be a twin. Everything about her was wrong. Her version of the Beatles haircut was too lumpy with her thick hair, and her hair color was too medium brown. She was all wrong to be a twin, very untwinlike, even if she was the actual twin.

Mom hadn't given up on Denise and Sherry being identical without a try. She dressed them alike for years even though Denise was a full head taller than Sherry throughout all of childhood, more dissimilar than any two sisters in our family. They had a lopsided gene pool, with Denise having 75% of it, ending up larger, with a bigger nose and bigger birthmarks compared to Sherry. Sherry, with 25% of the gene pool, was small and lithe, she had the same nose but in miniature, a birthmark so small that it appeared to be a freckle, and little china doll feet.

Mom had ignored all this because to her twins are twins. So there they were in all the pictures – at age four, in identical clothes but with Denise in the size six and Sherry in the size four, Denise a head taller than Sherry, Sherry a tiny pixie scampering under Denise's feet, both squinting into the sun behind the camera. Dad perching Sherry on his knee for the photo while making Denise stand behind his knee, like a prom date.

Mom doesn't understand that twins are supposed to be dressed alike because they are identical, not fraternal. She doesn't quite understand the concept of "identical," that identical twins are born, not made.

After a few more growth spurts by Denise, even Mom has to face the fact that this identical twin thing isn't working. She already has the incredible panache of having given birth to seven daughters in a row, now she wants her twins to be perfect too and they're ruining it. In 1965, when Mom lops off all of our hair into Beatles' cuts, she notices that Sherry and I bear a striking resemblance to each other even though I'm a big five-year-old and Sherry's a tiny seven-year-old. It becomes even more apparent when she dresses us alike. Then my mother, the Lithuanian immigrant childrearing expert, decides in a quasi-conscious way, to present Sherry and me to the world as her identical twins.

While I'm a twin, I'm thrilled to be a twin. It's not just that I'm assumed to be two years older than I am because Sherry and I have to be some type of agreed upon age and there's no way she's going back down two years. There's the added bonus that since Sherry is cute and petite, I'm considered cute and petite too, even though I have my doubts about both, since all I've been prior to that time is a gigantic kindergartner with grown up teeth that start growing in behind my baby teeth in two rows, like a shark.

It's also exciting to get promoted to twinhood when I'm not even born to it. Since I'm always looking for a way to move up in the birth order of our family, and hadn't even thought of this on my own, this is an unexpected boon. I figure in some weird way this puppet twinship my mom's forced me into has changed me from sister six to sister something else. Four and a half?

So we are at the wedding. There's me, the imposter, Denise, Sherry, and all my other sisters, along with a polyglot group of other inbred cousins and aunts and uncles, all milling about, drinking too much, cruising the tables for unlifted centerpieces and unclaimed party favors, when someone asks my mother the question that makes me cringe.

"Helen, these are your twins?" A beaming lady from the old country asks, looking at Sherry and I, nodding in approval at our matching red polka dot dresses with red sash ribbon belts.

Mom looks over at us. She never lies. This twin thing was done in some deep subconscious of hers. She needs to organize her girls into look-alike pairs just like she needs to organize socks into pairs, matching up the stray black with the almost black navy blue as close enough. She needs things neat and orderly. So she answers.

She says, "No, these are the twins." She waves at Sherry, "this one," and then she flicks her hand over to Denise, isolated in her yellow chiffon, "and that one." And the lady glares at me, The Pretender.

Besides Sherry and Denise being the most dissimilar fraternal twins ever, their dissimilarities extend to their social groups at school. They are never friends with the same people. Sherry's friends are all tiny like her. There's Lori and Lynn, the two most popular girls in junior high, the miniscule Susie Wolfson and Mara Spector. None of them will top 5'2 when grown.

There are a lot of boys calling the house for Sherry; boyfriends rotate in and out of her life and then are boomeranged back and forth between her and her friends, a constant pinball game of rotating boyfriends in the Junior High popular group.

Denise and her friends don't have these kinds of boy problems. Her friends are a more unpolished bunch. She has a lot of friends, but they're always the most awkward girls in our neighborhood or in her grade. There's Ruth from across the street, with her black frizzy hair and her cake-like breasts, even at age eleven. There's Jackie on the corner, with her Appalachian dishwater blond hair and *her* cake-like breasts. There's Elise from a few streets over whose mother is a different type of Holocaust survivor than ours, the more normal type. Overprotective, her mother monitors Elise around the clock and keeps her wearing little girl clothes. When Elise comes over to our house, her mother lurks in front for hours in her housecoat, stalking her.

Sherry and Denise may not look anything alike but they have this one disconcerting trait of all twins - they share some sixth sense in that when one gets hurt the other one screams. And Denise does get to dominate Sherry in one thing. She was the first twin born, older by a few minutes. In a family in which the law of the land is birth order, this is a very big deal. Denise is sister number four and Sherry is sister number five. This is something that Sherry's petite size can never take away from Denise and something that I, pretend twin or not, can never usurp.

Two years later, in the fall of 1968 I am sitting at a table at my sister Francine's Sweet Sixteen party. I am half her age, eight, a mini-Francine all dressed up at Piccolo Mondo, the fanciest restaurant in Skokie, a restaurant I have ridden past every day of my life but which has somehow never once been open for business, always admiring its rococo exterior and gilt cornices from afar.

This is a snazzy affair. There are tablecloths, a dance floor, dress up clothes, a band, a sit-down meal, and all my old country relatives, creaking and groaning as they unbend from their cars, making their way into this foreign-born phenomena - a Sweet 16. A Bas Mitzvah they could live with, a wedding they expect, but they don't know from a Sweet 16.

Due to some plot of my mother's, I am the only child at this table of grown ups at the Sweet 16; my other sisters dot the room, alone like me. The seating arrangement seems intended to maroon each child away from all the other children not just to avoid fighting, but also so there will be no talking, just the clink, clink, clink of the silverware, the hemming and hawing of the toasts.

Being seated next to Uncle Izzy, my grandmother's brother, and at the same table as the mute Tante, would be bad enough by itself for boredom and social mortification, even if I just sat there being ignored while the adults talked over my head. But, of course, Tante doesn't talk, not even to Uncle Izzy, leaving Uncle to make conversation with me, an eight-year-old. He does this by watching me attack my food with the table manners of a barbarian and so he undertakes training to prepare me for my eventual Sweet 16 and my eventual wedding at eighteen, neither of which ever occurs.

"Linda, mameleh, you know why the silverware is arranged like this?" Uncle Izzy asks me.

"Uh…"

"Close your mouth, mameleh. It's not nice to keep your mouth open so long."

During Francine's Sweet 16, Uncle regales me with endless dining rules. I am taught how to use my silverware from the outside in and chew with my mouth closed; I'm also taught how to cut my meat without screeching my knife across the plate, although he has to give up on my elbows jutting out and striking all the other diners when I do this. Worst of all, Uncle Izzy forces me to cut my salad, piece after piece of iceberg lettuce, instead of allowing me to pick it up in one great mass and nibble on it like a rabbit.

In 1968 Francine may be sixteen but I am forever eight, caught in a slow motion childhood that never moves forward, just stays in place, scenery passing by before me, watching the teen years of my older sisters with eager anticipation. I expect the same teen years when I get there, the same concern with mini skirts that aren't longer than my fingertips, with the Beatles vs. the Rolling Stones. But when I get there, it's gone. Francine remains an ideal I can never quite reach, something I always see glimmering in front of me like water in a desert, but which disappears when I draw near.

By the time Mom is pregnant with Mindy, Dad has lost all hope of ever having a boy. He doesn't think there's a chance in the world that the baby Mom is pregnant with will be a boy. And six girls is enough already. He wants Mom to terminate the pregnancy, to go before the Chicago Board of Medical Examiners and tell them that she can't withstand the rigors of another pregnancy and that, as immigrants, they just can't afford another baby.

So Mom goes but, of course, she wants this seventh baby because she loves her army of little girls and by then she seems to love thwarting Dad's plans for a boy, hoping the littlest one will be a girl too.

She goes before the board and they ask her why she's petitioned to terminate her pregnancy.

She says, "I don't want to terminate my pregnancy. I want this baby, my husband doesn't."

Down goes the gavel, and Mindy, the seventh daughter, is born several months later.

Despite my best attempts to murder her and every trick I could pull out of my three-year-old sleeve, Mindy survived. As a toddler she is round and cherubic, with curly black hair. She takes a long time to talk, or maybe she just takes a long time to get a word in edgewise between a mother eternally talking on the phone, six older sisters who won't shut up, and a father who wants complete silence when he got home. So she wanders around the house playing and smiling, kind of a built-in servant for all of us.

When she's not in the house, she's outside of it, in a full tilt run towards our neighbor Arnie Green's house where she knows the kindly Mrs. Green always has cookies baking and milk to drink.

This is an activity that involves a significant amount of danger since Mr. Greene hates children as much as his wife loves them. He's the polar opposite of his wife, and a curmudgeon so vile that he puts poison on his grass to kill animals that stray there, and once even slaps me for touching some glop he had smeared on his sick tree. Mindy risks running into him each time she goes over there for Mrs. Greene's cookies. And worse, she risks running into him while she sits stark naked at his table because the first thing she does before escaping our house is escape her clothes.

She runs naked out of our back door, through the alley, and to the back door of the Greene's, the sole evidence of her going the slamming screen door and a flash of socks and shoes. Mom insists on socks and shoes.

This is what happens after Mindy disappears each time. First the screen door slams when she runs out, then I yell to Mom in the basement, "Mom, Mindy ran away again!" Then nothing happens for a long time. Mom continues sewing and talking on the phone downstairs even though she knows Mindy's out in the neighborhood naked. The oven clock ticks and tocks.

Then the horrible sight of Arnie Greene's looming face appears outside the screen door, his hand grasping Mindy's arm as he yanks her along back to our house.

He yells in, "Mrs. Burt, Mrs. Burt! I have your daughter, Mrs. Burt!" There's no response because Mom's in the basement clacking away on the sewing machine, the phone glued to her ear. There's just me, staring at him with a poker face from the kitchen table.

He yells in one last time, "Here's your daughter" and he thrusts Mindy in the house like she's a prostitute he found wandering in the neighborhood.

Mindy continues to run out of our house and over to the Greene's house naked, joyous, at full speed, over and over again, and is dragged home by Mr. Greene each time. She does it until she learns it isn't okay to do it; that it isn't okay to be that happy or carefree or free.

Four

But Can We All Fit in Israel?

Because of Siberia, where my Dad had spent the war, and because of having parents who had spent their war years frozen like icebergs, they didn't naturally see the need to ever pay for cold air to be provided in our house in Skokie. As a matter of fact, there was some incredulous fascination on my father's part with the mere idea of our neighbors buying air conditioners as the 1960s draw to a close.

"Pay someone money to get them cold? I should have bottled the cold air in Siberia during the war!"

Because of this attitude, we don't have an air conditioner until 1970. Until then, an air conditioner falls into the category of "frivolous" and "not food" to my parents. My father has certain distinct attitudes about what he's willing to pay for in the world and, more than that, he has opinions about temperature and what constitutes hot and cold. He isn't one to bow to the elements.

Dad isn't afraid of some heat, some humidity; if Siberia hadn't beat him, is Chicago going to? Ego, not comfort, governs my Dad's decision making.

For years he scoffs at air conditioners. They're junk. Garbage. He wouldn't be caught dead with one; he wouldn't spit on one. Real men aren't afraid to sweat; in fact, real men *like* to sweat.

Because of this, there's one time each year that we all sleep together, every single person in the house all piling into my parents' bedroom. The hottest day of the summer. And that's because until 1970 their bedroom has the only window air conditioning unit in the house. Other than this tiny window unit propped between the upper and lower windows, threatening to smash it flat between them, and kicking out a trickle of cold air, we have no air conditioning anywhere in the house.

But when Dad finally installs air conditioning, he changes his tune. Then he says that only a person with a *loch in kopp* - a hole in their head - would sweat when they can cool off. Having an air conditioner becomes another way to prove he isn't a greenhorn.

But before that happens, we sweat. On the worst summer nights in Chicago, we give up. Dad gives up his privacy for the night, we give up our rooms for the strangeness of sleeping in theirs, and we drag all of our mattresses in there, our bedding, our pillows, and set them up like a jigsaw puzzle on the floor. And I see a blanket of sisters before me, sisters rolled out in each direction, as far as the eye can see. Sisters I've never seen sleeping, whom I normally only seen with their mouths open screaming at me. I see them dreaming, sleepy, unconscious.

In our family, we have our morning rituals. There's our wake up, which is rough because none of us simply hop out of bed. We alternate between difficult to get up, impossible to get up, and dead to the world. First we have a hard time falling asleep and a hard time staying asleep; then we're hard to hold down in our beds with our wandering sleepwalking feet and Holocaust-induced nightmares. But, somehow, when dawn hit, we sleep dreamily, moodily, comatosely. We can never wake up.

Sherry gets up quicker than the rest of us and then spends her time getting ready for her day as one of the popular girls at Skiles Junior High, putting on pale lip gloss, curling wings of hair, tweezing her eyebrows into thin arced lines, and brushing on blue eye shadow. Then, when she's done, she becomes the Kapo of our house, pouncing on me, Denise and Mindy, still sleeping in the room we share.

She uses a variety of tactics to wake us up, starting with light artillery and ending with atomic bombs. First she yells at us to get up then she turns on the lights. When that doesn't work she blinks the lights on and off about a hundred times until Dad yells out, his finger always on the pulse of the electric bill, "You think I'm made out of money? No lights on in the day!"

Then Sherry rips off our covers, which is bothersome and most of the time enough to make us get up. If that doesn't rouse us, she goes out on the landing and yells down to Mom - which summons Dad - "Mom! They won't get up again! I've tried *everything*!"

So Dad thumps up two flights of steps because at that point in our lives he's planted his shaving cup and shaving brush clear in the downstairs bathroom, as far away from the seven of us and Mom as he can, claiming it as his own twenty-five square feet of private space.

He thumps up the eight uncarpeted steps from the downstairs. Thumps across our supernova foyer. He thumps up the muffled, carpeted staircase to the second floor. And soon his mad, red, face appears in our doorway.

He yells out, "Get up, you lazy bums!" but to no affect. Then he disappears. At that point, it would have been wise of us to roll out of our beds and hide beneath them, but we don't, or at least, we don't the first time.

He returns with water and douses us awake. We are up, awake, and washed, all at the same time. And we never have that problem again.

Once we all clamber out of bed, it's on to the other rituals of our morning. Someone needs to make the breakfast for all seven of us. This is a rotated chore and no one is exempt.

For some reason, grilled cheese is one of our breakfasts, but it's grilled cheese as devised by my immigrant mother who doesn't understand the idea of buttering bread and frying it in a pan with cheese between the slices. We have our own recipe - seven pieces of Wonder Bread laid out on a baking sheet topped by seven slices of Kraft American Cheese, all thrown into our scary gas oven, the pilot light of which has to be lit by one of our skinny, childish, arms, which is then chased out of that black hole by the circle of flame.

When it's my turn, I get the bread in the oven successfully and manage not to pull my arm out a burning cinder. Then I peer through the blackened window of the oven determined to carefully watch the cheese melt and prove to my sisters that I can handle this chore. I take this pretty seriously because I don't want to hear the complaints of my six sisters if I make it wrong. And I don't want to be moved back down to my old chore: folding the hundreds of paper grocery bags Mom brings home each time she goes grocery shopping.

So I watch and nothing happens. And I watch some more and nothing happens. Then I look away, goof around, get distracted, leave the kitchen, get sent on ten errands by Mom, stop in the bathroom and examine my lower jaw which is growing faster than the upper, making me look a little like Dudley Do-Right from the side, only to return to the oven with smoke coming out of the door and one of my sisters removing the cookie sheet from the oven while yelling, "Damn it, Linda! You were supposed to be watching this!" And breakfast is seven blacked bubbles of cheese on seven burnt pieces of bread.

Because I am at the tail end of the family, number six, it's just assumed by everyone that I am going to be stupid and incompetent forever, so I'm given simple, repetitive household chores to do. The glamorous sisters, the oldest ones, get to wash dishes, a chore I hope to move up to one day. They get to make an assembly line which can use up to three sisters if they play it right, standing there by the sink, all of them clearly of one mind and one purpose so Mom can't send them off to do something else. Francine washes, Lauren rinses, Brenda dries.

My first job was, of course, folding the paper grocery bags when Mom returned from the grocery store. I proved myself so adept at that that I was given this next job, cooking breakfast. I'm quickly removed from the kitchen. I'm given another job, one much more dangerous - ironing Dad's hankies.

Even though we own a laundry and get our laundry done for free, that doesn't mean it's done well. If we were real paying customers maybe it would have been, but we aren't, so our laundry come back home clean but a wrinkled, clumped mess, stuffed in a white laundry bag. And even though Dad's a laundry man, sweating like an animal in that boiling hot laundry, he still clings to this one artifact of his days as a playboy in post-war Germany – he must have a crisp, white, linen handkerchief, ironed into a rectangle and then folded into a triangle and carried at all times peeking out of his shirt pocket.

I am given a mountain of hankies to iron, one by one, little square white hankies, flat on the ironing board, that I then fold and stack into a pile. There were other chores I could have done, like folding the mountains of our threadbare towels into stacks as high as the ceiling or vacuuming the house with our broken down, sputtering Hoover. But I'm so good with the hankies that Dad, our king, demands that I handle this chore alone. I iron them perfectly, fold them just right, and put them away in Dad's nightstand.

The seven of us have certain timeworn fights. Since we share two bedrooms among us for most of our lives, space is a problem. At any given time, there is some difficulty going on between one or more of us. In the oldest sisters' room, their difficulties might involve furniture hoisted at one another, lamps flying across the room, and torn clothes, until, invariably, one of them is thrown out of the bedroom door, ejected, the loser in the ongoing battle for space in a room that will never get any bigger.

During brief quiet periods, they try to get along, agree to decorate together. Laüren, the artistic one, takes out a box of Craypas and draws huge daisies on one wall with massive leaves until there's a giant garden in there; a huge, mod, Peter Max flower garden marching across the wall above Brenda's bed. People came in our house and express surprise that our parents let Lauren draw on the walls but, of course, our parents aren't completely aware of this. Mom can't quite get in there since the phone cord won't reach that far, so she stands peering into the gloom of their room, not quite making out the flowers; and Dad would never walk in, veering away on his way to watch TV each night.

Besides not enough room in the house, there's the telephone to fight over. Since Mom organizes everything by birth order that means that those of us at the bottom of the family have almost no phone rights at all. After she finishes with her phone calling for the day, a chore in itself, the rest of us line up for our turns.

The problem is that some of us needed more phone time than others.

Francine, the oldest, has to talk to her boyfriends for hours, to field requests for dates, and to set up practice times for the band in which she shakes the tambourine. Since Lauren hides the existence of her embarrassingly ethnic and Jewish family from her boyfriends, she hardly needs any time on the phone at all, just enough to arrange for the current boyfriend to pick her up for dates down the street so he never runs into any of us. Brenda and Denise also barely use the phone at all. Brenda's friends all live in a vortex around our house, and Denise doesn't need the phone because all of her friends show up at our house each night to wait for their love interests: a bunch of guys with heavy acne, hair that falls over one eye only, and cars with no mufflers that they park on our street until two in the morning, when the engines start up again, waking the neighborhood.

Sherry's the problem. Sherry's in the popular group at Skiles Junior High and so has a list of popular girls she needs to talk to, and earth-shattering emergencies to tend to, each and every day. She also has a series of boyfriends from the approved popular crowd list and so, as each year moves forward, she progresses through these boys, rotating them back and forth with the other popular girls, like ping pong balls. This takes a lot of phone time, a lot of rotary-dialing calluses. Also, she has to talk to the boys themselves when they're going steady, then less seldom when she's growing bored, and finally, during the break up, for a quick hang up or two.

Then there's me. I'm determined to use my phone time even though Jill, one of my best friends, lives across the street and I see her every day. So she goes home to her house across the street and we call each other just so we'll get some phone calls. Sometimes we switch it up a bit and write letters or send postcards to each other because, besides phone calls, we also want to get mail.

"How are things on your side of the street, Jill?"

"Pretty good. And yours?"

"Good. Did you get the letter I sent you yesterday?"

"Yeah. I wrote you one today. You should get it tomorrow."

And Mindy, the youngest, needs no phone time at all, too young to get into the fray.

Lauren has a schizophrenic relationship with our dad. Where most of us steer clear of him because of his bad temper, because of the endless, fruitless, searches for his shoes, his toothpicks, the minutiae of his life that will make him comfortable after he works in the laundry all day, Lauren doesn't. She gets in the lion's cage.

Sometimes she grabs him as he reads the paper and tries to snuggle with him, calling him cutesy names. Sometimes she sits near him on his recliner and crumples his newspaper while Dad grumbles and rolls his eyes.

Dad doesn't seem to like any of this. Despite the fact that she's the only one who shows that type of affection for him, he shrugs her off. But she's untouched by his indifference and the next night she does it again. It's mysterious, why she likes him so much.

So when Lauren finally gets in a fight with Dad, it's a conflagration, a nuclear war.

At the time, there are several things I'm aware of. It's a Friday night. Lauren asks Dad if she can use the car to go to the Pump Room, the teen bar in Evanston. Dad says she can't go but she apparently interprets that answer more liberally, deciding he means that she just can't use the car.

So the house should be humming along with a low level of Friday-night activity, with TVs droning, with telephone-talking and food-eating, but instead there's this strange burst of energy continuing. Lauren is getting dressed to go out, getting her makeup on. It's like watching a fuse burn on a stick of dynamite, waiting for the moment that she tries to leave the house.

Suddenly Dad looks up and there's a taxi outside our house honking its horn.

I'm kind of inside Dad's head, somehow, while this is happening, watching his delayed response. There's the sound of the taxi horn, the slo-mo panning of Dad's head as he looks out the picture windows and sees the incomprehensible sight of a taxi in front of our house. There's the dawning realization on his face that the taxi is there for Lauren. There's the sudden reddening of his face.

Then, behind him, there is a sudden flurry of movement. Lauren is trying to get down the stairs and out the door, past him and into the taxi before he can stop her.

There are a few more images that flash by, the film reel rewinding: Lauren running for her life up the staircase, into the bathroom, slamming the door shut and locking it. A tiny, little, push-button lock; a flimsy hollow-core door, all to withstand the force of Dad. Then Dad is on her heels, following, and slamming his shoulder into the door a second later, the rest of us standing transfixed at the bottom of the stairs, waiting for Lauren to be murdered. There's a splintering sound and then the door is open and Lauren and Dad are in that small space together. There's hitting and screaming - both ways.

She yells, "I hate you! You are such a crappy father!"

And he yells, "Oh yeah? I'll show you! It's my roof over your head! Next time you get out!"

The bathroom door never shut quite right after that, though Lauren went back to normal. It took a few weeks but after a while she was back to her regular relationship with Dad, sitting on the arm of his chair, crushing his newspaper, calling him cutesy names.

Because Dad dominates our TV set, he picks what we watch. We watch Jackie Gleason because he's Jewish. We watch Joey Bishop because he's Jewish, or at least we watch him until he stomps off the set of his talk show, or someone does anyway. We watch Jack Benny, Don Rickles, and Phyllis Diller because they're

Jewish, and soon we add the young Joan Rivers because she's Jewish too. We watch Ed Sullivan because he has a lot of Jewish comedians on his show. We watch Carol Burnett even though she isn't Jewish, but we know there's something strange in her family background so we think she's probably Jewish but just doesn't know it. We watch movies with Tony Curtis, Jack Lemmon, and Jerry Lewis. Jewish, Jewish, Jewish.

Soon Dad expands our repertoire, narrowing it from all Jewish to all bad-tempered. We'll watch anyone on TV who has a bad temper, anyone who slams off a movie or T.V. set, anyone who tells the producers to go stick it or who plays a character who tells anyone to go stick it. When *All in the Family* debuts on T.V. in 1971, Dad is in heaven. Everything he finds funny is right there in a single character; everything he ever wanted to say. He decides right then that Archie Bunker is his alter ego and that Mom is his own Edith-style *dingbat.*

Dad moves our TV from room to room too. Since he's the king of our household, he gets to decide where we watch. Does he feel like watching on his La-Z-Boy recliner in the basement, or does he feel like sticking to Mom's plastic-wrapped sofas in the living room? Maybe he feels like lying stretched out on his bed? As a result of this whimsical decision-making, the TV gets hauled up and down the staircase like a suitcase, plugged and replugged, my sisters adjusting and readjusting the bunny-eared antennas on top. It's always a fight between the seven of us, who will be stuck getting up, stomping over to the 19-inch TV set on its little cart, and turning the channel.

TV isn't all fun and games for Dad; he's a serious news watcher, fretting over the fate of Jews in faraway lands. First he worries over the local news, then over the national news, and last he worries over the international news, analyzing the political implications for the Jews in each region. He watches miserably, agonizing, impotently, assessing how the Jews are faring in the world at large, how entrenched we've become in each country, how portable our wealth is, whether we can leave each country at a moment's notice. And if we need to, can we all fit in Israel? He's ready for a rap on the door, a gun motioning us onto a train; Mom's ready to pile on layers and layers of coats, to sew diamonds in the hems of our clothes.

When the international news narrows down to news of Israel, as it always does, the room must be silent. There's the Six-Day War, the Yom Kippur War, the Munich Olympics. All these events confirm my Dad's assessment that Jews are outcasts in the world, and always attacked, even when we have our own country. Is there ever going to be a place where we're safe?

The 1968 Chicago Democratic convention comes and goes with its accompanying violence. To Dad, if Christians are rioting and waving guns, it's just a matter of time until they find a way to blame everything on the Jews. The election of that year comes around, and even though both my parents are Democrats, Dad votes for Humphrey and Mom votes for Nixon, their votes negating each other. Mom votes with an eye to international politics, choosing the candidate she thinks will be better for Israel and Dad votes with an eye to domestic politics, choosing the candidate he thinks will be better for American Jews, businessmen like him.

Dad wakes us up in the gray dawn as he watches the final election results unfolding on the black and white TV set, which is in our room. It's 5 A.M. and he's perched on the edge of Sherry's trundle bed, the TV glowing in the dark with no sound on.

He's swearing. "Damn, damn." Then, "Goddamned bastard is going to win. We'll have to move to Israel for sure."

And that's it, the thought that stands behind every other thought, behind every other word. Israel is just standing there waiting for us and if things get bad enough in the United States, we're out of there. But like the Jews in 1930s Germany, we have to keep our finger on the pulse of the country; we have to watch for the signs of coming trouble. We can't wait till the last second or we won't be able to get out. We're waiting for that irrevocable sign, that thing that will give us that extra little push, make us give up the suburban Chicago home, the laundry, our English; that will make my parents wander the world again, become refugees again. Is it Nixon becoming president? The assassination of Martin Luther King, Jr.? The unrest of the 1960s? What will make us go?

I'm concerned about a couple things. Can we all fit in Israel – all the American Jews? And maybe we should go now before it fills up and they shut the door.

I bring this subject up with my mother one day.

"Mom, why don't we move to Israel now, before anything bad happens?"

She looks at me like I'm crazy, like she'd never heard Dad mention this idea. "Move to Israel?"

"Yeah. You know how Dad always says we'll move to Israel if things get bad here?"

"With their inflation? And the army? You want to be in the army? They put girls in the army! And we'd have to live in an apartment, no house ever! And all those crazy Arabs everywhere around you, ready to march in with an army anytime! Move to Israel! On purpose!"

Dad is uninterested in Vietnam, despite the fact that it is the actual war going on at that time. He has no sons who could be drafted, first of all, and second of all, he's unable to conceive of any effect of this war on the Jews, so Vietnam is a non-issue to him. But when it starts affecting American politics, that's a different story. Watching Nixon squirm through press conferences, hemming and hawing about troop withdrawals – Presidential instability – that makes my father sweat.

Other than this, Vietnam is like an endless reality show from Southeast Asia on our black and white TV set at all hours. Sometimes by mistake I catch glimpses of these newscasts before I change the channel – aircraft buzzing a jungle, clouds of napalm descending over a beach, or the unmistakable sound of helicopters taking off, soldiers hanging off the landing gear, the thump, thump, thump of the propellers. Each time I change the channel as quickly as I can.

When the TV is off, everything is back to normal. It's World War II again, at least in our house. Not the battles, the hawsers, the maneuvers, or movements. It's the war on foot, the movement of refugees on foot, on trains, through forests and trees, through snow. And that war will never end.

Five
In Marched the Germans

No one wants to hear about the Holocaust.

My parents are both aware that the outside world is not interested in their suffering, in their stories of survival. In the 1950s and 1960s the basic attitude of the world is that they are to put it behind them, to get on with their lives, and to pretend it never happened. Since my Mom can't talk about it outside of the house, her story is saved for us inside the house, the words pouring out at all times, any time. There was never an unsuitable time.

My mother begins every one of her stories with the words, "In the Old Country." She never says Eastern Europe or Poland or Lithuania. In my family we designate huge tracts of land, huge political entities, by the words "Old Country" and "America." The implication is that she left the old behind for the new, she's lucky to be out and alive, and she's never going back, not even to show them that she made it.

In the middle of every one of my mother's stories, in march the Germans. Not the Nazis, as would be proper for her to refer to them and more politically correct. Rather, she uses the term Germans so she can condemn the whole German people, to wrap them up in a ball and label them all guilty. Germans equal Nazis in my house; my parents have no patience for some nonsense about those who might have been against the Nazis but who never spoke up. They condemned the entire German people, the entire people that allowed a Hitler to come to power, who went along with him. They didn't care for shades of gray; there were no shades of gray in Siberia, in the forest, in the concentration camps. There was just living and dying.

We have other methods of referring to our communal story, our own family shorthand. To us, there was just one war, which was World War II, and it was called "the war," and that word encompassed all the suffering my parents went through and the death of their loved ones. And that war was never to be confused with any other war, even though the war in Vietnam was going on at the same time.

The end of each and every one of my mother's stories is the same, and I cringe at these coming endings. As I grow up, I'll do anything to stop the inexorable march of her narrative. I'll interrupt, I'll change the subject, I'll interject; if we're on the phone I'll have to get off with no warning. Because the ending of every story is that they all died; she'll say, "and then the Germans killed them all." My mother has never told me a story that hasn't ended with these words. We have photos labeled just with those words on the back – from old men to young aunts to rosy-cheeked toddlers – all killed by the Germans. I understand that's how their lives ended, but is that always the way the story ends that she's telling me? I don't always have to know the ultimate fate of this person or that person; sometimes I just want to hear a small story. Tell me about just one day.

When she manages to get this ending out, when I haven't ducked it in some way, she stops talking and looks at me expectantly. I know that I am supposed to be crushed by these stories, as a normal person would be. I should be outraged and inflamed and repulsed and motivated to action and, maybe even fearful of being Jewish, of passing on my Judaism. But I've been hit with this stick too many times. I'm an emotional zero. It's too big for me to wrap my mind around, and, more than that, too different from Skokie. I look outside. There are no dirt streets, no burning buildings, no Jews starving in the forest. No forest.

In our family, the war had just happened, even though it had been twenty-three, twenty-five, years since it had ended. My Mom is still looking for a missing cousin, my grandmother is still looking for her dead siblings, and it doesn't matter that she'd seen them murdered right before her eyes; until her death she is still looking for them. She might seem to be involved in other things, like cooking, cleaning and mending, but these are all just distractions. Her real job is getting back to concentrating on finding the family members who are missing.

Even though they talk about the war and the old country and the Germans too much, I'm proud of my parents for their ability to speak of the unspeakable. Inside I jeer at the other Skokie Holocaust survivor parents with their taciturn expressions, turning away from any discussion of what happened to them. My family is loud with the Holocaust, in your face with the Holocaust, serving up the Holocaust to anyone who walks in our door, breakfast, lunch, and dinner with the Holocaust. The Holocaust forms the thread of our days.

My mother stays out of the discussion of why she survived and others didn't; more for her was the discussion of why everyone didn't survive. The miracle she was looking for she never got and the miracle she got she never recognized. God had died for her on a fall morning in Krivich in 1941. She looked for him, up in the sky, in the faces of murderous soldiers, but didn't find him. He turned one way and she turned the other.

My mother never tells anyone that she's from Lithuania. She'll barely admit to being Jewish once we leave Skokie, unless the person knows by accident, like by running into her at a synagogue or the Jewish Community Center. Instead, she'll claim that her Lithuanian accent is from some vague European country, like Liechtenstein, and that the Yiddish she speaks is French. And then, if something derogatory is said about Jews in front of her, she'll freeze up but she won't say anything. Later she'll say to me, "See they all still hate the Jews."

It turns out that my mother's town in Lithuania, Krivich, is a hard place to get your hands on; that Lithuania is a hard country to get your hands on. Sometimes Krivich was there and sometimes it wasn't; sometimes it was in Poland and sometimes it was in Russia, and sometimes, like now, it's in Belarus. Lithuania, after an earlier history in which it had been the largest country in Europe, had disappeared. In 1795 it was absorbed into Russia, but that didn't stop people from thinking of themselves as Lithuanian, my family included. It didn't matter that when my grandparents were born in Krivich it was part of Poland, or that when my mother was born there it was part of Russia. If you asked people in the shape-shifting, border-shifting Krivich, in the no man's land of my mother's town in 1941, right before the Nazis marched in, what country they lived in, they'd have answered, "Lithuania."

The Jews there referred to themselves as Litvaks, Jewish Lithuanians, a term that placed them to that exact strip of land in the heart of this virtual Lithuania, their exact piece of the Pale of Settlement, the swathe across Eastern Europe marking the area in which Jews were allowed to settle after 1791. This term is also elitist; the Litvaks consider themselves the crème de la crème of the Eastern European Jews; more educated, more cultured, even if my grandfather was a shoemaker. This elitism made them despised among the other Jews in the region.

Even after I know this history, even after I know that Lithuania will disappear from the map during certain years of world history, Krivich is elusive. Part of the problem is that my mother insists she's from a place called Krywiec, Lithuania, and she spells it for me with that crazy Polish spelling. Just to confuse matters, it appears on my birth certificate spelled "Krzywieze." A few more letters. Then one day she admits that, since I'm looking for the real Krivich and not just the one in her memories, the town just may be considered to be in Poland, though since she hates the Poles so much it's hard for her to admit that.

Although I search, I can't find this town, a place that once existed and should still exist, just emptied of its Jewish population. So I decide to spell it phonetically - Krivich, Krivichi - and I find it. I find an eyewitness account of the Nazi massacres of the Jewish population of the town, of even my mother's family, and I find out things much more horrible than she knows since she was hidden away. And I, in turn, hide that information from her.

Although my mother leaves Lithuania at age eleven,

returning briefly after the war, Lithuania never leaves her. It's like another person living in with us, an omnipresent eighth child. The war inside my mother never ends; she's always going to sleep in Skokie but waking up in Krivich. There's no way to bridge the two halves of her. There's the little girl growing up in a huge extended family in Krivich, the rolling hills and trees of Lithuania around her; and the little girl growing up in the Lithuania of the Nazis marching in; the freezing, the starving, and the dying.

And so like some kind of macabre Jewish Chicken Little, she is always running around telling us, "The Holocaust is coming, the Holocaust is coming," and we, those seven daughters who were not even supposed to be born because *by a hair's breadth she was almost killed*, we have to be prepared. Prepared for jackbooted Nazis, for train rides to nowhere, for snowy winters and no coats. She has to be prepared to lose all of us, in a flash, to a soldier carrying a hand grenade, pulling its pin out casually, and tossing it into our home. Since she can't prepare for this, she does the next best thing. She hides from the thought of this.

Mom always insists that Dad isn't a real Holocaust survivor, not like her, anyway. After all, he had spent the war years in Siberia - and there was no Holocaust in Siberia. The Nazis had just gotten to Russia when they were frozen out, routed by the Russian army and the snow. So Dad starved and froze, but with no Nazis in Siberia shooting them, how bad could it have been?

Sure, both Siberia and the forest she lived in held sickness and death, but Dad was lucky enough to have had only the Soviets to deal with, not the Nazis. And also, didn't he have a coat? And didn't he live in some kind of wooden shack, with a floor and walls, and even a roof? And didn't he and his whole family have jobs milking frozen cows standing in the Siberian tundra, herding horses across the ice? This, to her, stuck in the forest, underground like in a grave, lice falling on her head; this would have been luxury. *Siberia?* She laughs a Cruella DeVille-kind of laugh intended to raise Dad's hackles. *What I wouldn't have given for Siberia!*

She'd had no coat, no shoes. Just look at her frost bitten toes if you don't believe her. She remembers sitting there in her hiding place in the forest, its door a tree stump, and breaking off her toes, one by one by one, as they froze, she tells me. Yet there they are, Mom's toes - elongated, coming to a point that no shoemaker can fit, permanently numb from that cold.

Before that there had been what she had gone through in her tiny town of Krivich, trapped with the Nazis, sending the Jews of her town, of her family, this way and that way, one to this line and one to that line, confusing her, making her think maybe she should run from her parents, her sister and brother and go stand over there with her Uncle, her Aunt, her cousin, and her grandfather.

"This close I came to dying," she says to me, holding her fingers so close together I can't even see air. "The next second, they're all in the house. The soldier, he throws in a grenade and they're gone." And did Dad go through that, she asks? No. They heard the Germans were marching into Poland and Dad's family left. She nods like this makes her case.

It's a dangerous game my mother plays, this game of competing tragedies. Who suffered the worst? Who went through more? The game of competing tragedies is played with every survivor she meets, and not just by her - it's a game played by every survivor unwittingly or not. This one was only in the

Underground. This one had fake papers and spent the war passing for Christian. Or this family got out before the war when things were just getting bad but people think they're survivors because of their accents.

There's always the chance that someone will have suffered worse than my mother; she runs this risk every time she opens her mouth. She loses this contest every time she comes up against those who survived concentration camps, like my Uncle Barney. Didn't she have fresh air, after all? What no gas chambers, no crematoriums? In the forest they could run, nu? In the concentration camps, no running. You'd be shot like a dog if you ran.

My mother has an innate suspicion of Holocaust survivors who remain silent, who won't share their stories. Maybe nothing so bad happened to them or let them speak up and compete for the worst story.

"They weren't even survivors," she'd jeer, hearing of someone like Dad who was transported here or there, but away from the Nazis. There are different levels and it's important to her that she's able to compare them.

She not only has survivor's guilt, she has survivor's insecurity - she needs reassurance that this thing that happened to her was beyond belief, beyond the pale. The people we know, the people whose stories we're familiar with, they're okay. But, as a rule, we don't like other Holocaust survivors. It's hard work talking about this all the time.

And now the next generation has to take over. Which of us was born over there after the war and who was not? Who was born to mothers and fathers whose first children had been killed, and who had not?

There's never any doubt in my mind that both my parents qualify as Holocaust survivors; I don't care about the technicalities. They're both Jews, both run out of their homeland by Nazis, lost their homes because of the Nazis, lost family because of the Nazis. Whether one was freezing in Siberia and the other was freezing in the forests of Eastern Europe, this is all just nitpicking to me. Both end up in Displaced Person's camps in West Germany after the war in 1946, where they met.

Six

Drake Avenue

Our street in Skokie is filled with boxy houses, one across from another, with boxy hedges in front of boxy picture windows, up one side of the street and down the other. All the houses look across the street at other houses, with the ones on corners facing away towards the next street, like they're giving a cold shoulder to the ones on their own block.

Our house sat next to that of Trudy Gordon, the owner of the house on the corner, and one of the few non-Jews on the block. That's how my world was divided, into Jews and non-Jews. Like the uncola, the only thing I knew about non-Jews was what they weren't: Jewish.

Since Trudy's home was on the corner, she had a huge expanse of grassy lawn that she let us play on any time we wanted. She also mowed this monstrosity herself each weekend, something that no Jewish woman in Skokie would be caught dead doing. Of course, Trudy was a special case. Not being Jewish, she clearly didn't know one of the rules that governed Jewish women's lives: the men did the mowing. She was also divorced, so she obviously didn't understand another rule: no one got divorced.

Trudy had a tremor that made her head nod to one side in a rapid movement while we were talking to her. From time to time she'd get some treatment for this - a heavy neck brace to choke the tremor out of her, some dopey drugs to slow it down and that she'd describe to us in detail, but overall she just seemed happier nodding away.

She also always had a dog, always a Schnauzer, and always named Schnapps. She seemed to have an endless supply of Schnauzers in the wings somewhere to replace each Schnapps as they kicked off from a variety of dog ills, from car mishaps to bad dog food, to poison eaten in our neighbor Arnie Greene's yard.

Year after year we watched them, this endless line of Schnauzers named Schnapps, all starting out as puppies, aging, dying, and being replaced the same day with another dog named Schnapps, Trudy tirelessly tracking down the old Schnapps' soul into its new incarnation, like the Dalai Lama. We'd go over to her house then and pretend we didn't notice that her old decrepit Schnapps had died and been replaced by a new puppy Schnapps instead we'd just admire her dog like we'd done a million times before and talk to Trudy as she carried on one conversation with her mouth and another with her nodding head, a Morse Code with which we couldn't keep up.

Inevitably one of the Schnappses took a bite out of my little sister Mindy because Mindy looked like she'd be delicious. She was little and pudgy and had curly black hair and spent all of her time running naked through our neighborhood. What dog could resist that?

Trudy went into a veritable panic, believing that our parents would make a fuss if Mindy caught rabies and started foaming at the mouth. Like maybe they'd insist that Schnapps be put to sleep. She showed up at our house like a suitor, saying nervously, "Linda, can you give this to your sister?" and handed me a basket full of candy, just like it was Halloween, and all for a little dog bite.

Of course, our parents would never have gotten involved. Mom, of course, stayed on the phone after Mindy came home crying and bleeding with the bite marks marring her arm. This is a woman, after all, who had lived in a forest being shot at by Nazis when she was hardly older than Mindy, a woman who didn't get involved in neighborhood disputes. And she loved Trudy. Dog bite, shmog bite. So Mom didn't take a breath from her phone call. She grabbed a *schmatta,* a bottle of whisky, and some plastic wrap, and made Mindy a whisky compress. She wrapped Mindy's hand up tight in this stinky, liquor tourniquet, and once it was off and Mindy's hand was shrunken and wrinkly and smelled like liquor, she announced it healed and sent her back out into the neighborhood.

Until I was nine, the Simon family lived in the house on the other side of us innocuously, placidly, creating no trouble at all. Mom was happy because Sylvia Simon's house was smaller than ours, and because Sylvia only had two sons which, of course, wasn't as good as having seven daughters. But for some reason, Sylvia was happy anyway. They were the best of friends.

Then the Simons got rich; it appeared that Skokie wasn't their last stop on their march towards affluence. First Jerry

Simon's company car got traded in on a bigger, newer model, and then, after he earned his CPA, Big Eight accounting firms court him.

Then they house-hopped. First to a house bigger than ours in a different suburb and then they house-hopped all the way to Georgia for a new job.

As a result of the Simon's defection, a new neighbor, Roberta Rosen, moved in, and she was very different from the safe, dependable, Sylvia Simon, lifetime member of Hadassah, with her short, mannish haircut, her sensible shoes, her unostentatious jewelry, and her two average-looking sons.

The day after she moved in, Roberta Rosen walked out of her door wearing a skimpy bikini and pulling along a lawn chair. She proceeded to spend the day tanning in her front yard, creating quite a stir. Men cruised by in their cars or circled the block for another look, while the women on the block glared out of their windows, calling each other on the phone to discuss exactly who Roberta thought she was.

Roberta did this every day. She was permanently installed on her lawn chair, flipping over from back to front and front to back like God was holding an enormous spatula and turning her over when she was cooked just right. She spent her life like this, baking in her front yard under the Chicago sky, moving her lawn chair to avoid the shadow of the running man sculpture her husband, a plumber, welded and erected in the yard, and which fell over her tanning body like a sundial.

Just like Trudy Gordon, but in a different way, Roberta Rosen didn't seem to understand the rules of Jewish womanhood, and Roberta was Jewish. After you got married and had kids the rule was that you had to let yourself go, dye your hair blonde, and have it teased into a bouffant once a week. The other ladies didn't tan; they were pasty white and freckly and they wore housecoats unless they were leaving the neighborhood. But Roberta was young and thin and, by then, she was tanned to the color of furniture. She had choppy black hair cut in a shag before anyone had ever heard of shags, and she wore bikinis unless she was leaving the neighborhood. Even if the other Skokie ladies were forced, kicking and screaming, into a bathing suit, it would never have been a bikini. It would have been a one-piece with molded bra cups and a flouncy skirt at the bottom.

Roberta's husband Mike was wild for her, and they seemed to be a bit of a mismatched pair - Mike, a balding plumber, and Roberta, the bathing beauty. He was a sculptor on the side, of course. The eight-foot-tall running man sculpture he installed in their front yard was made in their basement in secrecy and with a lot of welding tools. It was built of pipes, vises, and faucets, all left over from his plumbing jobs, with a soccer ball for a head. After he hauled it up the steps from the basement he planted it like a tree in the center of the front yard, there to watch over Roberta while she sunbathed - maybe he had installed a primitive spycam in it. Instead it became the target of anyone who drove by and felt like knocking it down. They drove their cars right up onto the Rosen's lawn to take down that running man, all of us shaking our heads over it the next day: his downed, twisted metal body, his detached head. We secretly hoped he was destroyed for good, but Mike just fired up the welder, repaired the running man on the spot, and put him back up.

Mike and Roberta bought their children a swing set, candy striped red, white, and blue, possibly to keep them out of the front yard so Roberta would have it free for sunbathing. It had swings, but also a little carriage and a two-seat see saw and a slide and a pole. Mike cemented all the legs into the ground.

Our swing set was a little different than theirs. Rather than being candy-striped it was more half chipped green paint and half the rust that had eaten away that chipped green paint, so it was kind of a splotchy brownish green. It had no carriage, no slide, no two-seat see saw, just swings. It was taller than the Weiner's swing set in an unwieldy, unbalanced way, with the weight unevenly distributed. Dad never bothered to cement the legs into the ground, so when any of us swung too hard back and forth, trying to fly away into the sky, the front legs would tip up, as high as a foot off the ground.

Sometimes I fantasized that one day I'd wake up and we'd have the Weiner's new swing set in our backyard and they'd have our monstrosity; that maybe ours, with its uncemented feet, would have just clomped on over there.

I'm peering out one of our front picture windows one day, when I see a police car coming down the street and pulling to a stop at the Saltzman's house across the street. I watch as the officer gets out of the patrol car, handcuffs dangling as he rings the doorbell and Marlene Saltzman answers it. The officer takes out a notepad and begins to write.

Marlene, all 5'1, nose-jobbed, dieting, inky hair-dyed and tanned inches of her, is telling the officer something that she, at least, finds very interesting, all the while punctuating her narrative with jabs of her cigarette-holding finger towards down-the-street, towards the house of her enemy, Phyllis Pearlstein. I watch as the smoke from her cigarette loops in the air about her, forming smoke rings, maybe an arrow inching its way down the street, so the officer won't miss the perpetrator's house. I see the Saltzman kids crowding around her and I can hear their high-pitched additions to Marlene's story, the "and then he..." and the "I wasn't doing anything wrong..." and the "They started it when they..."

In Skokie, our Hatfields and McCoys are the Saltzmans and the Pearlsteins, but instead of fighting with guns they fight with the law, dragging police officers to their homes, there to boomerang up and down the street, back and forth between their two homes. They have to listen to the tedious versions of yet another fight between the older boys, between the younger boys, or even three on three, with Wendy Saltzman thrown in for good measure, the only girl in the bunch. When they're feeling more benevolent towards each other, they do less annoying things, like order pizzas to be delivered to each other's home and make phony phone calls to each other.

In the deep recesses of Skokie memory, we all have our opinions about how this feud might have started. Maybe with a tiny push in a single file line when the two oldest boys were in Kindergarten at College Hill Elementary School, with both going home crying to their mothers. I imagine Phyllis pausing in the daily drawing on of her eyebrows to gasp at the sight of her son so distressed at his first day of school, and Marlene, obscuring her son for a moment in a puff of cigarette smoke, doing the same.

Mom learns a valuable lesson from this feud. She will never get involved in any of our problems. We could come home bloody and beaten but we learn right away that there won't be any interference from Mom. Of course she'll treat our injuries, putting her whiskey compresses on anything, even broken bones, but otherwise, she is neutral, as placid as Switzerland. Because of all this Nazi shooting at her head stuff, Mom had come to have a distaste for violence, even that certain type of social violence that occurred between mothers who were trapped in Skokie in the 1960s peering out of their houses at each other all day and who then decided to overmanage motherhood.

So she didn't pick sides when war broke out on the street between Phyllis Pearlstein and Marlene Saltzman; she didn't even talk about it much, preferring to continue on the well-worn groove of her familiar topics - everyone in the world's weight, from movie stars to the teenage daughters of friends, and the companion topic: the week's newest diet. For a woman who had once starved, this was proof she had become an American.

It's a big deal when the Simons move out of Skokie. For many people in our neighborhood, Skokie is their last stop; this is the move-up home. My parents would have been satisfied staying in the apartment on Sawyer forever except that with my birth even they had to admit space was getting a little tight. Not to mention the eventual seventh. Our house in Skokie was the place we moved up to, the gigantic mansion of our dreams. The concept of moving up away from it was alien to my parents.

But then the Simons moving sparks my Dad's interest in the concept. Or at least he has some interest in the idea of being the big shot, the *macher*, the rich American. For a while right after they move Dad also starts flirting with the idea of moving, taking all of us out to new subdivisions in Northbrook and Naperville each Sunday. It's quite a concept to us since we do want to be rich, and having one of these enormous houses will definitely mean we are. I'm enthralled with the spacious bedrooms in the model homes we see, the gabled windows, the lawns that roll down to the street, Mindy and I rolling down to the street on those rolling lawns. But Dad doesn't buy a new house; he gets over this. His natural frugality wins out.

Once Sylvia Simon moves away, Mom has to go visit her, and this is a problem because Mom has just learned how to drive and hasn't taken to it very well. She seems to have a problem with the amount of incoming data. There are the traffic signals, the other drivers, the oncoming traffic, the same direction traffic, not to mention the pandemonium going on in the interior of the car.

She has a few near misses where she almost kills all of us in her first years of driving; the years after she gingerly approached her red Chevy Nova under the tree where it'd been rusting for a few years and eases into the drivers seat. First there's a small rear ender with her carload of kids, and then there's the time she drives us halfway to Sylvia Simon's new house in the oncoming traffic lanes of the freeway, until she realizes that all the cars honking and people waving at her aren't just being friendly.

When we get there alive, Mom figuring out how to drive on her own side of the median, we discover what Sylvia, her husband, and their two sons had moved up to. A two-story red brick house with a single garage down a sloping driveway; a house like ours but a little more spacious, the street a little more tree-lined. I try to recapture my friendship with the younger son but he's changed; he doesn't want to play with girls anymore. He takes me down to the playroom to see what we can find to play with but I back away in horror. The previous owner has left something behind that the Simon's have left up - an enormous, staring, decapitated elk's head mounted on the wall.

Then the Saltzmans move away in 1970. It was unheard of

in Skokie for two families to move away within the same decade. Unlike the Simons, the Saltzmans didn't go far, nor did they move up. They move to Wilmette, just on the other side of the Old Orchard shopping center, and into a smaller, more non-descriptive home, a squat, square box of a house on a street of little monopoly houses across a chain link fence from a school.

Marlene Saltzman had always seemed unhappy with one important thing about her house - it was different. Their house looked like maybe it was the original farmhouse that was in Illinois Territory back when it was part of the Louisiana Purchase; like maybe a builder had bought the land around it and built all our little box houses on a street enveloping this farmhouse.

It had a pointy roof and porches, both front and back. And it had floor confusion. When I walked in the side door, I ended up on a tiny landing with only an umbrella stand, and this required an immediate decision - did I want to go down to the family room or up to the kitchen, living room, dining room, and master bedroom? All of the main rooms were on the second floor.

There was even one more floor up a narrow wooden staircase from the main floor that contained the kids' rooms, right into the center point of that roof. Both Wendy Saltzman's bedroom and the bedroom shared by her two brothers had walls that sloped down and hit you with forty-five degree angles in the head, so that furniture couldn't be placed against the walls since the vertical part of the walls was about two feet high. Though Wendy was short, even she was no match for this room. The only place to straighten up and stand was in the middle of the room, along the crease that formed the peak of the ceiling.

When Marlene wasn't hatching plots to destroy the

Pearlsteins, she was smoking cigarettes and drinking coffee, sitting at her table in her little farmhouse kitchen just smoking and sipping. Did she imagine the houses up and down the block standing around her Victorian bordello of a house, laughing at it? Or just staring, their great wide picture window eyes open wide, unblinking? Marlene knew the house needed either a renovation that involved chopping off the point and the kids' bedrooms, making do with it as it was, or badgering Abe to death until he gave in and let them move, coughing his approval.

Or maybe it was none of this. Maybe it was the feud with the Pearlsteins that drove them away, too many unordered pizzas arriving on their doorstep? Maybe there were too many squad cars arriving to investigate complaints of a wild party and instead finding Abe Saltzman, a toothpick in his hand, sitting in a recliner in their darkened living room, watching TV?

My Dad wasn't the most popular father in the neighborhood. His overall personality guaranteed that he wouldn't be. In some ways he fit in fine. He left the house early each day, he came home late; he gave a jovial wave hello and goodbye to the men he saw on the street. But those waves weren't enough to make him fit in. And it wasn't just the blue-collar job, the accent, the rough mannerisms, or the pants that rose just a little too high, showing just a little too much white sock.

My Dad had a superiority complex. Even when he saw all the men in the neighborhood leaving with briefcases while he was hauling huge white laundry bags, he pitied them for their corporate servitude, for not being their own boss. He'd shake his head, amazed at those poor louts, that their appointments during the day were in conference rooms all over Chicago, running a race against the clock, while he was his own man, his own boss. He answered to no one. His word was the law. Dad pitied those men their stuffy, practical company cars, all sedans, while he got in his station wagon each morning like it was a flying carpet. He loved driving, even to our laundry.

In the fall it was even more noticeable how different Dad was than the other neighborhood Dads.

One day our street was green and leafy, the leaves forming a canopy over the street so that everything was in shadows, and then the next day they turned brown and orange and gold, and then they fell - pounds and pounds of crashing leaves falling, fluttering, cascading until there was no street, no sidewalks, no bushes, no me.

The neighborhood Dads all decided to kill the fallen leaves, to burn them in great barrel drums, to smoke out the neighborhood. But not my father. He had to be different than the neighborhood Dads. He was a non-incinerator; he's a raker. He raked and raked. He raked the leaves to form miniscule piles, little continents of piles, piles within piles, piles intersecting piles. Then he combined his piles, dividing our yard into quadrants, the front half, the back half, and the two sides. Then he amalgamated them all together into a mountain of leaves, a pile bigger than our house, a pile I stood before in confusion, looking for him.

Then he bagged it just like he bagged our laundry. He stuffed and stuffed and stuffed some more until his garbage bag was bursting. When that bag was stuffed into our small steel garbage can, Dad condensed the leaves until they were mashed together, smaller and smaller, into a tinier and tinier space until they were one leaf, everyman's leaf, and it fluttered along behind the garbage truck rumbling through the alley, next to the garbage men hanging on to the edge of the truck; until one of them reached out to grab it and it was gone.

Mom also didn't fit in with the other neighborhood moms, though not as poorly as Dad did, and for different reasons. Unlike my Dad, my Mom had an inferiority complex, believing that her accent and foreign birth set her apart from all these American women. She knew she could look like them on the surface, but once she opened her mouth, the illusion was over. It wasn't just her accent; it was that she was also self-conscious. Mom doesn't just come out of the war with missing family, with a missing tooth; she was missing other essential things, like a sense of well being and of being right with the world that the other women had.

The biggest difference, however, between my Mom and the other neighborhood women was that my Mom spent her life downstairs in our laundry room at her sewing machine clutching a telephone between her ear and her shoulder and talking nonstop in Yiddish to every woman in our family while the ladies in our neighborhood lived outside their homes, marching like a parade in front of our picture windows. I looked out those picture windows like they were a crystal ball of my future and what I saw wasn't very inspiring.

There appeared to be two types of moms, and my Mom wasn't either type. Across the street, Mrs. Blum epitomized one kind. She sat on her front porch step in rollers, a housecoat, and worn slippers, her kids running circles around her, taking tired pulls from the cigarette in her hand, while saying, "Eli, Bella - children - stop your running." And then her sentence would peter out and she'd just sit there pensively smoking while Eli and Bella ran.

But that was just the first Mrs. Blum, the more tired Mrs. Blum and, as it turned out, the cancer-riddled Mrs. Blum. After she disappeared one day from the doorstep, dead of that cancer, her husband went back to Israel and married her younger, and nearly identical, sister, the second Mrs. Blum, and brought her home to fill that same spot on the doorstep.

Then there was the other extreme, the energetic Coco Raskin, also across the street, marching by our house in tiny high-heeled slippers, taking small steps so she wouldn't fall over, since her body was dangerously top heavy. Coco was shaped like an upside down pyramid, starting with a mass of fluffy blonde cloud hair teased so high that I could see through it. She had a jowly, over-made up face, breasts - three, maybe four of them - standing in the middle of her chest. Those breasts were cantilevered out by some miracle of engineering that ended in a sheer drop, a calamitous fall, off the edge of her square baby-bearing belly to her tiny prancing feet.

Coco marched down the sidewalk in those high-heeled slippers many times a day. Without a real job, she had two main tasks to attend to each day. One was to patrol the neighborhood in order to gather gossip for the evening's phone calls between all the ladies up and down the block - her sister lived at the other end and patrolled down there - and the other was to search for her tiny dog, which was forever running away. She'd call out his name in her raspy, cigarette smoke-ruined voice, a kitschy Jewish name like "Kugel," "Schnitzel," or "Strudel."

It would have been impossible for Mom to sit on our doorstep like either of the Mrs. Fishers, and even more impossible to imagine her with a cigarette drooping in her hand. She would never chase our dog down the street - she would have had to leave the house. And anyway, that's why she had the seven of us, so we could run down the street and chase the dog for her. We were our parents' emissaries out there, their English-speaking agents, leading the way in assimilating our family with the American neighbors.

Besides the garbage men and the garbage trucks, we, too, spent a lot of time in our alley just walking our dog. After a while, we noticed that what some of our neighbors considered garbage wasn't considered garbage to us.

Our garbage was real garbage, easy to identify. Food garbage. But our neighbors threw away things that were hardly used, even toys that looked better than those that had passed down to me through five older sisters. Chairs and games and workbooks barely filled out, and balls just because they had lost a little air, and crayons just because they had lost their points but weren't broken in half and still had paper wrapped around them.

One day, unbelievable for Skokie, we find is a little, frosted, white, plug-in Christmas tree with ornaments attached. The kind that blinks on and off, on and off, like a migraine headache, but cheery, reminding me every other second that it's there, lighting up the gloom of, let's say, a Holocaust-tainted household, with the opposite: merriment, forgetfulness, cheer.

Mindy and I take it out of the garbage and sneak it inside like a load of heroin. We haul it into the laundry room, and set it up on its little x-shaped wobbly wooden stand. We plug it in; it blinks on and off, on and off, just like it's supposed to. Why was it thrown out?

We know it's forbidden; we know that even though we're allowed to watch every Christmas special on TV, wondering later if Santa will bring gifts to Jewish kids who don't have chimneys, we know that a Christmas tree, no matter how small, is beyond the pale. We know we're Jewish and what *they* had done to *us* and all generations of *us* in perpetuity, and that we're supposed to stay Jewish - Christmas tree rejecters - to spite Hitler. Our parents, their accents strong, all their stories that stop in the middle, or don't stop in the middle, their sighing about what should have been, what could have been. That looming hatred of the enemy, and my confusion about who the enemy is. Is it every non-Jew?

While Mom is peeling potatoes, cracking eggs and crying over onions upstairs in the kitchen, Mindy and I fidget around her, hem and haw around her, trying to broach the subject of the Christmas tree. Just a piece of plastic and a plug, after all. Nothing more than that.

Finally I say, "Mom, we found this tiny little tree outside. It's just a tree with a plug, not a Christmas tree because those are big and green and this is just a tiny white tree and can we keep it?"

First, since she's barely listening to me and I'm being so oblique, she has no idea what I'm talking about. She gives her offhand permission, which I know won't stick once she realizes it's a Christmas tree. So I have to get more specific, saying, "Well, maybe it is a tiny Christmas tree, but hardly a real one at all because the lights are attached and it's just a foot tall."

Then she understands. She's adamant at first. No tree. Then she comes down the stairs to see the tree and likes it. She joins in on our secret, to keep it in the laundry room, to hide it from our grandmother, to let it blink on and off while she's sewing down there.

So we have a secret that winter, at least until the day Dad discovers it. Furious, he rips its cord from the wall, breaks it in half and stuffs it in a bag so none of our neighbors will see it, carrying it back out to the alley to the garbage, but puts it in Trudy Gordon's garbage can - her Christian garbage can - so no one will ever know.

We had some normal parks in Skokie, dotted here and there on the edges of streets, along major avenues, and then there were the ones that no one knew about except us kids on bikes, maybe even just those of us who were garbage pickers because of all the time we spent in the alleys. A park in the middle of a triangle alley, where three streets met, outlined by a chain link fence, a pile of old rusty, lead painted equipment eroding in the sun, just sitting there. All of us whooping and hollering with joy the first time we find it and each subsequent time we manage to re-find it, like it's Brigadoon and not always where we left it.

When I'm a kid, the playgrounds at the parks are sheer expanses of metal. The jungle gyms are metal hexagons, triangular formations exploding into the air. The monkey bars are horizontal ladders; the swings are flat metal shelves suspended from metal chain links. We have wooden, splintered seesaws with metal handles to jar one another and to boing our frog legs off the ground over and over again. There are spinning metal coasters. Here and there pieces are missing or are broken; there are sharp metal corners; there is rust.

One day Wendy Saltzman is swinging an empty swing back and forth, back and forth, when Mindy walks by too close. The flat metal swing hits her in the forehead and she falls to the ground in slow motion. Blood appears on her forehead from the cut that suddenly appears there and, just as quickly, we are running to get Mom, then running to the hospital, and then stitches are running across Mindy's forehead. This after we stand at the four corners of Mindy's hospital room cot holding down her limbs, which had tried to run away.

Afterwards the doctor stood, his fingers held apart just a hairsbreadth so we couldn't see air between them at all, and he said, "If that cut went a little deeper, if that swing hit her skull, she wouldn't have made it." And I know I've heard that before, that survival as a matter of whimsy, of accident, of death being so close but missing, still just an iota away.

Seven
Shopping Like An Eastern European

I'm fidgeting by the meat case at the Jewel Food Store on Dempster in Skokie near my Mom, standing on one foot then the other, listening but not listening, as she holds a detailed consultation with one of the butchers. He is hurried, harried, his apron is stained with blood, but my mother has all the time in the world. Nothing is more important than her leaving this store with good meat in her arms. I know this because this is one of my mother's core philosophies, that we must have good meat. That's why I have all hand-me-down clothes, why I share a dresser with three sisters, and why I'll soon be living in the basement, storing my clothes in the downstairs coat closet. This is why we rarely buy new cars. Food is our number one priority.

Mom asks the butcher, "Do you have any *flanken*?"

He looks confused. "*Flanken*?"

She rolls her eyes. Obviously she expects him to know Yiddish. Then she translates.

"Flank steak. Flank steak, in English."

My mother seems to think that everyone should know the Yiddish words for everything, even Christian butchers in the United States. And if they don't, they're anti-Semitic, probably Nazis.

"All out, Ma'am."

She heaves a sigh. "Well then, a nice brisket?"

He points to the far end of the meat case. "Briskets are over there, Ma'am."

"I'll pick one and you'll trim it up for me? Cut off some of the fat? And this," she hands him a sirloin roast, "I'd like sliced into steaks. Not too thick, not too thin. Oh --" And I watch him when she says this, waiting to see if he'll balk, "I'd like a few pounds of your left over beef fat. Just the scraps. No charge, right?"

Even though we eat bacon in our house, even though we're standing in the non-kosher meat department of a non-kosher grocery store, my mother still shops as if she's standing in the kosher butcher shop in the Old Country. Beef fat, indeed.

The butcher's brows draw together like he's about to ask her what on earth she needs a bunch of beef fat for but then, before he opens his mouth, he decides against it and nods.

My mother shopped for food like an Eastern European, which she was; like a person who nearly starved to death at one point in her life, which, of course, she nearly did.

Mom didn't know how to shop like an American. She didn't understand the concept of dessert. She didn't quite get packaged food. So she bought whole chickens, never chicken parts; she bought briskets, she bought egg noodles, she bought eggs; she bought loaves of bread and froze them. She liked to buy things in their pure form, or as close to their old country form as she could find them.

On the one hand, Mom was trying to become American as fast as she could. She knew the seven of us would have to be Twiggy-thin to attract American husbands and that her ultimate pride as a mother would be in marrying us off. On the other hand, her Eastern European hand, Mom had a deep emotional longing to see plump children, the better to ward of malnutrition for when the Nazi's come again. So which to have? Plump children or thin children? American-looking children or Eastern European-looking children? She ended up with a few of each, fat and thin.

She can never find any meat pre-cut or pre-packaged to her liking in any meat department anywhere. She always has to insistently ring the buzzer in the meat department in order to have a personal consultation with the butcher, waving her hands, making chopping motions, stirring motions, to punctuate her desires and her plans for the meat, and so they'll understand the cuts she wants. She can never make do with the *goyische* cuts of beef like ground or round; she needs the Jewish cuts like short ribs, the ever-present *flanken*, skirt steaks.

Once she gets home, Mom whittles the meat further down into something else. She sets up her heavy steel grinder on the edge of the counter, grinding the meat into tiny pellets until she's made her own ground beef, then mixes it by hand with eggs and breadcrumbs to make burgers. She puts some meat in a big wooden bowl and hacks away at it with a short meat cleaver until she's tenderized her own steaks. My Mom has to actually touch the meat, get in the bowl with the meat, stomp around with the meat. She has to transform the meat from its original form into something better. She makes meat into magic.

She doesn't trust the butchers at the supermarket to do any of this for her, not in their white aprons, behind their glass window, not with their union that lets them shut down the whole meat department well before the rest of the grocery store closes, casting that whole end of the store into darkness. Mom grew up with Jewish ritual slaughterers, not just a union, a closing time, and they're gone, like these Americans.

It's impossible for them to understand that to her it's not just food - it's spiritual. If she believed in God, He'd look like a steak in heaven.

"If they had starved in the forest like I did," she tells me after one of these encounters, "they wouldn't be throwing away so much perfectly good food."

Because it turns out that even fat is food to us, it's not garbage. Beef fat mixed with flour, sugar and sautéed onions, and then stuffed in casing, makes kishke, a staple of our holiday diet.

We get our packages, all in white-wrapped butcher paper, and head down the other aisles. I look scornfully at the other shoppers in their housecoats, their hair in curlers. My mom is dressed in the height of fashion, even though she sews her own clothes. She's wearing a brown corduroy jumper with a paisley blouse underneath and crinkly, wet-look boots that zip up the side. She has on a short frosted wig that normally sits on one of the wig stands in our upstairs bathroom. She's wearing the wig because she's between her regular hair appointments and had no time to take out her pick and force her hair into a floating halo around her head. Since there was no time, she slapped the wig on her head, jumped in her jumper, and out we went.

I am also dressed in the height of style, for a ten-year-old in 1970. Mom, thank goodness, doesn't make my clothes, so I'm wearing my favorite outfit from my favorite store, Turn Style: red, white, and blue pinstriped pants with a boy-slide fly, and a red, white, and blue balloon-sleeved blouse. My stripes are all vertical going down my body so that I look like a visual disturbance as I walk beside the cart on my way through the store. In the freezer aisle, I break up the visual line by throwing my favorite piece of clothing over my head - my tan-colored, suede, fringed poncho. It lies heavily on my shoulders during the rest of the shopping trip but I keep it on anyway: I know I look cool.

Although World War II had ended by the time I was born, apparently no one had told my mother. She was still hoarding chickens, storing loaves of bread, and freezing pots of soup, all against the starvation that could return at any time. She filled our freezer and refrigerator with nondescript bulk packages, with poultry arms and legs and beef tongues, all protruding from butcher-wrapped packaging, so that a peek inside our freezer resembled a frosty slaughterhouse. No ice cream bars in there, no Popsicles, just the staples: soup, chicken and bread, like she ate growing up in the old country.

She only bought the big categories of food - proteins and starches, and then nothing that had been processed. These were the foods that would fill a person up during a cold Lithuanian winter, even though we were in Chicago. These were the foods that would keep a person alive in the forest if, say, Nazi bullets were going to whiz over your head for a few years, forcing you to live in underground shelters, forcing your teeth to rot from malnutrition, forcing your toes to freeze and then turn different colors from gangrene. Just in case.

I'd come home from school starving for a snack and check the refrigerator. Nothing. Well, two apples, a dish of cucumbers floating in vinegar, which was Dad's appetizer for the dinner he'd eat later than us each evening, and a big, double-handled pot of clear soup, nothing floating in it at all, just soup. For the life of me, I couldn't imagine why anyone would make soup with nothing in it. Disgusted, I'd move on.

I'd go over to the cabinets. No crackers, no chips, no snack foods. I'd peer into the cereal boxes. All the charms had been eaten out of the Lucky Charms and all the raisins out of the Raisin Bran. I'd open the broom closet where there was a nail on which we hung salamis and, sure enough, there was always a shrunken, shriveled, kosher salami hanging there on a twisted cord. I'd file this away in my brain as a potential source of food, and then go back to the refrigerator, bracing myself as I opened the freezer.

After the blast of cold air clears, I'd find that wall of butcher-wrapped packages – meat and more meat – in the freezer, and behind those, more of those, and maybe one or two packages defrosting in the sink for Dad's elaborate dinners. If I wasn't too hungry to wait, I could grab Mom's dull carving knife, use it as a chisel, carve out some frozen soup from the freezer, throw it into one of the dented pans she stored in the unlit oven, and wait for it to melt. There was nothing to eat in this house that wouldn't take a week to defrost.

Finally, defeated, I'd go back to the broom closet for the salami that, in our house, qualified as a snack food. I'd slice off a few pieces with the knife Mom keeps forever, having Dad sharpen it on another knife, its blade worn down to a sliver, and that would be my after school snack.

We continue our grocery shopping, a battle in every aisle.

We fight over breakfast foods.

"What for do you need special food for breakfast?" she asks.

I learn that in the Old Country, breakfast wasn't different from any other meal: an onion and a dry piece of black bread. And if she doesn't understand the cereal thing, she's never going to understand the prize in the bottom of the box thing.

In the produce department, she can't stand wasting money on things that they used to grow for free in the Old Country, like fruit and vegetables. So she buys sparingly, leaving the seven of us to fight over a few apples.

Mom has adopted a few American foods into her repertoire, but just for convenience and just enough to get through the seven lunches she has to make each day in the days before hot lunches: Oscar Mayer beef bologna, Campbell's tomato soup, and Holsum bread. From these she will not waver. When Spaghetti-Os suddenly appear in the grocery store I beg, plead, and whine in the canned food aisle, but she holds firm, marches past me. After all, she knows noodles, and these are not any noodles she's ever seen. Egg noodles are noodles.

My parents used a mixture of English and Yiddish to refer to the food on our plates, creating a pidgin form of English, a patois, with which I ventured forth from our home to my friends' homes to eat meals. In our house we never heard the terms "leg" or "wing" when discussing chicken parts, just *polka* and *fleagle*. Potato pancakes were *latkes*, stuffed cabbage were *kapushnikas*.

At my best friend Linda Winkler's house for dinner one night, I appear to be a normal American child. I was dressed like other American children and I spoke English with no accent. There was no reason to believe, as I sat down at the table, that English was my second language.

Then dinner is served and it's chicken. To chat with me, Mrs. Winkler asks me what my mother cooks for dinner and what my favorite meal is.

I say, "Well, I like chicken bread a lot." Apparently, even *I* hadn't understood my mother's accent when she pronounced a dish "chicken breast."

Mrs. Winkler looks puzzled and she's not the kind of mom who gets sweetly puzzled; she gets irritated.

She says, "Chicken bread? I've never heard of that dish." She looks over at Mr. Winkler. "Sidney, Linda Burt's mother makes 'chicken bread.' Have you ever heard of that?"

"No Sheila, I haven't," he says. "Maybe we should ask Linda Burt more about it."

I hated when they called me by my whole name, over and over again, "Linda Burt this" and "Linda Burt that." They referred to me as "Linda Burt" and their daughter Linda as "Our Linda," so that the conversation became peppered with constant "Linda Burts" and "Our Lindas" until even I got mixed up about which one I was.

Then Mr. Winkler looked over at me, his eyeglasses shining in the light so I couldn't see his eyes. He said, "Is it bread or is it chicken, Linda?"

By then I was frozen in my seat by all this attention. I

mumbled, “I’m not sure,” so Mrs. Winkler moved on to offering me a piece of the chicken she had made, telling me to pick whichever piece I’d like.

With my best manners I said, “May I have a *polka*, please?” Her forehead creased again. She looked over at Mr. Winkler then back at me. I didn’t even know I was speaking Yiddish.

“What?” Mr. Winkler was now handling all communication with the foreign girl.

I tried again before he could answer. “Well, a *fleagle* is fine too.”

When Mrs. Winkler looked at me like I’d fallen off a spaceship and even Weenie Weenie Winkler, Linda’s nerdy brother, was suppressing laughter, I realized that I’d been booby-trapped by my parents. I didn’t even know the English words for chicken leg or wing. My parents had left me stumbling outside in the real world. Stumbling even in another Jewish household.

Finally I was forced to use a combination of pantomime and charades as Mrs. Winkler pointed to each piece of chicken on the plate. She came to the leg. I nodded.

***

We spent our lives shopping at Turn Style, a Walmart-style store located in Skokie, sweeping in there at least once a week, planning on a long stay. After all, we had a lot of territory to cover. First there was the sheer volume of us - Mom, the cart, the gang of us straggling along. We’d pass by the Brach’s candy display and Mom would grab a few candies, like they were free. Then we’d fan out. I’d go to the Barbie aisle, Sherry and Denise to the record album department, Mindy over to baby dolls. There were enough departments for everyone. There was Home and Garden, Home Fashions, Foundation Garments, Women’s

Fashions, and even Fabrics, where I knew Mom could disappear for hours.

The first time Mom lost me shopping I thought it was a pretty big deal. I had started off having a good time. I was alternating between the Barbie aisle and the Liddle Kiddle aisle and had gathered up enough in my arms to nag Mom into buying me maybe one or two dolls because I already knew the fine art of negotiation - start high and end low. But after a while, even I was bored with the dolls; even I started looking around thinking that I'd had enough time alone in the toy aisles.

But Mom didn't show up. I started wandering blindly through the store, like Helen Keller, careening from area to area, looking for her among the bolts of fabric in Sewing, among the swinging polyester pants in Fashion, through the daisy-patterned Corning Ware in Housewares. But no Mom. I started crying and calling for her down each aisle until finally some other grown up took me by the hand and led me off to customer service at the front of the store. There I milled about with all the other lost children whose mothers had gotten too caught up in bargain-priced shopping and lost their children too.

When it was my turn up at the counter, the weary store clerk fired up the microphone, and tapped on it, saying, "Testing, testing." She looked down at me with a bored expression on her face, and asked me my mother's name, which I said with a sob, "Helen Burt," like it was the name of my now-defunct mother, my disappeared mother, like maybe I was savoring the collection of consonants that made up her name on my lips one last time.

The clerk paged my mother and, that first time she lost me, Mom showed up there in an instant, like I'd conjured her up. My sisters showed up too, hearing Mom's name across the intercom, appearing from various nooks and crannies around the store, and then we were all there, walking towards check out the way we walked in, the cart piled high with striped pants, balloon sleeved shirts with pointy collars, and identical clothes for me and Sherry, the fake twins. We checked out, zooming past the Brach's display one more time, where Mom stole more candy, and we left.

From then on, losing me is just what Mom does. It's intentional and it's not just me. She shops alone, like a wolf, and she expects all of us to shop alone too. One of us is expected to eventually make our way to customer service, like it's our family's paging service, and that intercom announcement calling her to the front of the store is the call for all of us to rendezvous at the front of the store and make our way to the check out stand. We all shop alone this way, like solitary hunters.

My mother has several annoying shopping habits. Of course there's the way she eats all the Brach's candy in the front of the store without paying for it, like the store is providing hors d'oeuvres for its customers. There's the way that she eats something in a grocery store until there's nothing left but the package and then she pays for the empty package, like she's some kind of ravenous animal who can't wait to eat until after we pay. This is a big problem when the item she's eaten has to be weighed, like an apple, and she just has the core left. There is, of course, the issue of her losing me all the time at Turn Style. But one of the worst things about shopping with Mom is the way she forces me to try on clothes.

Here's what she does. We're in the kids' clothes section at Turn Style, perhaps in front of a square, deep display table piled with my favorite red, white, and blue striped pants. And perhaps

I'm wearing shorts. Mom picks up a pair of pants and they appear to be my size, at least as much as she can tell by holding them up first horizontally and then vertically and hemming and hawing over them.

And then it comes. Her demand. "Linda, mameleh, you need to try them on."

Well, now, this is exciting – to try something on. So I look around for the elusive dressing room sign because I'm already ten-years-old and I have these little flat breast bud things on my chest and who knows what's going on around the rest of my body? Maybe a pubic hair is growing in. So of course I need a dressing room. But my Mom doesn't know from dressing rooms and she has no intention to discover them at that late date in her shopping career. She also is not going to leave her outpost there in children's clothes, her shopping cart full of things that she's fought out of the hands of other women, to schlep me all the way to some dressing room on the other side of the store.

So she holds open the pants, scrunching up one pant leg into a miniscule cuff so I can slip my foot into it and boom, the one leg is on and then the other and somehow - I'm not sure how - she's gotten my shorts off me at the same time and the next thing I know I'm standing in the middle of the store wearing the pants.

I couldn't resist these scrunched up pants legs that my mother held up to me. I had been slipping my legs into them my whole life. I would have put my leg into one made of hot lava, I trust her so well. It's pure instinct. As I head into adolescence, my mother's practically stripping me naked in the middle of Turn Style as if we're invisible and all the other shoppers are blind. I'd stand there, shirts thrown over my head, culottes shimmied up over my hips, training bras somehow fastened around my chest, and Mom would cast a critical eye at me - her judgment was infallible. She'd say, "Perfect," then strip them off me, and we'd add them to the cart.

I am standing in line inside the bookmobile sitting in the park near my house and clutching my cardboard library card. Other kids are on the see saw, on the jungle gym, and on the dangerous metal swings, but I have left the sunshiny park to stand in the dim interior of the bookmobile and check out another Henry Huggins book. We don't have any books at home, just a pile of Dad's hidden *Man* magazines, a bunch of Chicago Daily News', and textbooks that my sisters have forgotten to return to our elementary school.

Eventually the books I check out will be returned late just like all the other books I take out, the fees of five cents a day stacking up, unpaid until Mom cracks open her mysterious purse and pays up. She never could seem to get me to the Skokie Public Library to return these books on time nor could she figure out when the bookmobile will be arriving again at this park. Anyway, Mom seems to have some idea that I should make off with the books, that it's a pretty good bargain even for the lost book fee, which she has no intention of paying.

She says, "So we'll lie and get cards in other names!" but I'm mortified; I beg and plead to go to the library to return the books, eventually sneaking them onto the librarian's desk, too embarrassed to explain why the books haven't been brought back sooner.

Our house ends up filled with stolen library books, purloined textbooks entrusted to our care from our homeroom teachers, pilfered musical instruments on loan from the school's music department never to be returned. By 1968 we have a cello, a flute, a trombone, and several violins. The music teacher is just lucky that I take up piano and that even Mom would have found it a little cumbersome to wheel the rickety piano out of the school's basement music room and down all the streets of Skokie to get it home. And also, lucky for them, we already have one.

Mom seems to think that America is full of wonders; that there's free stuff available at your corner elementary school for the taking. To Mom, this is not stealing. She seems to consider it a matter of civic duty to outsmart schools, stores, public swimming pools, government officials and all civil authorities. Things are just owed to her. They are Holocaust reparations.

There's more than just the issue of "do not steal" that Mom doesn't understand. She doesn't understand the concept of getting us to school on time, marching us in any old time she wants, as if seven-year-olds can be fashionably late for spelling. And she doesn't understand the American concept of parental involvement. She doesn't attend recitals, performances or graduations, all the way from kindergarten through high school. She's always busy with something else, something unavoidable; something that has her tied to the house - like if she left she'll dissolve into a million tiny pieces, a figment of our imagination.

Eventually, the stealing gets carried away. Here and there, my sisters are driven home in police cars when they're caught shoplifting, the neighbors watching us from behind the curtains at their front picture windows. One sister is babysitting a neighborhood kid one night when she lets a friend in the house and he steals the mother's credit cards, causing some kind of police investigation. Then there's the run of the mill stuff that, to me, just seems routine: forging notes from Mom authorizing my sisters to buy cigarettes at the corner drug store, forging notes excusing them from school. I had very grown up handwriting by third grade.

I have an ingenious criminal mind from a young age. I decide I want one of those Pillsbury Dough Boys so I write to Pillsbury and claim, in my grown up handwriting, that I'd sent payment some time back and where was my Dough Boy? They face me down, stating they had no record of my payment. Another time I write to Marvel Comics telling them I am too poor to buy comic books but I'd seen kids at school reading them, specifically the Archie comic book series, and did they have any old ones they could send me? I come home one day to a two-foot stack waiting beside our door wrapped in shipping paper.

I'm particularly obsessed with comic books, and Archie comic books in particular, because of their depiction of teenage life. Somehow, inside of me, I think my life will be like that of the comic book characters when I get to be a teen. Really, I'm just hoping I end up as curvaceous as Betty and Veronica, that someone - maybe God? - will draw me like that, with a pert sloped nose, big vacuous blue eyes, and fashionable hair up or down or in a thousand curls. I hope I'll have that tiny waist and ten thousand miles of legs beneath it and a bosom that stands so high that some mornings I won't even be able to see over it, and that I'll need a bra to hold those breasts down instead of to hold them up. And a head emptied of the Holocaust.

So, even though I was a quick study, even though I had been trained at Mom's War Reparations School of Thievery, I got arrested early, at age twelve, as an accomplice to Linda Winkler, even though I didn't know what the word accomplice meant. I had gone from being a nice little girl who bought blue daisies for my mother at the corner flower shop on my way home from school each day, to riding in the back of a police car.

Before The Paper Place opened up in the two empty store spaces next door to the flower shop in 1970, I was just a small-time shoplifter. I'd steal candy from the Skokie Pharmacy and watch as the owner's wife, Mrs. Rosenberg, wrote down everything I took and added it to Mom's account. Surprisingly, I never heard about any of this from Mom. She just paid the bill.

Of course, we had a long history with this drug store. It was run by the elderly Rosenbergs and their middle-aged son, also a pharmacist. His son, the youngest Rosenberg, just out of pharmacy school, got a Ford Maverick like he could escape from the pharmacy and from his fate in it. It was lime green with a checkered cloth top and a curly-qued behind - up to date, the newest thing.

There were three generations of the Rosenbergs then, all pharmacists, all as alike as if they were looking in a magical aging mirror, a curmudgeon time machine, but only one wife among them. The elderly Mr. Rosenberg got bone cancer but kept on working, though pieces of him were soon missing: no leg, no hair. The elderly Mr. Rosenberg's days were numbered, then his legs were numbered – two then one, then he's gone.

My shoplifting was under control when it was just the Skokie Pharmacy. How many bags of pistachio nuts could I eat, after all? But when The Paper Place opened, I was overcome, helpless over my desire to have everything in the store.

Brimming with paper dresses, smiley face stickers, paisley journals, feather pens, and Peter Max posters, the store was a cornucopia of hippie-era *tchotchkes.* There was no way my haphazard allowance could cover purchases. Dad's theory on allowances was that since the time he had begun to work, he had always handed over every cent he earned to his parents, so what for did I need money? Wasn't there food on the table, a roof over our heads? That left me with stealing money out of Mom's wallet - one of seven girls doing this with her tacit approval - so by the time I got around to it each day there was nothing left. There were two options left - I could stop wanting or start stealing.

I was sure it was okay to want. In my family, we were professional wanters, having been taught to want by our mother who wanted to be American, to be blonde, to be thin, to never be hungry again.

Hours after we were caught, after Linda was picked up at the Skokie Police station by a shrieking Sheila Winkler and I was picked up by my sister Francine, I was hiding in our basement waiting for Dad to come home to mete out my punishment.

I thought of the punishments he'd given so far in our lives. I'd seen him hit, I'd seen him threaten to take his belt off and whip, I'd seen him chase Lauren up the stairs that time, break down the door to the bathroom, and nearly kill her. He had two punishment personas, either impassive in his recliner, a newspaper with legs, or chasing us in a murderous rage. The good thing was that my sisters were all still alive, ignoring me as they walked past the staircase to the basement. None of them had died at Dad's hands yet.

He came home, his silhouetted figure passing back and forth in front of the stairwell. He didn't yell or threaten to take off his belt. Instead, he was scornful, disgusted, thinking nothing of me at all.

There were other thieves in the world besides me. It was especially onerous to me when someone stole from me, taking my purple Schwinn bicycle when I was six. At least there should have been honor among thieves.

It was a special bike - I knew that. When I rode down the street on its nubby fat black tires, steady and fast, I knew it was. When I looked at the color, just the right purple, not too red and not too black, I knew it was. When I felt its heft, hauling it around like a foal, edging it inside our one-car garage at night next to my sisters' yellow ten speeds, feeling the weight of that frame, I knew it was.

When it was time to register the bike at our elementary school, I did, weaving in and out of the concourse of orange cones, to prove what a master rider I was. I rode home validated, certified, licensed, sealed.

It got stolen anyway. One time, in a rush, I laid it down outside the house and ran inside. It lay there supine, purple, its glitter banana seat gleaming under the Chicago sky, the tall handlebars waving to passersby.

I came back and it was gone. The bike, the serial number, the glittery banana seat, the perfect purple. I got a replacement, which, just like all replacements, was never quite the same. It was a blue Schwinn, and not a perfect shade of blue, a little too blue. Although it had the same heft, a glitter banana seat, and a set of come hither handlebars, it could never erase the memory of the first bike.

Because I had registered the purple one so well, it showed up again, or at least the frame did, its registration number etched on it that day at my elementary school. The seat was now the small two-tone one from a dorky, fendered, three-speed Schwinn. The handlebars were big, spread out, one going north, the other west. It was jacked up, souped up, on stilts. I tried to tame this rodeo pony but it was now a bike on hormones, a jacked up megalo-bike. I rode down the street on it - or it rode me - and it was impossible to hang on, the handlebars went one way, the wheels another; the seat was askew. It was like riding a unicycle.

It was good to have a few bike riding options each day because I loved to ride away from my house. When I was overdone, inundated, overcooked, hardboiled, I could ride away. When I couldn't listen anymore to Lithuania, to Poland, I could stand up, walk out, ride and ride and ride, down the street, down all the streets. I could ride away from the railroad crossing of our hallway that the Allies should have bombed to save the Jews. Ride away from the Poland, Russia, and Lithuania of the three upstairs bedrooms. Ride from the forest stretching out behind and around the Krivich of our house, towering over everything else. Look, no hands, no eyes, no ears, no touch, no sight, no sound.

I could ride the normal bike each day, the wheels in perfect alignment, the wind blowing through my hair, wondering if any moment would ever be as perfect as this one again. Or I could ride the bike that once was stolen, try to hang on like a bucking bronco, show my skill by staying in the saddle, and hope there were no sudden emergencies that might force me to dismount, fling myself off, and let the bike go crashing into a fence. It had no brakes.

Let's put it this way: Linda Winkler was stuck with a Huffy but I always rode a Schwinn.

Eight
The Forest

When my mother talks about her life before the war, she talks a lot about school. The political history of Krivich can be tracked in her educational history as a young girl.

When she was little, since the Krivich Jewish community was too small to support its own Hebrew School, she attended Polish schools. She doesn't remember any prejudice from that time, just learning alongside her Catholic classmates, except for one important fact - all the Jewish students received one letter grade lower than all the non-Jewish students, no matter the quality of their work. This was no accident, she tells me, and not a reflection of the work being produced. The Polish school system was designed to keep Jews out of higher education.

When the Russians took over in 1939 the schools changed. The education became rigorous, with schooling taking place six days a week and including the Jewish Sabbath, and the prejudicial grading ended. The teachers that the Russians brought in, besides being more demanding, were also quite adamant about their state-sponsored Atheism. There was no God and that was that. My mother had endless arguments with them about how wrong they were, how there was a God up above and she knew it; conversations she recalls now, wistful at her naiveté, at her youth, at her faith.

The third phase of my mother's school memories start when the Nazis marched into Krivich in 1941. The schooling stopped, at least for the Jewish students since Jews were no longer allowed to attend school. My mother and her sister and brother went to a house in the ghettoized part of town every day to sit there all day long, watchful and wary, with nothing to do but play cards. My grandmother would bring them there on her way to a work detail to clean an officer's rooms, each day leaving my mother with these words, "Chasia, if shooting starts, you're big enough - run to the forest."

Of course, there was more to this pre-war life than education. There was the tiny town itself, with just several hundred Jews, its wooden houses and dirt streets unchanged for centuries. There were no cars in Krivich, no movie theaters, no restaurants, and no hotels; people there owned horses with wagons, and barns for the horses behind their homes. There was a train station but it was five miles outside of town. The most modern thing my mother's family had was my grandfather's bicycle, which she knew how to ride before the war, but didn't know how afterwards. My mother alone disproves the belief that a person never forgets how to ride a bicycle.

She lived in the center of town in a house built the year before she was born, in 1929, and which cost seven hundred dollars, money her grandfather's brother sent from New York. Originally built out of logs, a few years later the exterior was planked in to cover up the logs and give it a more modern look.

Every Thursday there was a market in the center of town, which was right in front of my mother's house; but out in back stretched five acres consisting of vegetable gardens, an orchard, a barn with horses, cows, chickens, and turkeys and a pond with ducks. The inside of the house held two bedrooms. One was for my mother's family, who slept in two large beds along with a crib for my Uncle Herbie, and the other was for her Aunt Chaya, Chaya's husband Itzche Velvel, and their small son. My great grandfather Mordechai slept in the living room where there was also a high worktable at which my grandfather and Itzche Velvel, both shoemakers, worked all day.

My Mom says this was a luxurious house, a grand house by Krivich standards but, when pressed, she admits there was no heating, no cooling, no plumbing, and no running water. There was an outhouse set away from the house and chamber pots within each bedroom. There was a wood stove in the kitchen and a stove in the corner of the living room just for heating and which was kept burning year round. They had basins for daily washing and a tub for the bath she took once a week, my grandmother boiling water at the wood stove to fill it.

The house was right next door to that of a Polish policeman whose son she used to play with but most of the time she played with her little girlfriends, some of whom ended up surviving the war as well, women who grew old on opposite sides of the world from her. They played on the tire wagons at the fire department nearby; they collected broken shards in a field nearby and other treasures they could find, collecting them and pretending they had retail stores. One time her father went to a larger nearby town and bought her a doll head and hands and feet; then my grandmother made the body and attached them all and my mother had her first and last doll.

My mother isn't very animated when she tells me about her pre-war life. She tells me about it with no spark, in a droning tone. She has to be prodded for details, for specificity; she calls me again and again with more mundane details she forgot to tell me each time we talk. This is different than when she tells me about the war years, where it's like a film playing in her memory all the time; the conversations run in there, intact, verbatim, like she was taping them. It's hard for her to talk about any of the innocence of the pre-war time without mentioning what happened afterwards, and what happened to all those people afterwards. Her story is lackluster; it's hard to scoop it up, to understand Krivich as a real place before 1941, before the Nazis. But I'm not going to be able to get any closer to it than she can.

There is this one rueful thing she does remember. My grandmother had a dream for my mother. She wanted her to leave Krivich when she grew up and go to America, to her Uncle Izzy and her cousin Miriam, and get an education. My Mom shared in that dream, the dream of getting to America, the dream of the exciting, unknown future. She gets there, but she doesn't know that first she'll have to leap over the Nazis.

The pivotal events of my mother's life are these: One day in September 1941, an army of Nazis marched into Krivich. Unlike most of the other towns they marched into all over Eastern Europe, once they finished counting the Jews and tabulating the Jews, interviewing the Jews and stealing all of their belongings, they decided not to transport them. Instead, after living among them for seven months, making the ghettoized normal the new normal, they murdered them there.

Krivich was a tiny town with so few Jews they tended to marry within the community, so when my mother's parents married each other, their siblings, my grandmother's brother, Itzche Velvel, and my grandfather's sister, Chaya, married each other too and lived in my mother's house along with their small son, and with my great-grandfather, Mordechai.

The family I knew growing up, consisting of my grandfather and grandmother, then Yankef and Goldie Katzowitz, and my mother, her sister and brother, and those family members I never met, all hid in a crawl space above their kitchen for two and a half days during the first massacre, in April 1942. The Nazis had been in Krivich seven months by the morning they stormed the ghetto. Some people had felt the massacre coming that day. They could feel the change in the air; there were no regular sounds, the soldiers weren't at their regular duties. My mother saw the Nazi soldiers striding toward their house wearing black jodhpurs. She told her parents they were coming, giving the family time to hide in a crawl space above their kitchen. The soldiers entered the house, saw nothing alive inside but a cat, and so they killed it.

Some of the Jews the Nazis found in town they killed execution style, but most were gathered outside of town, after first being told to hand over all their hidden wealth to the soldiers. When none was forthcoming, the soldiers beat, raped and tortured them for hours. Towards evening they put the rest of them in a barn, hundreds and hundreds of Jews. Then they nailed up the windows and doors and burned them alive.

This all happened the first day, when my mother's family was hiding in the crawl space, a howling wind covering the noise that her little cousin made and that of her grandfather, who was rambling in his old age. At the end of that day, the town glowed with fire and when it was done burning, they knew everyone was gone. They came out into a different Krivich.

The Nazis were happy not to have killed my grandfather and my great Uncle Itzche Velvel. They were shoemakers after all, and the Nazis had a lot of boots that needed work after marching and murdering their way across Europe. They allowed both of them to be a slave laborers, repairing those boots, until right after Yom Kippur, October 1942, when they decided to kill the rest of the Jews of Krivich.

There was something about the Nazi's choices of dates for these massacres – April and October, Passover and Yom Kippur – that makes it more difficult for my mother later. She especially has a hard time with Yom Kippur, with the idea that all these people massacred so soon after the holiday somehow weren't written in the Book of Life, like their deaths were somehow meant to be. This is unacceptable to her, and a god who would do this is unacceptable as well.

In October the Nazis picked another form for their massacre. They lined the remaining Jews of Krivich in two lines. They stood there, my mother worrying over the lines. Should she switch lines? In her line were just two small families - hers, consisting of her mother, father, sister and brother, and the family of the town tailor. In the other line were the remaining Jews of the town, along with the other members of her family, her tiny cousin, her much-loved aunt, uncle and grand-father. *This close* I came to switching lines, she tells me sixty years later, stunned by her brush with death.

Her line was released to return to their homes. The other line, the tiny fragment of the Jews of Krivich who hadn't been killed in the April massacre, including that tiny fragment of my mother's family, were confined in a house that my mother and grandmother watched all that day and evening, waiting for something to happen.

And finally something did happen. Later that evening, a German soldier with a good pitching arm walked over and stood in the road some distance from the house. He took a grenade off his belt, pulled the pin out of the grenade, and threw the grenade in a looping arc toward the house. It hit and the house exploded.

I have always been told that because my grandfather was a shoemaker and the Nazis needed him to repair boots and shoes, they kept him alive; that it was because of this that the family wasn't killed. But then my Mom tells me that Itzche Velvel was also a shoemaker, and then I don't understand, because Itzche Velvel and his family were killed.

I say, "You mean that the Nazis didn't know that Itzche Velvel was a shoemaker?"

But my Mom says, "No, they knew everyone's occupation."

So I say, "You mean that the Nazis knew that Zayda was a more skilled shoemaker than Itzche Velvel? That's why they kept Zayda alive and killed Itzche Velvel?"

And she says, "No. Itzche Velvel was a better shoemaker than my father."

And the ramification of this hounds me because I always

thought there in that last line they were in, that last *selection*, there was some reason for my mother's family surviving. Of course they were spared - my grandfather was needed to fix shoes. But if there were two shoemakers and the Nazis knew it, and one was more highly skilled than the other, and the Nazis knew that too, then not even that mattered. It was a complete whim. A Nazi soldier's finger points this way or it points that way and one family lives and another dies. *This* close we came to dying.

My mother carries the image of the exploding house with her through every dogged step of her life from that moment on. The horror of that sight froze her there, in that village, on that dirt road, for the rest of her life. Asleep or awake, my mother is locked in that one central scene of her life, a frozen film frame.

With the Jewish population of Krivich down to two families and the boots and uniforms that need repairing dwindling, my mother already knew their days were numbered. A Christian neighbor warned them, telling them that in three days the Nazis were planning to kill the two remaining families.

By this time, my grandparents were a little shell-shocked. They had just seen their siblings murdered; my grandfather had seen his father die. They had witnessed two massacres of everyone they had ever known. Maybe their minds had snapped a little in all the horror.

But my mother's hadn't. Then eleven-years-old, she went to them after the neighbor left and said, "We aren't going to wait here to be killed, are we?" And when she tells me what she said, she always gives me her exact words in Yiddish even though it's been over six decades. She said, "If we don't run away tonight,

I'm going to run screaming outside this house right up to that soldier out there holding the machine gun and let him shoot me," and she motioned to the window. And so my grandparents woke up from their stupor, alerted the tailor's family and they left that night.

It wasn't easy to run away from a Nazi-occupied town when there were just a few Jewish families left and one Nazi soldier was guarding each house; patrolling that house, from front to back, back to front, circling the house. But in the middle of the night they snuck out their back door, barefoot, because they knew the Nazis would be suspicious of shoe prints in the snow but not of bare footprints, since the Polish beggars were often barefoot. And so they left, barefoot, their shoelaces tied around their necks, the shoes suspended like necklaces. They met up with the tailor, Binyomin, and his family, in the miles and miles of hills stretching out behind their village and headed to the forest.

Since they ran away from Krivich with no real plan to do so, a lot of things went wrong. My mother's family, which included her parents, her four-year-old brother Herbie (then known as Chaim) and her eight-year-old sister Reva, left Krivich walking straight toward the forest over hills that had been cleared for crops. There was no plant covering, nothing to hide them. All the Nazis had to do was spot them, take aim and shoot. But somehow, their disappearance wasn't discovered or not discovered while they were still within shooting distance, and so they continued walking over these barren hilly fields on their way to the forest.

My grandfather and Binyomin, the tailor from Krivich, were in charge of the major decisions for the two families, but since my grandfather had spent his life making and repairing shoes, and Binyomin had spent his life making and repairing clothes, they weren't very experienced in running from their village, in how to get from here to there, and how to avoid getting killed.

Their first instinct was just to put as much distance between their families and Krivich as possible, so they walked away, in a straight line through the forest, due east. They walked east when they should have been walking west, and they walked during the day when they should have been walking at night. Somehow the Nazis didn't see them, the collaborating farmers didn't see them, the villagers didn't see them; no one ran to alert the authorities. So the two families covered a lot of ground in their fear and inexperience. They were hoping to find other Jews living in the forest somewhere, people they could live among, share information with; people among whom they could survive the war.

They continued walking for three weeks without finding any other Jews. The weather was getting colder than they expected since it was May and summer should have been coming. That's when they realized they were going in the wrong direction; they were walking straight into Russia. They stopped and made a plan. They decided that the men would take five days and circle back around Krivich to see if they could find some Jews in the forest there. They left the women and children hidden at the place they had walked to, near some water that they could use for drinking and cooking.

It took the men ten days. Even though they were traveling light, and without their families, they still were covering ground that had taken them three weeks to walk before. My mother, my grandmother, Binyomin's wife and her older daughters thought the men had been caught and shot. Circling back to Krivich! How had they agreed to that? And what were they going to do now that the men were dead?

The women were staying in the agreed-upon place, waiting for the men just in case they weren't dead, in case they did show up by some miracle, when, one day, they were discovered by a boy from a nearby town. The boy saw them and then ran away but the women were sure he was going to alert the authorities that there were Jews hiding in the forest. So they ran in the opposite direction, going five miles further, hiding deeper in the forest, hiding from their hiding place. They were no longer where my grandfather and Binyomin would expect to find them.

Then, of course, my grandfather and Binyomin returned and found no one there. Like a macabre Romeo and Juliet, they thought their families had been caught and perhaps killed, but they were all there, looking for each other, five miles apart. My grandfather decided that since there was water nearby and everyone has to have water, he and Binyomin would stay there, hidden away, and that when the women came to get water then men would find them.

A few days later, Binyomin's daughter Leah, who was killed just months later by the Nazis, killed behind a tree where she was hiding, along with her mother, a sister and her brother when Binyomin decided to hide from the Nazis instead of run, this daughter was creeping out of her hiding place, going to get water, and they all reunited.

They made their way backwards then; back to the forest that stretched out behind Krivich, which was also part of the vast forest that covered Poland, Lithuania, and Russia, with the Soviets at one end and the Nazis at the other. They went back among the other Jews and the Partisans who were hiding in that forest, back there to spend the winter.

Things had seemed tough already for the two families when the men had gone back around Krivich, circling the town, looking for other Jews living in the forest. Things seemed tough when the women and children had walked the extra five miles to hide from the little boy who spotted them, and anyone else he might have alerted because, after all, at that time and in that place, it was illegal to be a Jew. Even a little boy could get you killed.

Things had seemed pretty tough to my mother while she sat there hidden with my grandmother and Sarah, Binyomin's wife, crying, wailing and worrying about how they would live without the men if they were dead. How would they get through the coming winter?

But then the men and women were reunited and the winter came.

My mother says that by this time she had no shoes. The shoes she had tied around her neck when they snuck out of their house the night they ran away from Krivich couldn't withstand the three-week walk in the wrong direction. Her feet swelled up and she couldn't put them in those shoes after a while the shoes got wet and destroyed from the snow and ice and the swamps. They had no coats, no blankets, and they were outside in Eastern Europe in the winter.

On the way east, they had gotten food by climbing over walls into gardens and stealing a potato or a vegetable, eating whatever they could. Once they returned to the forest surrounding Krivich, however, they became beggars.

There were many villages in that area filled with a lot of poor Poles. These people had no great love for the Jews but a new element had entered their lives - fear of the Partisans. If one of the villagers dared to turn in a Jew, or to aid in any way in the destruction of a Jew, the Partisans struck back. One time, my mother tells me, a village had colluded in murdering many Jews and the Partisans burned them out, killing all the villagers. So after a few of these retaliations, the Polish villagers, even those who hated Jews, had learned to treat even the lowliest, even those like my mother and her family, with some respect, to share some small amount of food, even if it was out of fear.

My mother and one of Binyomin's daughters, either Leah or Rachel, would walk out of the forest each day, and go to one village or another, begging food from people who also had no bread, but who would sometimes give the girls a potato or a blini, a small, flat, flour pancake they made each day.

My mother was ragged; a starving, skinny, filthy girl, covered with lice – so much lice and filth that she says has never felt clean again. One day she knocked on a door and a Polish woman opened the door, saw her and began to cry and cross herself. She fell to her knees saying, "I've never seen such a skinny girl like you," and gave my mother the shoes from her own feet.

For the first three months in the forest, my mother's family, Binyomin's, and the other Jews who were not part of the Partisans, constructed *zimlankas*, or dug-outs. These were underground shelters that were invisible to a person passing through the forest, with entrances known just to the inhabitants, sometimes through a rotted tree stump, sometimes through built up brush. To warm the zimlanka up, my grandmother would build a fire in rocks, fill the dug out with smoke and they would all wait outside till the smoke dissipated and then return while it was still warm from the fire.

My grandmother, a woman born to be a simple Jewish housewife, rose to the task of keeping her family alive. It's easy to be a Jewish housewife - a balabusta - when you have something to work with. Jewish folklore is full of tales, of the wives who could run successful businesses, raise huge families, and prepare elaborate meals for everyone who showed up at their door each night, magically, all out of one scrawny chicken.

But my grandmother no longer needed four walls to make a house. Their house was the forest, their roof the open sky, their walls the trees. Who could have imagined that she wouldn't need a kitchen to cook; not a stove, not a fireplace, not even a pot?

They found a German soldier's discarded and broken metal helmet by the side of the road and this became my grandmother's soup pot, propped up between rocks so it wouldn't fall over on its rounded bottom. Twigs were her spoons, melted snow was her broth, and whatever she could dig up by hand out of the snow, blistering and chapping her fingers, those were her vegetables. She'd search the forest floor for edible plants and then turn all that into food for the five in their family and the six in Binyomin's. In better weather she found mushrooms, and she knew how to tell poisonous plants from edible plants by sight. She took whatever they were able to beg from the Polish peasants and farmers and divided that between them all. And all together that was food.

I question my mother about this no shoes thing, this no coat thing. How could someone survive a winter in Poland like this? How could her feet not have frozen into a sheer block of ice? And she thinks back, which isn't hard for her to do because the memories are fresher for her than what happened yesterday, and she says, "My mother always had us keep walking no matter what, to keep the blood circulating in our feet. She always had us sit with our feet close to the fire or to hot stones, if that was all she had, to keep us warm."

And I ask about those fires; how could my grandmother have lit them? With flint and a rock? With two pieces of wood and days to spend rubbing them together? And my mother says no, that when they first ran away from Krivich, my grandfather had a lighter with him, a flip top lighter, and they used that until it ran out and by then they were with the Partisans who had plenty of such things. I forget, of course, that it had been 1941. Of course there were flip top lighters.

The zimlankas were built on a small hill next to a swamp. If the Nazis came, they figured they could all run into the swamp to either drown or hide; anything was better than being killed by the Nazis. The soldiers wouldn't follow them; they knew that, not into a swamp, not with their shiny, polished boots. But to go into the swamp, my mother and her family had to know exactly where to step so they wouldn't drown. So my grandmother and grandfather memorized the geography of the swamp, the rocks and the clumps of vegetation. They learned how to jump from one tree stump to another, from one rock to another.

And one day the Nazis came. They somehow heard about the zimlankas, five of them dug in the forest there. They knew the exact locations. People ran and ran. My mother's family ran into the swamp, the children running; my grandmother, my mother insists, ran clutching an egg, making sure not to break it, saying to her, "We probably won't make it, but if we do, we'll need to eat."

Binyomin decided not to run. In a split second he decided that his family would hide from the Nazis in the forest, staying near the zimlanka, hiding behind the trees.

My grandfather said to him, "Binyomin, you do what you want but we're going to run. They're going to have to kill us running."

But the Nazis didn't just destroy the zimlankas; they sprayed the forest with machine gun fire. By the time Binyomin realized he had made a mistake and began running, there were only two left from his family of six, he and his daughter Rachel. Four had been killed: his wife and three of their children, among the seventeen people killed from the zimlankas that day.

My Mom says that Binyomin was never the same. After running and running through the swamps, he realized that his wife, his daughters, and his son hadn't made it out of the forest, that his decision to stay and hide had lead to their deaths. My grandfather found him and his one surviving daughter and they rejoined my mother's family, staying together just as they always had.

They went back to where the zimlankas had been but there were no bodies. There was no possibility that the Nazis would have bothered with burying them, so they had to think about what did happen. And I have to think about this too, honestly puzzled when I'm talking to my mother. I have no idea what could have happened to the bodies. Maybe they weren't dead and they dragged themselves off out of the forest? Maybe Partisan medics picked them up? Maybe other Jews living in other zimlankas that hadn't been discovered made a makeshift morgue and stored the bodies there?

But my mother has no tolerance for my shenanigans, for

my naïve, American musings. She says one word. Animals.

Twice the family was separated, and both times by accident.

Before the zimlankas were destroyed, the Russian Partisans had approached the Jews in the forest, asking for a volunteer from among the men. They needed someone who knew the area well to come with them and help them make their way east.

Someone volunteered my grandfather, saying, "Yankef should go. He knows the area well." And so my grandfather was forced to leave with the Partisans, separated from his family, knowing if he didn't he'd be shot.

He stayed with them for several weeks, putting thirty reluctant miles between him and his family. When they stopped watching him closely, he ran away, back to the forest his family was in, worried too much about whether they were alive or not to care about traveling alone through the forest.

He found them there, alone and unprotected. They'd had a hard time finding shelter since no one would allow children into their hiding places. Finally they were allowed to lie beneath some swinging hammocks on hard ground, where lice fell off the other people's bodies and onto them all night long.

My grandmother lived through another accidental separation, searching for my mother, lost after Nazi gunfire opened on the Jews hiding in the forest and everyone ran.

She pulled the other two children along, asking each person she came up to, "Have you seen a little girl? Skinny, with rags on, alone?" Until she found her sleeping in the snow.

After the family was reunited, they waited for spring to come, which in northeastern Europe can take until May. Then there's a tiny little spate of what passes for spring and summer and then it's winter again.

With the zimlankas were destroyed, the family had to find a place to live until the snow started melting. They had two methods of building shelter - on top of the snow or burrowing into it.

To make a shelter on top, my grandfather would chop down some small trees and build a small structure, like a lean-to, one for his family and one for Binyomin and his one surviving daughter. For the burrowing into the snow shelters, my grandfather dug into the snow drifts with his bare hands, scooping out an upside down igloo, a concave hole that they would then climb inside and which would protect them from the worst of the winds.

Their second winter in the forest they had it easy, at least in comparison to the first. Somehow they heard that the Jewish partisans living in another forest needed a shoemaker and my grandfather was chosen to be that shoemaker, another time that his practical occupation saved their lives.

The partisans sent a driver with a horse and cart to take my mother's family from one forest to the other. The horse and cart clipped and clopped down country roads and up country roads, my mother's family out in the open for the first time in a year, not used to this, the exposure of it. My mother, her senses now acute, kept hearing the rumbling of trucks and, sure enough, as they rode into a village, Nazi trucks were driving out; as they rode out of a village, Nazi trucks were just driving in - a moment separating them from discovery each time. Each time she heard the rumbling of the ground, the sound of the trucks, the engines. Each time she told her parents, "Ma, Pa, don't you hear something? Some trucks?" but they just sat there in the back of the cart.

That winter was one of plenty. My grandfather had learned his lesson well. He and the other men built a zimlanka that was undiscoverable. An army tank would have had to sit on top of this one on the forest floor for it to break through and crash on top of the people hiding inside. They dug for weeks, hiding the sand that was removed from the ground by sending the women and children with it down to the river and pouring it in there.

They dried beans and peas and stored them in huge barrels so they'd always have something to eat. Knowing they had huge casks of dried beans and peas was unbelievable to my mother, more precious than gold, just knowing that they wouldn't starve, that there was all this food between them and starvation. And there were two big barrels of water. The zimlanka was large enough for 200 people inside and built two miles away from the Partisan encampment, not wanting to be too close in case the Nazis came. They were ready to live there for the rest of their lives.

But the Nazis came again. Early in 1944 they came to get the Partisans who had been attacking them, bombing German targets, retaliating against collaborators, the Partisans who proved that Jews could fight, and even that they could fight the Thousand Year Reich, which turned out to be the Twelve-Year Reich. So they came and when they were done killing, the bodies of the Partisans lay eight deep on the forest floor. Two miles away, my mother's family was safe with 200 other people in their zimlanka.

They didn't find out right away that the war had ended

when it did. Word filtered into their zimlanka; after all, the Partisans were dead and they'd always provided all the news.

Here's how they found out the war was over. One day there were German soldiers running through the forest, breaking ranks, running, chased by the Russian army. Some of the Jewish women cornered one soldier but couldn't stomach killing him. They spit on him, taunted him, and then let him go. How do you kill that kind of evil so it never comes back? Will killing one boy do it? From him they found out the Germans were in retreat and then, finally, a man who used to bring them news from the villages brought them a newspaper and showed them the headlines, the war was over.

After that, those still hiding climbed up out of the zimlanka, unsure where they were supposed to go. Were they all supposed to return to the towns where all their friends and family had been murdered? Should they go there to wait for word from other survivors? Were they supposed to ignore the fact that their neighbors had collaborated with the Nazis against them?

My mother had just spent two years in the forest and was now thirteen-years-old. Her immediate family was alive. Since they didn't know where to go, they went back.

Even though my mother talks nonstop about the Holocaust, even though she fills our every waking minute with it, there are some things she saw that she never talks about, even some things she never told her parents. These things have one important thing in common. Each episode points out something rotten in the souls of human beings. It's her secret that she's glimpsed these things.

She never tells her father that the one time she was alone,

separated from the family, Binyomin was nearby, running alongside her with his wife, his three daughters and his son when they were all still alive.

She said, "Binyomin, I've lost my family. Will you take me with you until I find them?" And he looked at her there, frozen there, shivering in the forest, alone, eleven-years-old, the daughter of a man who had saved his own life time and time again.

He said, "No. I have my own family to think of. I can't take you."

That's when my mother had laid down exhausted at the edge of the forest and fell asleep in the snow; that's when my grandmother came looking for her, dragging my aunt Reva and my uncle Herbie by their hands, looking for her in the snow.

Later when most of Binyomin's family was killed and he couldn't stand to go on living, my grandfather kept him alive through the winter, made sure that he and his remaining daughter were fed and sheltered and lived with our family. But my mother never told him that she knew Binyomin would have let her die.

That led to another thing that my mother doesn't talk about. That she and her family, minus her father, were left alone in the forest when they had no man to protect them when my grandfather was with the Russian Partisans. None of the other Jews in hiding would hide them; they insisted there was no room in their zimlankas for four more people especially since one was a little boy who might cry out and bring the Nazis upon them. They left my mother's family sitting out in the forest. After a while, one woman came, a woman wearing boots and a coat in a time when no one had boots and a coat, my mother remembers that the most. This woman knew that one of my grandmother's non-Krivich cousins was in a zimlanka nearby.

She said, "I'll take you to your cousin," and started leading them through the woods, but halfway there she must have changed her mind because she started walking faster and faster until she was running in her boots and coat, leaving my mother's family out in the forest.

One of the worst images that has stayed with my mother, beyond all the vulgar things that she saw and just got used to, like Partisans making love right in front of the children, where and when they wanted, and a thousand tiny cruelties and indignities, happened that second winter in the forest among the Jewish Partisans. The Partisans refused to allow a man and his wife to join them because they had a two-year-old daughter and in the forest young children were always a liability. But the man had an easy solution to this problem. He picked his daughter up by her feet and swung her in an arc against a tree, head first, killing her instantly. Childless then, he and his wife were taken into the Partisans but died anyway, killed by the Nazis two weeks later.

It's important to me that there be a happy ending to the stories Mom tells me. I've been programmed for happy endings and fairy tales by school, by my teachers and by living in the United States, which I've always been told is the greatest country in the world and which has won every war its fought. When my Mother's story doesn't mesh with my happy ending template, the story must change, not the template. The story must be mashed and smashed and shortened and broadened and flattened to fit in there; and when it does just for a second - before it springs out again - that's when I stop listening to what happened. Our Holocaust past is unlistenable.

Since my mother's alive and well and we're in America living in safety, I wonder why she can't just jump to the end when she tells me a story. Why can't she say, "Then we got to the United States and we lived happily ever after"? But that's impossible because the true story has miserable, horrible endings stuck right in the middle of it - things like the Jews all being massacred in Krivich; like what it took to get my mother's family out of Eastern Europe - that leave her unable to comprehend that there has been a happy ending at all.

I hear the pride in Mom's voice when she talks about her family being the only Jewish family to come out intact from her town, so I grasp at that; I want that to be my happy ending. I build my own distorted version of my mother's history inside my head, in which their initial miraculous escape into the snow is exciting, and the drama of living in underground shelters is adventurous. At best, I'm able to give the story a beat: good, bad, bad, good, bad, bad.

At the end of the war, I magically liberate my Mom from the forest; I float her, my tiny Uncle Herbie, my Aunt Reva, and my grandmother and grandfather safely to the American Zone of the divided Germany and into their DP camp the minute the guns have stilled. The Nazis are still on the run, still being cornered by angry Jewish women in the forest who still can't stand to kill the frightened young boys the fearsome Nazis have turned into, while my mother's family, safe and protected, is floating away in my imagination to their new home.

I have selective amnesia for what my Mother tells me. Their return to Krivich, which had become a death town; a handful of surviving Jews trying to pick up their lives, avoiding that area right outside of town where everyone they knew was burned alive. Leaving then and the train ride across Poland and what it took to get to their destination. There's a litany of bad things that happen; there's a halt to their westbound trip, a delay, bribery, harassment, my grandmother taken away by the soldiers who harass them and then suddenly returns. I ask my mother - *was she raped?* She's stolid in her denial. "Oh no. She would have told me." *Then* postwar Germany.

I'm not quite listening to all of this. I'm still waiting for the happy ending.

After the war, they returned to Krivich, thinking that it was their home, that because their family lived there for centuries before the war, that it would be their home once again.

They found the place where their house stood but it had been dismantled, taken apart piece by piece by their neighbors who thought money was hidden there. In the barn, which was still standing, but where no one had thought to look, my grandfather had buried six pieces of gold, worth ten rubles each, and large pieces of leather to make shoes - a fortune in leather. Poles would pay a lot for leather shoes and boots. These he dug up and then they went to find friends to stay with.

They stayed in this shadow Krivich for two years, from June of 1944 to April of 1946. Ten to fifteen Jews returned after the war and lived there; not even enough men for a minyan. They had no kosher meat, no synagogue, no torah, and there was no Jewish education for the younger children, like my Uncle Herbie. The children went to Russian schools and were never spoken to by their Christian classmates, treated like ghosts.

By 1946, my grandmother and grandfather had decided it was time to leave. My mother was turning sixteen in June, my aunt

Reva almost fourteen. There were no men for the girls to marry, no future for them there. They decided the best way to get to Germany and freedom was through Poland. They hid their gold pieces and rubles in their clothing, my grandfather packed some of his leather, and they left.

The Poles stopped the first train they took heading out of Lithuania the minute they crossed the border, ordering all the Jews to get off, saying, "Why didn't you all die in the war?" They waited in the rain, sleeping on tables for three weeks, when another train came to the railroad station on its way to Lodz. Other Jews poured off the train, yelling at them, trying to get them off the dry tables, yelling about them being Litvaks. When they slept at last, they woke up and there was no food. After a while some was provided by a Zionist organization.

In Lodz there were new problems. The mice were as big as cats. There were no sewers, no bathrooms; all the waste ran down the street. Poles were raping Jewish women on the train, but my mother said she was in no danger since she wasn't perceived to be a woman. Even though she was sixteen, she looked like she was twelve; after all of her experiences in the war, she still hadn't menstruated.

They arrived in Shtetin, which was bombed out and filled with roaming animals, now not just mice, but rats and cats, and they spent three days there. My grandfather found a loaf of bread and then he also found someone to take them illegally across the Polish border into Germany on a truck, twenty-five Jews. But one of the men who was going to drive them across the border got caught and shot the night before they were to be taken so the other men told them they would take them in barges filled with coal, that they would cross over the North Sea even though it was almost frozen solid with snow and ice.

This is what my mother remembers of the crossing. She remembers that there were five barges and the first one had a Russian in it, and that it took five days to cross. There was one loaf of bread provided to each family and a barrel in the middle of the barge where they went to the bathroom in front of the other families. Otherwise they hid in the coal. Even though it was postwar. Even though the Nazis were gone.

The barge pulled up on a shore in the Russian zone of Germany but no one wanted to be first to get off, sure they would be shot when they stepped on dry land. Finally my grandfather led the way, getting off the barge with no cover - no forest, no trees, no swamp to run into.

But there was no gunfire, just the quiet of the water and the night. They met their contact person, and were taken to a bunker where they spent the night. The next day they were given knapsacks and walked for a day and a half to get to the French zone where they took showers and ate donuts and drank chocolate milk. Then a truck came and took them to the American zone.

Nine
Family Fictions

In our family, we grew up with several reassuring family fictions, all of which surrounded our father. One was that he was the smartest of his brothers, not just the oldest but also the brains of the outfit. We heard these stories through our mother, that our Dad was the one who first thought of leaving their home in Poland when the Nazis were heading towards them from one direction and the Communists from another. We grew up believing that our Dad was the leader of his family, the trusted son to whom his own mother turned for opinions, for help. He was the one who would screw light bulbs in if they'd had electricity; the one who would unclog clogged toilets if they'd had plumbing; the one who would replace the filter on the furnace if they'd had heat.

I always imagined the two armies meeting right on the soil of my grandparents' farm, shooting at each other from behind my grandfather Gershon's rusty tractor, sniper soldiers creeping through the vegetable gardens, soldiers throwing down their sleeping rolls in my grandparent's barn, and that Dad's family got smashed between them, squeezed between two immovable objects - the Soviet Army and the Nazi Army.

The truth is that I've got it all wrong. There was no farm and no tractor or barn; another casualty of never listening completely to my parents' Holocaust stories, of always trying to be someplace other than the same room when the stories were being told. The truth is that my Dad's family owned two trucks which formed their small trucking company and with which they drove a very short route - from Wyshkow to Warsaw and back again.

The truth is that the Nazis were marching on Poland and when my father's family fled in the other direction, they fled into the arms of the Soviets. In one direction stood certain death, either a cattle car to a concentration camp or death on the spot in a grave they'd be forced to dig for themselves. They ran the other way, right into the Soviets, who just happened to be marching across that part of Poland, seizing eastern Poland as part of a deal made between Stalin and Hitler to divide that country between them. The Soviets offered citizenship, but Dad's family knew that Soviet citizenship was just a different kind of death for a Jew; they wanted freedom. So they ended up on a train to Siberia.

The truth is also that my Dad was the crazy older brother, always leading his younger brothers Meyer and Sid into some kind of trouble and, since this family was patriarchal and Dad somehow was the patriarch, he expected that they would follow him into all his scrapes if he told them to.

He had a lot of advice he shared with Meyer and Sid. Sometimes it came in the form of suggestions for how they could be real men, and sometimes it was just marital advice, how to lay down the law in their own households.

"Who's the man of your house?" he'd yell. "Who wears the pants in your family? Are you going to let your wife tell you what to do?"

When faced with this pressure from Dad, Meyer and Sid would slunk along with Dad on whatever adventure he had planned for them - sometimes good, sometimes bad. As the years passed, they became more cautious, going along with their wives more, Dad less.

It's also part of our family fiction that Meyer and Sid want to be just like our father, because he stands at some kind of pinnacle in the family. We have many examples to back this theory up with evidence. Dad immigrates to the U.S. and so do they. Dad gets his first job at Sinai Kosher in New York and so do they. Dad moves to Chicago and so do they, bringing along their mother, father and two sisters. Dad buys a laundry and so do they, first going into business with Dad, and then striking out into dry cleaning and dry goods. Dad moves us to Skokie in 1960; Meyer and Sid follow soon after.

This is what Dad told us about the old country. He talked about learning to drive when he was just ten years old - someone had to drive the two family trucks, after all - but he turned down my requests to hop behind the wheel of his Oldsmobile and take it for a spin when I was ten-years-old. He insisted things were different when you grew up in Poland and were the oldest boy in your family and needed to drive one of the two family trucks from Wyshkow to Warsaw and Warsaw to Wyshkow, back and forth, for your family business.

"It's different," he said, "when you have a trucking

company. Then you have to drive when you're ten."

When he talked about Siberia, all he told us were temperature stories. We got the bucket-of-water-thrown-in-the-air-comes-down-as-an-ice-formation story, the Chicago-was-never-cold-in-comparison-to-Siberia story. From his stories about Siberia, we may just have assumed that his family had decided to spend some time there from 1939 to about 1943, perhaps on an extended ski vacation but without the skis.

About Germany after the war and the Displaced Person's Camp, we heard a lot, although censored. He was the best at everything he touched: commerce (the Black Market), socializing (a ladies man), and transportation (he rode a motorcycle.) A quick look at the pictures shows much of this. Dad looked sideways at the camera in many of them, a cigarette held between two fingers, some with him sitting on a German motorcycle or with one propped nearby. Many photos were with his friends, a group of other skinny, shivery, Holocaust survivors in ill-fitting suits that hung like drapery, puffing away, pretending to smile for the camera. Later he filled out; the suit filled up.

What he didn't tell us was that in Russia, his sister Etta's baby boy died of malnutrition despite the best efforts of Etta and my grandmother to steal bottles of milk, hiding them under their coats. He forgot to tell us that when he, Etta, and another sister, Faige, came down with Typhus after the war, my grandparents traded their gold rings for a horse and then they balanced the three ill children on a door laid on the snow behind the horse, like a sled, and walked beside it for sixty kilometers to get to Tashkent where they could find medical care. And that's where Faige died. He didn't tell us about Faige.

Although he told us about having Polio as a child, about

how it ruined his eardrums and resulted in our TV always being set to a blaring volume, he never mentioned that he'd had Typhus, or that he'd once had a sister named Faige. I did know this: That my oldest sister's Yiddish name is Faige and that's all Dad ever called her. And I have a picture of Dad holding her as a baby, staring with adoration at her little face in the light of their apartment window.

There were a few other things Dad forgot to mention.

He never mentioned that there had been five dead babies born to his mother before he was born, all born without rectums. He also never mentioned that he was involved with one girl in Germany and got her pregnant. In addition to never mentioning this, he also never mentioned that we had a half-sister in Germany, Anna, born soon after my parents' wedding. There was no mention of whether he knew right away about this first daughter of his, this eighth daughter, and no mention that once he knew; he sent letters to Anna and money to her mother.

Of course, Dad never talked about any of this. We learned of this through our grandmother spitting out the name of this woman as an expletive, as *that shiksa* and Mom telling us; and through Anna searching for her seven younger sisters on her own, years later.

Instead, my grandfather Gershon told my mother the rest of their story during the Sundays he would visit us before he died and sit in our shady backyard, sitting on a thousand broken lawn chairs, adjusting his eye patch when it got uncomfortable, talking about Faige, about Tashkent, about Siberia, about Etta's baby, about his and my grandmother's five dead babies. He sat there talking while Dad mowed the lawn, front and back, trimmed the hedges, swept the patio, destroyed a wasps' nest over and over again, fixed the screen door, and then when he was done, laid down on a patio recliner and slept.

The Jews who survived the war from Krivich, Vilna, and the surrounding areas after WWII, were cast into the Displaced Persons Camps dotting Germany, Austria, and Italy, along with hundreds of thousands of other Jews from all over Europe. After killing so many of the Jews, Hitler had somehow become an inadvertent matchmaker. Jews who would never have left their home villages if not for the war were instead thrown together in the DP camps, Jews who would have married whomever was chosen for them before the war.

My parents and their families land in Displaced Persons Camps in Germany after the war because, of course, they're displaced. Mom's family could no longer bear to live in Krivich and couldn't make a Jewish life for themselves there, and Dad's family began making their way back to Poland after the war then abruptly changed their mind when they heard the Poles were shooting the Jews who tried to return.

Overall, my parents were considered pretty lucky – they survived with their families. Both had their parents, both had siblings, and both had family in the United States. Of course, this didn't tell the whole story, the starving, the freezing, the terror for my mother in hiding for so long, of not knowing if she'd die like so many others, and the murder of her aunts, uncles, cousins, and grandfather; and, for Dad, Siberia, Tashkent, Typhus, and the loss of his sister and his nephew. Nothing can quite tell the story of living through a war in which anyone could kill them any time they were Jewish. But in the DP camp, where tragedy was measured as a numbers game, my parents learned that they didn't have it so bad. After all, there were Jews who had lost not only their parents but also all their siblings; there were Jews who had lost their own husbands, wives, and their children. So what did they have to complain about? Survivor's guilt was built for my parents.

Since my parents both had family living outside of Europe, their stay in the DP Camps shouldn't have been long, but my mother ended up staying three years and my father six. Dad's two sisters, Pearl and Etta, were already in Panama, one before the war and one after, and he had relatives in New York; and Mom had Uncle Izzy in Chicago and Uncle Nathan in Pennsylvania, my grandmother's brothers. My grandmother knew she could depend on Uncle Izzy because from the moment he discovered that her family survived the war, he wrote to her every day until she arrived in Chicago. A letter every day when the family returned to Krivich. Every day in the DP Camp. Every day on the way from New Orleans, where their ship docked. Everyday on their way to Chicago.

The DP camps were scattered throughout the three European Axis countries, some in military bases, and some even in the former concentration camps. Since they were far apart, just being in one was no guarantee of my parents meeting. They were living in DP camps one hundred miles away from each other, my mother in Lichtenau and my father in Hofgeismar near Kassel, both in the German state of Hesse. One day my mother's father heard that there might be some survivors from the area around Krivich in Hofgeismar so he and my mother traveled there by train to find them. They didn't find what they were looking for, but my parents met.

Photographs of my mother - then Chasia Katzowitz - from 1946 show her with thick, black, unruly Jewish hair standing out from her pale, frozen face in coarse waves, what I've come to think of, in a type of Holocaust shorthand, as "Forest Mom." She never smiled in these pictures, either because her gums were destroyed from the malnutrition she suffered during the war, or because, at first, she was missing a front tooth. Soon a shiny gold false tooth, considered quite a status symbol at the time, filled in that space and then she smiled again. But because the tooth was gold and the photography was black and white, in those pictures that tooth showed up as a blank space. Worse than before.

She transitioned quickly, though, from this frightened child-person with brambly hair and pursed lips into a fashionable teen. In later photos she and her friends stood in matching floral dresses linking arms, their hair done in the intricate waves and curls of the late 1940's, smiling despite the fact of what they lived through, smiling despite the fact that they seem to be permanently living as displaced persons in the former Nazi Germany.

Since there were hundreds of thousands of Jews in the DP Camps, there were a lot of dating opportunities for Mom; Jewish men and women were pairing off, getting married, having babies, leaving the past behind. Some men she ruled out right away - the ones who were the type she always thought she'd marry when she was growing up religious. Things had changed; she had changed. She couldn't be that kind of Jew anymore. She needed someone who felt the same way that she did about being Jewish; that she'd stay Jewish because she was born Jewish, but that was it. Was there a type of payback to it? That since she felt God had abandoned her, she was going to abandon God? It was tricky dating criteria, looking for someone who felt the same way but who, like her, hadn't articulated it.

In her Displaced Persons Camp, Hess-Lichtenau, my mother lived in luxury compared to how my father lived. Her housing unit was made up of five single rooms with a bathroom in the middle. Each room, measuring twelve feet by twelve feet, contained one family. My grandmother did all the cooking for their family on a tiny, electric, plug-in cook top, eight inches square. My mother did no chores; my grandmother wouldn't hear of it. Instead, she was busy taking classes all day, learning to speak Hebrew and how to sew. She learned English from a local German professor who wrote to her after she came to the U.S. imploring her to continue her education. She didn't.

The DP Camp my father lived in, Hofgeismar, was much more primitive than my mother's. It was converted from a metal barracks, essentially a series of large rooms housing multiple families on cots infested with bed bugs, and nearly two thousand in total at the camp.

My father - then Hersz or Herschel Bursztyn - came out of Siberia different than he had gone in. The Nazis had marched on his native Poland in 1939; it was six years later when he got to Germany and it would be six more years before he arrived in the United States. He arrived in Germany thin, but grown up, sleek, and handsome. He's always wearing a suit in the pictures I have, always seducing the camera. On my father, poverty somehow looked like wealth, a metal barracks like a swinging bachelor pad, ignorance like silent charisma.

There are photos of my dad on a motorcycle - about a thousand pictures of dad on a motorcycle, a thousand motorcycles, a thousand dads. My father, a cigarette dangling from his lips - a headshot - looking sideways into the camera. Posing in a suit too big for his skinny, starved frame right after Siberia, after Tashkent, the youngest boy in a group of young Jewish men. Later he became the coolest one of them all, part of this group of young men, their suits filled out now, their hat brims angled down low. His eyes looked a little blank, sometimes a little defiant.

My father's post-war photographs always contain a prop of some type. There are a lot of cigarettes smoldering away in his hand, the smoke spiraling off to the ceiling of some unknown roof in the room he was in. There are a lot of 1940's fedoras; in one picture there's a trench coat worn on a rainy day. But there is especially Dad's motorcycle.

Mom says now that Dad didn't have a motorcycle, he just had a motorbike, and that he'd hop on that thing on the weekends when he was done with work and ride the one hundred miles between his Displaced Persons camp and hers, just to see her. But in these pictures, I see a motorcycle, the weird spoky, vintage-type of motorcycle of that era, but a motorcycle just the same.

My Mom was swept off her feet when she met Herschel Bursztein in the DP camp in Hofgeismar. He was the flashiest Jewish guy she'd ever seen and she was beautiful by then, her hair tamed, her missing tooth filled in, the gold of it an asset not a liability, and she could satisfy what my Dad's parents wanted: a good Jewish girl.

My Dad was already having name problems in the Camp. In a type of Holocaust Survivor gallows humor for a while Dad told everyone to call him "Adolf Bursztyn," but that didn't last long. When their relationship was getting serious, he told my mother that he planned to drop this Jewish name of his, this Bursztein, Burstyn, Burstein, *who needs such a Jewish name anyway?*

She agreed.

She picked trouble on purpose -- motorcycle riding, unfaithful Dad suits her just fine. Even when they were dating and he was making commitments to her, he was working his way through all the Christian girls in Frankfurt. Even then, Dad was planning on marrying Jewish but cheating Christian.

When my mother arrived in the U.S. at the Port of New Orleans in 1949, she was the only immigrant on her ship who could speak English, though this was the textbook English taught to her by her German professor who had her translate whole pages of German into whole pages of English and then sound it out. She, the nineteen-year-old with the gold tooth and the Jewish hair, who had been seasick for days during their ocean crossing, stood by as the mayor of New Orleans welcomed last shipload of refugees, and represented the passengers with the English she had learned from a dictionary. Once landed, her family headed to Chicago, to Uncle Izzy and Tante.

When they landed in New Orleans, Uncle Izzy handled everything. He had sent eight hundred dollars to Germany to pay my mother's family's ship fare to the United States, and he had sent papers for them all. There was an apartment waiting in Chicago, fully furnished, the rent paid for a year. He had also found a few places for my grandfather to apply for work as a shoemaker. My grandfather found a job the first day, earning thirty-nine dollars a week making hockey skates.

Dad followed Mom to the U.S. in 1951, although he arrived in New York. He stayed there for a while, earning money by working at Sinai Kosher, then made his way to Chicago with his brothers. His parents were still in Germany; his sisters were in

Panama.

My parents married right after Dad immigrated, on March 24, 1951. Mom already looked like an American, except for her ruined teeth and gums, so in the wedding pictures she smiled mysteriously, her mouth closed. She wore an off-white satin dress with a long ruffled train; Dad was in a tux. Serious looking men in yarmulkes surrounded them, along with short, beaming women dressed in tight, fitted dresses. Besides part of Dad's family missing the wedding, scattered in different countries by the war, my Mom's sister Reva wasn't there either, sick on the day of the wedding.

They started their life together in that apartment on Sawyer, the one that was big enough for them alone, and big enough for them and all of my five older sisters, but not big enough for all of us once I was born. Mom still had black hair, done in a salon once a week, wore swingy 1950's dresses, and shopped for food by pushing a wire basket to and from the corner grocery store. And Dad opened Washtenau-Division Laundromat on Division Street.

My parents had some things in common after all. They both ran from their towns, ran from the Nazis, ran from the Poles after the war, and then ran from Europe, never wanting to see it again. They ran from their war dead and everyone's war dead and then they ran to America ready to start over as a newlywed American couple.

In 1946 they met as Chasia Katzowitz and Hersz Bursztyn in Displaced Persons Camps in the region of Hesse, in Germany. By 1956 they were named Harry and Helen Burt, and by 1966, they owned ten television sets, and lived in Skokie, Illinois - halfway around the world from where they had been born.

Ten

Mismatched

Dad comes to resemble our house over time, which is unfortunate because our house is square both in its macrocosm and its microcosm. It isn't just square in its outline; the bricks that made it up were squarish rectangles, the picture windows – square. The garage door, square, the unimaginative bushes beneath each picture window – all square. The squares of sidewalk, of driveway pavement, all form a box outline cut into the air of Drake Avenue in Skokie that was unmistakably our house. A square topped by an isosceles triangle that was our roof. Dad's body fills out just like a square too.

He wasn't always. In those pictures from post-war Germany he's first thin like a willow, his suits floating around him, clad also in cigarette smoke, a wary look in his eyes, and a brush of brown hair falling across his forehead. Later he's perched on that motorcycle and he's a little fleshier but not square, not yet. He's young and dangerous – at least to women in Germany – and still growing vertically, still tossing hair out of his eyes, waving smoke away from his face as it circles out of his cigarette.

But by the time he rumbles forward to Skokie, to the 1960s, to his marriage with Mom, to being my Dad, to the squareness of his suburban existence, of owning the Washtenau-Division Laundry on Division Street, of thinking always inside the box and never outside, he has filled out horizontally. By then, layers of steak fat surround his heart and other organs. He wears pants that stay up on his widened waist through some magic of factory tailoring, pants that ride up high enough to see his white socks, his shiny tie-up shoes. He's 5'8", or at least lies and says he is.

Above his neck, the squareness of him stops. His head is round, the lower half of his face either bristly or shadowed with facial hair always trying to take over, his nose a nondescript lump. None of us want this nose. From the time we learn the basic facts of genetics, we wonder if that nose is our destiny, if one day our little kid pug noses will explode into that potato nose of Dad's. We'd prefer Mom's razor sharp one instead, her high cheekbones to Dad's fleshy ones, her long head to his round one.

His hair is oiled and thinnish, parted straight like a road, carved out by his ear, one side or the other. His eyes are nondescript, although they are unique. One is light and the other dark.

Mom and Dad have many physical cues to their incompatibility. There's Mom's volubility, Dad's taciturnity; there's Mom's wardrobe, always changing, always up to date, and

Dad's wardrobe, every day in the same laundryman uniform, those khaki working man pants, collared cotton button-down shirts, black belts, his worn out black leather wallet, those white socks and tie-up shoes. He's the drab of this relationship, the colorless moth.

If Dad's essentially square, Mom's essentially pointy. Her nose stands in the middle of her face, the aquiline, non-Jewish point that we all covet but none of us get. Her fingernails are trimmed to points over their wartime malnutrition-destroyed nail beds. Her feet with her extra-elongated hammertoes, those double-A narrow feet, are always too pointy to fit in shoes; the shoes are always too square.

Living in our laundry room downstairs, she always holds a pointy needle in her hand, sewing and sewing, the material in her hands in from one direction, out in the other. And while she sews, she clutches a phone between her pointy chin and her pointy shoulder blade, having pointed conversations with my round, circling aunts, conversations that seem to me to have no point.

Since Mom spends her life on the phone, her movement is limited by the length of the phone cord, like she's a plug-in appliance. Even stretched out, the phone cord allows her to reach the doorway of our bedrooms and no farther, so when we fight she stands there waving her arms ineffectually, narrating the fight like a sports announcer; she isn't able to put the phone down and pull the combatants apart.

Our phone cord ends up stretched out so far, I wonder why she and her friends even need to call one another – can't they just shimmy up and down the stretched out phone cord from coast to coast or even across oceans, from Israel to the United States, to continue their conversations? I spend my childhood tugging on this bell pull waiting to be acknowledged, waiting for Mom to come up for air. I shift in front of her from foot to foot, watching my life pass by, waiting for her to take a breath.

Sometimes when I see how Mom winds herself up in that phone cord like a mummy, it's hard to remember the best parts of having her for a Mom. She pays no attention to us, which means we have almost no rules: no TV watching rules, no homework rules, no hand-over-your-report-card rules, no be-nice-to-your-sisters rules. She will put any atrocious artwork of ours in a dominant place in the kitchen, held up in between the cabinets, at least till she's on one of her manic cleaning binges and then down it comes. She pays attention to us just long enough to get bragging material for all those phone calls to all those relatives, and then we're free agents. And because of the Holocaust, she has a laissez-faire approach to parenting. If we're alive and breathing and there are no Nazis, everything's okay.

My parents are not complete opposites, they do have their connection to fabric in common, with Dad cleaning clothes and Mom sewing clothes, both somehow attached to clothing, and both, because of their experiences not having enough warm clothes during the war, attaching a lot of emotional weight to that clothing. Mom makes it, Dad washes it, we all wear it.

No matter their differences, my parents have quite a social life. They dress up and go out a lot, mostly with Dad's brothers and their wives, or they have everyone over to play cards. A few times they even host big, elegant parties with mink stoles piled up in the bedrooms and our full bar put to use. Mindy and I sneak around the house during these parties, peering through the staircase banister until I get my head stuck between the spokes. Dad plans to leave me there, pilloried - *a lesson to you all!* - but he ends up pulling as hard as he can, one hand this way and one hand that way, and my head slips out.

***

In the years before the kindergarten school bus took me off to school I stood by mesmerized as my mother did her calisthenics. This wasn't something she approached lightly, nor did she do these all the time. She entered her murderous workout regimen when pushed to the limit, in desperate times. Maybe if Dad had made some comment about her figure, or she suddenly woke up one morning and noticed she hadn't gotten her shape back after the seven of us were born.

So on would go her tights and off would come her bra. For some reason Mom just couldn't work out in a bra - too confining perhaps - so she'd take it off and her breasts would fall to the floor like two limp water balloons. But then, to my relief, she'd cover them up with a half-slip, a camisole, or a small shirt of some type.

When she was dressed just the way she liked for exercising, on would come the TV with a 1965 exercise show. Mom's head would disappear as she bent over to do the first exercise, the criss-cross toe touching, and then all I'd see was a whirlwind of arms, a windmill of arms, rotating in front of me, left hand to the right foot, then the right hand to the left foot. Then she'd plop on the shag carpet, prop me on her feet like a sandbag, and count off her sit ups, lifting me in the air with each one, until she found my weight inadequate to hold her legs down and instead shoved her feet under the couch, which she was unable to lift.

After that, she'd flip back upon her upper back and elbows and start bicycling her legs, running upside down in the air, going nowhere, faster and faster, running from her imaginary fat, with me behind her, always running, trying to catch up with her. There'd be jumping jacks, her arms and legs slicing through the air like scissors but cutting nothing, and even more variations on toe touching like there was something magical about what touching one's toes could do for a woman's figure.

In the middle of her straight up and down version of this toe touching, sometimes she'd be reaching straight up into the air when she'd notice a cobweb on the ceiling, and then she'd have to take a break while she pulled out the dust mop, held it up in the air like a pole vault and knocked it down. Sometimes she got back to exercising, sometimes she didn't. Sometimes other cobwebs beckoned.

When she was done, my mother would fall to the floor, exhausted and schvitzing. Then she changed back into her regular clothes, put back on her bra and one of her smart handsewn dresses, and waited for my sisters and father to come home.

I didn't know then that these calisthenics were all a vast improvement over her 1950s version which was basically an abdominal routine that involved holding in her stomach while pulling up her girdle, and a chest routine that involved scooping up her breasts and shoving them into an eighteen-hour bra.

My mother longed for the perfect body, but it was always just out of her grasp, a mere five or ten pounds away. This five or ten pound flaw did serve one important purpose - it joined her psychically and spiritually with all the other women in the world who felt they, too, were imperfect. It allowed her to start a diet each Monday; it allowed her to worry about slimming fashions, to shop for girdles, and full-body bras that looked like corsets.

She was good at dieting. Possibly because of her forest years, my mother was a natural-born starver. She joined Weight Watchers when it was still owned by Jean Nidetch and the diet was so primitive that it was one endless variation on tuna and carrots. Compared to Mom's wartime diet, carrots and tuna were a feast. She joined TOPS and won each week's kitty for the most pounds lost because she didn't know how not to follow the rules, how not to lose the weight.

To my mother, losing that five or ten pounds was like having a fairy godmother wave a magic wand over her head. It had the power to change the way she fit in her clothes and the size she wore; it also had the power to change the way she spoke to Dad and to other women. There was power in looking just right, in knowing that there was one less thing about her that other women had to talk about.

It wasn't just the successful dieting, after all, that mattered. It was the anticipation of the successful diet, the wishful thinking and fantasizing about the perfect body - this formed the crux of my mother's telephone conversations with the aunts in the days leading up to the actual dieting. And it wasn't just the perfect body she wanted, it was the perfect body at the perfect event - the wedding or Bar Mitzvah she and the aunts were all dieting for. This required endless planning and strategizing almost on a global scale - the diets they each chose, the undergarments which would hide any final flaws, the shopping for the perfect dress, a size too small but expected to fit by then.

My mother was magic. One day my she left the house with her regular black hair towering upon her head in a tall bouffant and a spit curl in the middle of her long forehead, but when she came home she was a blonde, with a modern blonde updo instead;

even the spit curl was dyed blonde. She apparently had seen the commercials about blondes having more fun.

Dad didn't notice or, if he noticed, he didn't say anything. He also never mentioned it when she lost her five pounds, or her ten, when she whipped up a new wardrobe for almost no money at all - smart Jackie Kennedy suits, fully lined. She did those calisthenics until she carved a waist out of sheer baby-bearing flab, out of sheer determination, and, still, Dad didn't notice.

When Mod fashions hit, Mom was ready for it. She tossed out her imitation Jackie Kennedy suits and dresses and she bought patterns for floral bellbottom pants and belled tunic tops. She ended up dressed in polyester flowers, polyester stripes, polyester checks, paisleys, plaids, in her corduroy jumper. She wore high heels and those crinkly wet-look boots that she bought in black and white with matching wet-look purses. Her seams always matched - up and down each leg, up and down her waist; some were even lined. With the new wallpaper we had gotten in the kitchen, Mom in her new clothes was a camouflage, disappearing into the background. She matched it, blended into it. She was always dressed and ready to go, even if she never left the house. She was beautiful.

Other families had overweight mothers, out of style mothers; mothers who didn't put on make up, mothers who wore housecoats and rollers all day long. But my Mother was hip, Lithuanian-chic, with a pouf of ash blonde hair on top of her head as hard as a rock, and a little flippy thing down by her neck, all glued in place. My Mom was always made up, always dressed, always had shoes on, was always presentable.

Mom's makeup was not applied with as much care as her

outfit was put on. She put on her lipstick expertly - lipstick she understood. But then she used the lipstick like a paintbrush, putting two red dots on her face, one on each cheek like Raggedy Ann, and rubbed them in for her blush, and then another dab on her too-long forehead to shorten it. She pulled out a huge powder puff with loose powder falling off and powdered her shiny, lipsticked face into the matte persona of a mask. Her eyes got some liquid eyeliner, imperfectly drawn; whatever eye shadow happened to be lying around got slapped on above her eyes, and, voila, she was done.

My mother wasn't just working on her body; she was also improving other things about her appearance. My Mom sewed, an activity she could pursue while talking on the phone and while monitoring the comings and goings of all of us each day.

Of course, if she was going to learn a family trade, it should have been shoemaking. She was raised with the prejudices of a shoemaker's daughter that included the importance of fine leather shoes for her feet; after all, a person only had one set of feet. She had also seen how her father's occupation had saved their lives after the war, how quickly he was able to earn a living in the U.S. after they immigrated. But they didn't have classes in shoemaking in the DP Camp after the war and they did in sewing.

My mother had sewn many sets of curtains, even blood red bordello curtains for her bedroom. She had sewn her own smart polyester dresses and polka dotted dresses for all of us to wear to our Uncle Herbie's wedding. She sewed even though somehow Dad hoodwinked her out of buying one of the new, beautiful Singer sewing machines that made its own buttonholes, put in darts, fixed seams, attached patches, and got up and danced a Hora, all by itself. Instead, in another one of his laundry barters, Dad had gotten her an antique Singer sewing machine, a black Victorian model, that belonged in a museum of technology. It had been jerry-rigged with electricity controlled by a foot pedal, and stuck in a new, square, fold-down sewing desk.

Then, in 1970, Mom decided she needed even more to sew, so she decided to go into business making fancy department store dresses with her friend Miriam Weiss. And so bolts and bolts of fabrics showed up in our house. There were see-through chiffons and dotty poplins, nubby raw silks and slippery satins.

Mom picked these fabrics at Singer Fabrics, lost among the sea of fabric bolts, her pouf of blonde hair ruffed up a foot above her head visible above the bolts. Each time she went there it took her a day of wandering in the store to make her purchases. It took an hour each among the buttons, the zippers, the ric rac trims, and the patterns; two hours among the fabrics; and one hour to chat up the store clerks and the manager, trying to ferret out information on upcoming shipments, on the remnants that hadn't made it yet to the floor. I'd wander with my eyes glazed in boredom, following Mom along as she searched, charging from fabric to fabric, grabbing up tiny square swatches of material until she carried hundreds, with more piled in my arms.

Mom and Miriam named their company Burt & Weiss or Weiss & Burt; I wasn't sure. They had tiny fabric labels custom-sewn for them, placing one in each dress they designed but I never looked that closely; I just saw the plastic bags for the dresses and Mom's model mannequin standing around the house like an extra sister.

They got the samples done and then they called

department store buyers in downtown Chicago to get appointments to show their line. I guess if they got any orders they planned to turn our entire house into a conveyer-belted factory. Dad would, of course, handle the hiring of the Puerto Ricans, since that's what he thought was the key to every successful business - hiring Puerto Ricans. Then he'd give them all scissors, some material and thread, and have them churn these dresses out by the hundred.

They got a few appointments with department store buyers and then, even though they were terrified, my mother and Miriam had to drive into Chicago. Even though they were afraid of freeways and of making left turns, even though they had to schlep armloads of dresses into marble department store lobbies where aloof doormen sniffed in disapproval at Mom's boxy red Nova. They left Skokie hours ahead of time for these appointments to handle all the eventualities, their car inching along side streets on their way downtown, puttering in the right hand lane along the sweep of Lakeshore drive.

In September they got a pre-holiday season order for an unlimited amount of their most popular item, a reversible holiday blouse, as many as they could make and as soon as they could make them, all to go to Marshall Fields. They were in business. A delivery truck from Singer Fabrics had to bring the material this time and Mom and Miriam had to hire a mother and daughter team to sew, though Mom did all the cutting until her hands were numb.

The business trickled on, somehow getting smaller instead of larger. Mom retracted when she should have expanded, expanded when she should have retracted; she didn't update her designs, just used the same ones over and over again with a nip here, a tuck there. She ignored the cover of *Life* magazine, *Look* magazine, she ignored midis and minis and see-through clothes and paper clothes. Mom was a classicist in a mod world.

She and Miriam hung up their professional shears some time later; they saved the extra bolts of fabric for other projects. Mom made new, elegant kitchen curtains and then more curtains for every room in the house. She sewed zippers on pillows, put snaps on our clothing, lace on her bras and garter belts. Then, when she had reduced all the material down to remnant size, down to a manageable level, she packed the rest away in her puffed green sewing box, closed the lid, snapped it shut and put it away.

When Mom ended her business venture, she had the time to become a lady of leisure like the other moms in Skokie who all kept busy enough without running businesses. But my mother couldn't stand to be idle. She kept on sewing, just on a smaller scale. Pants suits, dresses, more curtains. She kept on cooking dinners every day, one at five o'clock each day for the seven of us and a separate one for Dad at seven. She redecorated the house, looking for just the right shade of red for the windows, just the right wallpaper, or she ripped it all down and started all over. Her time was occupied; she never had a moment to rest.

She was industrious, always busy with her hands. If she put down her sewing for a while, she'd take up something else. For a while this was knitting and crocheting and our house was filled with prongy knitting needles in metallic colors and balls of yarn rolled around the house by our cat. She knit berets and scarves and mittens on strings, snaking them up and down the sleeves of our coats. Then she took up crocheting, for what dual purpose I had no idea, and crocheted some more – potholders I think. She didn't have enough patience to work designs into her objects but she was methodical enough to just keep working - like a factory - producing more berets, more potholders, more gloves, than the seven of us could ever use.

In the middle of all this, she decided to teach those of us who were interested how to crochet as well, but succeeded just in teaching us how to crochet a long line of crochet stitches. I ended up quite proficient at crocheting miles and miles of this string, imagining that maybe one day I could sew it all together to form my own beret, or maybe into a rough shape for my own set of winter gloves. Or maybe I could use it to lasso Mom, rope her down like a steer as she set off on a new project, to try to keep her by my side.

Eleven

Dad Jekyll/Dad Hyde

My Dad had his good side and his bad side.

First of all, he made a good living. We were constantly being told this fact by Mom, by our uncles, and by all the other people who spun in and out of our orbit. This was a very important asset for a man in the 1960s, more important than the other details of life. No dads remembered their children's birthdays; how could he be expected to? There were seven of us, after all. No dads were ever home. We should be happy he made such a good living. Some fathers were gone such long hours and were still such big good-for-nothings that they didn't bring in any money. And I agreed; it was good not to have to worry about food on the table, a roof over our heads. I knew I was lucky I didn't have to live in the forest like Mom did or in Siberia like Dad.

Dad was always willing to work hard. He was never sick; he got up everyday like a machine, working, working, working. Compared to how hard it had been to make money in the Old Country, he seemed amazed at how easy it was to make money in America, astonished at the things the foolish Americans would give him in trade to get their wash done. We got cheese steak sandwiches from an Italian deli; once we got a case of Chunky bars. But Dad's favorite trades were the TV sets he lugged home, the obsolete, 1950s, tiny-screened, huge-consoled TV sets that formed a virtual TV museum in our basement, all traded for cleaned laundry. In a macabre twist on the old country where wealth was measured in livestock, Dad measured his wealth in television sets.

He enjoyed a few things thoroughly in the world: The Chicago Daily News, not the Chicago Tribune; his favorite chair, which started out being some moth-eaten ratty armchair but got exchanged over time until he had a deluxe La-Z-Boy recliner. He loved his round, not flat, toothpicks; and he loved his cars, all Oldsmobiles - first his 1954 sedan and then the station wagon he got in '64. He could live with the Ford Country Squire he bought in 1969, but it wasn't an Olds.

He loved to drive and when he wasn't driving he loved to look at his car, to kick the tires, to fill it with gas and children and take us all for a spin, *see what this baby can do.* He made his once a week allergy shot appointments in Evanston an event, loading us all up, leaving the car double-parked and idling outside the allergist's office while he zipped in for one, two, three shots. When he came back out he'd take us on a celebratory run to Dairy Queen as if to congratulate himself on agreeing to medical treatment of any kind.

My Dad loved an ice-cold can of Budweiser and a nice shot of Schnapps. He liked to stand around with men, preferably his brothers, slapping them on the back, reminiscing and drinking that Schnapps and those cans of Budweiser. He loved to be one of the boys.

He loved the weather in Chicago because it was so much warmer than Poland and Siberia and Tashkent. Chicago was a heat wave compared to Siberia. If he wore a coat at all, it was thin cotton canvas and came to the waist. He was very happy with his perception of Chicago as a sweltering resort town, at least until we started taking family trips to Florida and California. Then that perception was ruined and he realized he'd been had.

Sometimes, when even Dad thought it might be a little nippy - let's say a wind chill factor of twenty below zero - he'd say, "It's too cold for you girls to walk to the bus stop. Get in the station wagon!" Thrilled, we'd all hop into the car, happy that we wouldn't have to walk at a 45 degree angle against the wind and the freezing snow, our feet frozen blocks of ice, down a mere block that, in the summer, we could run down in a minute.

So we'd be in the car but it was still cold. The car was a hunk of frozen steel with ice cold vinyl upholstery and windows that were not perfectly air tight, but it had spent the night parked in our one-car garage so it wasn't iced up, so that was good. There'd be a boatload of us on our way to school, a pile of little girls from age five to ten.

Dad would back out onto our snowy driveway, back out onto the icy street; a careful, cautious driver, he'd make his way down Drake, somehow never skidding, never careening into parked cars, never ice skating the car on its four wheels onto the curb, up over the curb and into someone's house.

Then we'd come upon our bus stop and we'd see some snow covered, wooly mammoth-like creatures standing there shrouded in hats, scarves, coats, mittens, snowsuits, boots. And Dad couldn't resist; he just couldn't. He couldn't just leave them standing there. So he'd pull over, somehow slide the car over to the curb without sliding right on top of the children, and he'd open the window and say, "Hop in, kids - I'll take you to school." And they had no idea who he was, if they were getting in a car with Mr. Stranger Danger or an axe murderer. But then they'd see us all bundled up in back and hop in.

Then the fit would be tighter in the station wagon and we'd be on our way again. But then Dad would come upon another bus stop, and another, and stop again and again. He'd do this at the top of our street first, then the top of St. Louis, the top of Trumbull, at each bus stop, until he had picked up all the kids freezing at all the bus stops along the way to school, till we were smashed in there, faces against faces, against windows. Some in seats, some in the back of the wagon, some on laps.

He'd pull up at school, the nearly empty school bus inching along behind us, and we'd all stumble out.

My father had a great public personality. He was always looping a big, hairy arm around salesmen, getting chummy; he was friends with everyone everywhere he went. He knew all the attendants at every gas station, yelling out, "Fill 'er up with Ethyl!" every time we pulled up at a pump. Wherever we went, he pounced out of the car, sharing cigars with restaurant staff and kicking tires with used car salesmen.

He was also a great salesman. He saw the potential for commercial laundry accounts everywhere, signing up hospitals and nursing homes and then swinging by each day to pick up their lines so he could do their laundry and get rich. He was always ready to help other immigrant Jews he came into contact with, telling them to open a laundry like he did, like it was the perfect business for an immigrant to learn.

He'd say, "Rent a place in the South Side of Chicago, buy some big machines, separate the whites from the colors so you don't ruin the clothes, hire some Puerto Ricans," then his hand would smash down on the table for emphasis, "and then you're in business."

The other Dad was a little different and he was around a little more often than the easygoing, affable Dad.

Just to be sure that Mom knew he was home each night, Dad would toot the horn on his car as he pulled in the garage. This was her final warning to get his appetizer and soup on the table and a secret signal for the seven of us to hide or stand around like statues and hope he didn't notice us.

He'd walk in with the bag of laundry he had taken with him in the morning, now clean, and lean it against the wall. And then, every night, Mom would run up to kiss him, but she'd never make it. She'd get pushed away, playfully at first, like for the first five or six years, like maybe Dad was a big, kind of quirky, bear who didn't like public displays of affection - even in private - and so he'd swipe at her with his big paw.

After a while, it wasn't cute, and it wasn't an act. Mom was running at Dad all the evenings of my childhood full force, barreling through our oversized Skokie kitchen, oven mitts on, apron on, hair done, lipstick perfect. She was aiming for a cheek, not even lips, for a bristly, cold, large-pored cheek which would be turned away at the last second, leaving her arms grasping nothing, her lips kissing nothing: no Dad, no arms, no bristly cheek. And each time she was pushed away she remained in good humor - it had no effect on her. She continued her bustling work in the kitchen, schlepping and hauling out the many dishes for his meal; she'd get on her evening cycle of phone calling.

On his way up the stairs to change his clothes, Dad would bark out orders at any of the seven of us that he could spot.

He'd say, "Toothpick."

"Slippers."

"Newspaper."

And we'd scatter.

Soon we could hear the quiet sounds of him eating alone in the kitchen, of his paper rustling, of his fork tapping on his beer glass to get Mom's attention if she slowed down between his courses or he needed a refill of his beer. His meal was organized. Appetizer; Soup; Cucumbers in vinegar; Main dish, Dessert. When he was done he stood up, pushed his chair out and walked away from the table without saying a word to Mom, who was on the phone anyway, leaving the pile of dishes on the table.

Mom made up a lot of excuses for Dad. He was in a bad mood - for about a decade. He was worried about the business; he was planning for the future; he was working too hard. To allow for all of this stress, we'd tiptoe around the house when he got home, allowing him his quiet solitary meal. But by the time he stood up, done, he was human again. He was unwound; he had a few beers in him that had mellowed him; he was ready to join the family.

In our world, certain things were normal. Even though we

were Jewish, it was normal to eat bacon; and when we ate it, it was normal to eat it barely cooked. It seemed normal that Dad never had dinner with us; that we ate at five p.m. and he ate at seven. I thought it was normal, even funny in a weird way, but not in a *ha ha* way, that sometimes Dad would joke around about trading all seven of us to an Arab Sheik for one sturdy little boy.

Also normal in our world was the fact that things would move along in their regular manner for months, even a year or more - Dad worked, Dad came home, Dad worked, Dad came home. But then there would be a sudden glitch - Dad would work, but Dad wouldn't come home - and we were all set awry. Mom's dinner would sit on the stove simmering all night. We'd watch whatever TV shows we wanted all night, the volume normal instead of blaring for Dad's Polio-ruined eardrums. Mom would plant herself on one of the dining room chairs right in front of the picture windows, looking out all night, waiting for Dad's headlights to pull into the driveway. In front of her she'd have lined up all the bank passbooks she could find to add up the balances, to see how she'd survive if he was lying dead somewhere.

He'd come home late at night, a little too loud, and smelling of alcohol. She'd try to have it out with him, saying, "Where have you been, Herschel? You couldn't call? You couldn't call so the girls and I wouldn't worry?"

But he'd refuse to tell her where he'd been.

"I'm my own boss!" he'd shout in the quiet of our midnight house. "I'll do whatever the hell I want." His word was the law of the land around our house; why should he answer questions? Sure there was that one Harry, that married suburban family man with seven daughters, but sometimes that wore thin.

Sometimes when the Puerto Rican guys at the laundry said they were going to play cards, go wherever, he just felt like going too.

Then we all knew that his patience and tolerance for us was limited. One wrong word, one crossed eye, and he'd be out of there in a flash.

"Damn it, Chasia! Where are my shoes?" Dad's yell can be heard through the house, out the window, around the world.

Mom spots me. "Linda! Go get Dad's shoes from our closet. The black ones – hurry!"

I give my Mom an incredulous look. She knows Dad has ten identical pairs of black leather shoes in his closet. It's impossible for anyone but him to know the minute differences between them to figure out which pair he wants to wear today.

I go upstairs and come down to Dad's thunderous disapproval, the pulsing vein in his neck, a matching one in his forehead, his red face, his shaking head.

My Dad has a bad temper. We all tiptoe around his temper, giving him alone time when he gets home from work, alone time on Sundays when he's resting, alone time in the car when we're driving somewhere. Basically, alone time all the time unless he doesn't want it.

When I first become aware of the fact that death exists, I'm afraid of dying myself. But then I get more worried by something much bigger than that: Mom or Dad dying. I'm willing to trade anything to put that off forever. I'll trade whole sets of grandparents, who are old anyway, to forestall this event, but Dad ticks away at home like a bomb. He's mad about dinner and mad about breakfast, mad about shoes and mad about winter; he's mad about politics and mad about Joey Bishop.

I figure out that death exists not because of Mom telling me those legions of horror stories about the Holocaust; not because she has filled my head with so many stories of starving, deprivation, brutal death, and horror that I think it's a wonder to be alive - not for any of those reasons. I know it because in the summer in between Kindergarten and first grade, Denise, Sherry and I hear that Kenny Hansen, a boy we never paid enough attention to, drowned on vacation in Florida. To confirm this, we never see Kenny again, except for maybe his ghost, causing us to sleep even more tightly piled up together in our room for a couple of days, to leave even more lights on than usual, to recite even more "Mary Worth" chants while staring at blank walls.

Despite this first tangle with death, I'm sure my parents are immortal, especially Dad, who is a virtual monolith. He's picks up huge laundry bags every day and carries them like they're cotton candy; he never wears hats or scarves; he scoffs at wind chill factors, jeers at icicles, and laughs at all seven of us, bundled up in snowsuits, peaked hats with pom-poms, mittens with string connectors snaking through our sleeves, and rubber boots. So it is odd when Dad disappears for a few days in the middle of the summer, then he shows up again, like he didn't miss a few days.

"A mole," is all he'll say.

"Thyroid cancer," is what Mom whispers to Francine, my oldest sister. The younger ones are not to know, not to worry. We have to shimmy through the kitchen on our bellies to catch phrases with the truth, in order not to be seen. We have to carry around Yiddish to English dictionaries to make any sense out of what Mom is saying to Francine in Yiddish, and English to Yiddish dictionaries to figure out what Francine is answering back. Even after we hear it, we don't know what it means.

The bandage comes off. Dad goes back to carrying the white, fluffy, laundry bags out of our house everyday and pretty soon everything's back to normal. He's coming home late again and Mom's sitting by the picture windows with all the bank passbooks laid out in front of her, peering down the street.

Because Dad is always ticking like a time bomb, he's easy to rile up. We can pick a topic, any topic, and it will have the potential to get him mad. Sometimes even just talking instead of allowing him to read his newspaper in peace and quiet will get him mad. But certain topics are always tried and true, guaranteed to make his face go red, his eyes widen, bulge, narrow – moving them from disinterested to something else.

Dad is not a Polack, we learn this early on. We aren't to say it or hint it. He may be from Poland but he is not a Polack. Why he is not a Polack is explained to us once and once only, through gritted teeth, and, if we knew what was good for us, we'd better remember the answer. It appeared that the term "Polack," which, in Chicago in the 1960s meant a backwards buffoon, in pre-War Poland instead meant a person of Polish descent, a good thing when he was growing up there, and something the Jews were not. The Jews were not considered by the Poles to be of Polish descent, rather they were considered to be generations upon generations of aliens living there. Never Polacks, Dad says.

If someone outside the house calls Dad a Polack, there isn't an intellectual analysis of why he isn't one. There's no reasoned explanation of how the word "Polack" referred to some type of belonging or citizenship, like the word "American" in the U.S. Instead, there's be the typical Dad reaction - he turns beet red, his eyes bulge out, when he gets home he slams around the house for an hour, a day, a week, muttering under his breath. And then, when he runs into that guy again who'd said it - always in a jovial, joking way - Dad pastes on a fake smile, slaps him on the back, throws an arm around his shoulder and pretends nothing happened.

Sundays, which should have made Dad happy, instead got Dad mad. He had high expectations for Sundays since he worked at the laundry Monday through Friday and then worked at our apartment building in West Rogers Park on Saturday. So his anticipation was high for a relaxing Sunday but it never panned out.

First he'd try to sleep late, but this was ruined every Sunday by our neighbor Arnie Greene waking up at the crack of dawn to mow his lawn. Since Dad refused to buy an air conditioner, all of our windows were always open. Arnie may as well have been mowing our carpeting the sound was so loud.

Dad would yell out the window at Arnie, saying, "Mow your lawn at a decent hour, you dumkopf!" but Arnie never heard him over the noise of his own lawnmower.

Dad would then slam all the windows shut in the house leaving us sweltering, but Arnie Greene's lawnmower droned on and on just beyond the glass of our windows, making them rattle in their casings. Arnie would tease us with false stops and starts when he finished one swathe of grass and, pushing his mower to another, start it up again. We were fooled by those momentary silences, thinking it might be safe for us to close our eyes again, for Dad to close his eyes again. After this happened three or four times, we knew it was no use. Dad was up; he wouldn't fall back asleep. He was restless so we'd all have to rise and be restless too, then jump in the station wagon for the obligatory Sunday ride to get bagels and lox; eat breakfast for two, maybe three, hours, and then wait for Arnie Greene's lawn mower to finally stop sometime around noon. Then, like an odalisque, Dad would lay down upon his broken lounger on our cracked patio, the straps ripped here and there, so that there are bits of Dad poking through, and sleep.

Once Dad was outside on the lounger, he didn't want to be interrupted. I heard it from everyone. *Your father works hard. What? You don't want he should have one day to relax?* And so while all seven of us would also migrate outside to play in the sprinklers or play on the swing set, we knew we had to steer clear of Dad. Sunday was his day to "get some color" as he called it, as opposed to what it eventually became on his face and back, getting some basal cell carcinomas, getting some pre-melanomas, all growing here and there like freckles or beauty marks. He'd lay there, sometimes with one of Francine's empty record albums coated in tin foil and opened under his chin, his forest of body hair forming a black shadow over his body.

Sometimes we'd call out to him, *look how high I can swing, Dad,* or *try and find me Dad,* or *will you turn on the sprinklers, Dad?* But he stayed silent, like the hair growing out of his ears had muffled all sound. Or maybe he had checked out and he wasn't our Dad for those few hours, he was back in Germany after the war, sunbathing around swimsuit-clad women rather than his daughters in their flowered bikinis, their hair cut in Beatles' haircuts, like there were seven, miniature 1960s-era Paul McCartneys running through the yard.

When he had enough, of the sun, of the outdoors, of being interrupted trying to read his paper, he would stand up, done. He'd fold up the lounger and walk in the house, forgetting we were there. And we'd watch the screen door slowly close behind him.

Dad was a stranger in this country, an accented foreigner. He's never mistaken for American. And this was another thing that got Dad angry: the people who couldn't understand what he said, who couldn't understand his accent, or, what he suspected, those people who said they couldn't understand him when they could, just to make him feel more foreign that he felt already.

Dad's problem wasn't just that he spoke English with an accent, it was that by the time he was learning English it was his fifth language and he'd just about given up on the details. Dad just didn't have time for proper English, the nonsense of verb conjugation, correct pronunciation, or agreement between tenses. To Dad, English was a language of near misses and of imprecision; his English-speaking daughters foreign language-speaking strangers. Yet by the time Dad immigrated to the U.S. he already knew Yiddish, Russian, Polish, and German - all fluently. He had lost patience with the rules, the syntax, all the miniscule issues of learning another language, even if it was the language of his final destination - America.

This, too, got my father angry, how people talk loud to him, thinking his accent meant he was hard of hearing. The way they hung up on him if he answered the phone, thinking he spoke no English. The way he was mistaken for an immigrant, like he'd just got off the boat, even though he'd already been in this country for decades.

Just like he moved the TV over and over again throughout

the years, my Dad also switched bathrooms from time to time, staking out territory, declaring it his in this otherwise all female household.

He didn't want the upstairs bathroom. Mom had made sure of that, decorating it with shell pink tiles, a tinkly chandelier in the ceiling and the mysterious accoutrements of female life in the 1960s: wigs on faceless foam head stands, birth control pills in round punch-out containers, huge mattress-like sanitary pads with belts and safety pins, pink sponge rollers. Enough things to send Dad packing and clomping down one flight of stairs and sometimes two.

If he stopped on the main floor, he'd be in our powder room, an ordinary box with green painted walls and minuscule tile set in the floor, a rickety sink standing on two steel bar legs, a toilet, and a window looking out onto our patio. But if he went all the way down to the basement, chose to distance himself as much as he could from females and femalish things, then he arrived at the three-quarter bath, a place he could call his own, be the king of the castle, take a shower.

In either bathroom he had his rituals and his ritual objects. His showering itself was very simple - he required only a bar of Lava soap. With it he not only washed his body but also shampooed his hair. In one medicine cabinet or another perched his ancient cracked cup of shaving soap and the accompanying brush, stiff from years of use. For some reason, this cup was never altogether full or empty and it was never thrown away. To use it Dad would pick up his lathering brush, wet it, stick it in the soap cup and stir it up like soup over and over, till there was enough lather for the black bristles uniformly covering his round Polish face, his neck, and under his nose. Then he pulled out the silver shaver, the kind that had to be unscrewed at the bottom to load a new double-edged razor blade, then he'd screw it back up, and he'd shave.

This was not an event without incident. I watched him shave throughout my childhood, especially when he claimed the downstairs three-quarter bath and the downstairs happened to be my bedroom. I didn't talk to Dad while he was shaving because I didn't want him to cut his jugular vein or anything. No fighting, no excitement, no melodrama. Just that stropping, slicing blade, gliding over the stubble, around the moon-pitted landscape of Dad's aging and weary cheeks, his hanging jowls, gingerly shaving under his nose, then rinsing the razor in the sink. Black stubble disappearing and leaving beige flesh in its wake, at least until it started growing again.

Dad didn't come away unscathed. He emerged from the bathroom still in his pajamas, ready to trudge up the first flight of stairs and then the other, and he was washed, brushed, smoothed, and shaved, but angry. Because Dad always cut himself shaving. And not just the run of the mill shaving cuts other fathers get, a nick here or there from the dangerous blades they all used, those double-edged razors. Dad got plenty of those, emerging from the bathroom with pieces of toilet paper - makeshift bandages, starkly contrasting with his tanned brown skin, stuck here and there, to stop the bleeding. The toilet paper stayed on somehow through breakfast, through his getting dressed, all of us watching in fascinated horror as he left the house with toilet paper stuck to his face.

Dad had a bigger hazard on his face that made his shaving experience unique. He had a cleft chin. It served no purpose that I could ever see except as a sinkhole for his razor. It was plunked down in the nowhere land of Dad's chin - a little crevice, a live mine in a minefield. It sat there like a third eye, but upside down.

Dad could somehow never stop his speeding razor from catapulting into the cleft in his chin, and it was a painful, bloody mess when it happened. It didn't bleed like the rest of Dad's face, easily staunched by some toilet paper; rather, it hemorrhaged. A tiny piece of toilet paper would not staunch it; Dad needed to wind a roll around his head like a mummy to make it stop bleeding.

Shaving and the bleeding that accompanied it were the bane of Dad's existence and there was no respite for him in this. The minute he was satisfied with his image in the mirror, the minute he slapped on his Old Spice and washed off his razor, the minute he turned away from the medicine cabinet mirror, his five o'clock shadow was already growing in.

I learned how to shave from watching my father because I'd never see my Mom shave. Maybe she shaved secretly in the shower, or maybe her legs were as bald and hairless as a moonscape, like they looked, and needed no shaving. Was Mom's missing leg hair another casualty of the war, like her damaged teeth, her splintered fingernails, her numbed and frostbitten toes?

Watching Dad cut himself to pieces and bleed to death each day came in handy when I sprouted long, black hair on my legs at age ten. I probably wouldn't have cared so much about it except that the Black girls at school noticed before anyone else, just like they always noticed everything, noticing almost before I did.

Having the Black girls around to keep such a close watch on me was, by this time, just a fact of life. It was impossible to get away with anything around them, and not just for me, but for anyone, regardless of race. The most minute character flaws, transgressions and personality quirks were noticed by them and, like a choir, everything was commented upon, then elaborated upon, then made more and more magnificent and hilarious - right in front of me as if I were deaf - until something I perhaps thought was invisible or not a big deal when I went to school that day had become the stuff of legend.

Like the leg hair. I had noticed it; I wasn't blind after all. But my five older sisters had assured me that no one in our family started shaving until we were twelve; to do so before then was not The Burt Way. I had a strong need to head into adolescence just like my five older sisters before me, despite the black fur on my legs. But I was sitting in the auditorium at an assembly when they noticed my leg hair.

"Do you see what I see, Pamela?"

"What, Kimberly?"

"Look at Linda Burt's legs!"

"Whoo-ee! Someone ought to buy that girl a lawnmower before she turns into a werewolf!"

And they laughed and laughed while I grew steadily more flushed in my seat and tinier - until I was gone and there were just those legs sitting there, that long, black leg hair sitting flopped down like a pelt on the hard wooden orchestra seat.

I made it out of there when their conversation moved on to other targets: Jill Farber's new pimple, Philip Gordon's dandruff, and other matters of community interest. I went home and took Dad's steel shaver, popped a new double-edged razor in there, twisted the sides shut, and began to shave, neglecting that whole thing that Dad did with the soap cup and his shaving brush.

Here's what happened. The shaver left a trail of smooth, pale skin, blood dots, and hair in a strange zig zag line here and there, like a newly-mown swathe of grass, since I didn't know how to shave a straight row. Although the pain was unexpected, I knew what to do about the blood; after all, I had watched my Dad many times. I reached down for toilet paper and made delicate, tiny squares out of one piece. I placed them on the cuts like confetti, and I walked out.

Twelve

Knowing Goldie

In my grandmother's apartment was a couch, about a mile long and hard, turquoise blue. It wasn't a comfortable couch, it was a couch meant for people to sit upright on, perched up high, floating, their feet barely touching the floor. It was a couch that would look forever new because it was wrapped in plastic.

When the family went to her apartment, my grandmother lined up all the relatives on the couch like bowling pins. Sometimes they'd seem organized, men at one end, women at the other, or a little less organized, grown ups interspersed with children, one after the other - tall short tall short tall. She could fit ten, maybe twelve, people on there in a pinch, smashing them up against each other, legs sticking to the plastic.

They'd sit there, my Uncle Barney, my great Uncle Izzy,

my great Aunt, the mysterious Tante, all uncomfortably close, staring into each other's pores and molars as they talked about the events of the day or tried to understand each other across the yawning differences of their Yiddish dialects. There was no room for hand movements, no excited gesturing; their arms were stuck by their sides.

Hours went by with this frozen tableau stuck there on the couch, side by side and up and down. Once there, they couldn't get up. The couch was too deep, they were crammed in too tight, the angle was too hard. To get up, they'd have to mobilize the whole line of sitters, up in one direction and down in the other, coordinate a mass movement, a vast groaning, creaking and bending of knees, a vast heave ho. No one had the energy for this until it was time to leave, and then they'd be up, the entire line at once, in their coats, wrapped up in scarves, zipped up in boots, hats on their heads, purses clutched to their middles, all of them marched out the door.

But, stuck on the couch, having run out of conversation and looking for amusement, they'd grab slow children as they'd pass by, sometimes me, and then I'd have to sit on one of those knees and answer questions about school or about which one of the seven daughters I was – *number six* – and what my favorite subject was in school.

I'd escape as soon as I could because I had circling to do, circling to join in with my sisters, a blur around me. I needed to circle my way through the apartment – through the kitchen, the dining room, the living room, then out the door, down the steps, around the building, to the game of handball that my cousins Markey and Louie had set up in the alley, back up the creaky wooden steps in the back, and then back into the kitchen, to do it all over again.

When my parents would think of it, when they'd suddenly notice all seven of us circling in and out of my grandmother's cramped apartment, weaving around the grown ups, in one door and out the other, they'd yell, saying, "Stop running!" Or, "Sit down and eat some food before you starve to death!" So I'd do what they said, shuffling my feet for endless minutes, my tights-clad legs stopping on their eternal run, my dress coming to a rest, my matted fake fur winter coat warming up in the hot apartment air. And then, when they looked away, I'd be gone.

When I was born I had a full set of four grandparents, two from my Mom and two from my Dad. All my grandparents were apartment-dwellers. None of them would dream of becoming so American that they'd own a house even though both apartments were crammed with enough furniture for one. They were also crammed with doilies, Yiddish newspapers, and mountains of mothballs to preserve the collection of coats swinging in the closets. They never threw out a coat no matter what.

I thought I knew everything there was to know about my mother's mother growing up. She wore only dresses. She didn't drive. She lived in West Rogers Park in Chicago but visited us each Saturday, throwing on an apron the second she walked in the door and not taking it off till she left. When she'd light her Shabbos candles she'd use anything for a head covering, even a paper napkin or a dishrag, and then forget it up there so that we'd walk in the kitchen an hour later and find her walking around like that, like she was crazy, with a dishrag on her head. She didn't smile much and then she didn't smile at all for seven years after my Aunt Reva died in 1969. She had a heavy accent in English but

I assumed she didn't have any accent in Yiddish.

I knew this about my grandmother, Goldie Kay. In Chicago, her apartment always smelled like food. In the hallway, she had a rotary-dial telephone sitting on a rickety hallway stand next to a wooden chair where she'd sit holding the heavy receiver and talking to my mother for hours in between their weekly visits. She had a pantry stocked with dried food, with lentils, peas, beans, and egg noodles, and a freezer filled with frozen meat, but she just cooked enough each night - in a cast iron skillet with a plate over it, no lid - for my grandfather and herself, never an ounce extra, never anything in case someone stopped by, and never enough to overeat. She ate sparsely, meagerly, seeming amazed as my grandfather's weight climbed through the years. She parceled out the food sparingly. There was no monkeying around with the food. Food was serious business.

What I didn't know about my grandmother was that she'd had less before. No couch, no apartment, no West Rogers Park, no cast iron frying pan, no lentils. No egg noodles, no rotary phone, no rickety hallway stand, no hard hallway chair. At that time, what I didn't know about my grandmother was that she could make something out of nothing and sometimes she could even make something out of thin air.

Before World War II, she was just a regular balabusta, trained by being born to nothing to be a little more frugal, maybe, than a regular balabusta. Born Golda Alperovich, and one of nine children, she was fatherless at seven and an orphan by fifteen.

She'd had a few devastating things besides the Holocaust happen to her earlier in life that had taught her that maybe life wasn't going to be so easy.

When she was seven, her father, Abraham Alperovich, a woodcutter who was as big as the trees he cut, as solid as the tree trunks, and a happy, vibrant man, dropped dead of a massive heart attack. The worst thing about this wasn't just the horror of a little girl losing her father, of him going from vitally alive to frozen in death in the blink of an eye; the worst thing was that since he died on a Friday and Shabbat was going to arrive with sundown, he had to be buried within hours. She ended up believing that a horrible mistake had been made - that he hadn't died at all; that they had buried a living man.

Eight years later, when she was fifteen, her mother, Rivka Chodesh Alperovich, died after years of untreated diabetes. First her legs went, then her eyesight, then all of her, leaving eight living children and one dead. Rivka's death was, at least, a catalyst for two of the children, Nathan and Izzy, to leave Krivich and make their way to America, Nathan to Pennsylvania and Izzy first to Cuba then Chicago.

The rest stayed in Krivich. There were my grandmother's sisters: Baileh, dead before the war of cancer; and Tzipke, killed by the Nazis trying to escape over the border into Russia; and her other brothers, Yankel, Mottl, and Itzche Velvel, all dead.

It was understandable, then, that my grandmother didn't smile much - she was in a constant state of Shiva, a 365 day-a-year Shiva. She didn't seem to just be mourning the day her family members died, she also seemed to be mourning all those days they had lived that had been leading up to those horrible deaths, and mourning the days since then that she had gone on living without them. And even though my mother had filled her world up with little girls all named after those dead relatives, in some ways we weren't as real to our grandmother as her siblings who had died decades before. After all, each child was a new, extra person to worry about. So she didn't smile much, my grandmother, Goldie Kay – she was a serious person and there was a lot to be serious about.

Like luggage waiting to be moved from one location to another, these grandparents of mine would wait in their apartment in West Roger's Park each Saturday for my mother to pick them up in her 1965 Chevy Nova and bring them to Skokie. My mother was a good daughter. She hauled them around, even though to do so she had to overcome her fear of driving and her fear of her own car, which had been parked outside under a tree for a few years before she got her license and learned how to drive it.

Once she got to our house, my grandmother would walk in, take off her coat, and within seconds have an apron on over her nice Shabbos dress, ready to help Mom around the house and in the kitchen. She'd busy herself there while my grandfather wandered around. Because of his arthritis, his diabetes, and because of having legs that had just plain sprung, he couldn't ascend or descend the stairs, so he was stuck. Powder room, kitchen, dining room, living room, foyer. Around and around in a circle in his old man's shuffle. Getting some exercise.

His black horn-rimmed glasses with lines marking off the areas of unifocals, bifocals, and trifocals, would gleam reflections at me as he'd say, "Linda, mameleh, you want we should walk up to the liquor store, get some beer nuts?"

Of course, I was six, maybe five, maybe seven, so I thought he was just asking me to go to the liquor store like he said. How could I know what it meant to him to have living grandchildren, not grandchildren dead in a mass grave somewhere in Lithuania? Yes, let's take a walk.

I would skip, hop, and gallop my way up the street next to him, as he walked along, a black fedora on his head, planting one old, stiff, arthritic, diabetic, leg down in front of the other, like moving tree trunks clad in black gabardine. I wound inside of those legs, got tangled up in those legs, skipped ahead of those legs. If I saw a hopscotch drawn on the ground, I hopped. If I saw someone playing jump rope, I jumped in.

We made our way down Drake, across Crain, and down St. Louis, to the corner at Dempster, to the liquor store, the one just past the border of Evanston, where liquor wasn't sold, into Skokie, where liquor was. When we got there, we walked in, went over to the nut aisle, found the beer nuts for me, nothing for him. He'd pay, and we'd walk out, back the way we came. St. Louis, Crain, Drake.

On the way, my grandfather would make conversation. He quizzed me about school, feigning surprise that I took Language Arts.

"This is language or this is art?" he'd say.

All the way up those blocks, all the way down, we talked. Me, a little out of breath, a little jumbled with all the skipping and jumping and dancing, the twining around those heavy, labored legs of his.

I'd never make it back into the house. I'd see some kids outside playing Statue or Red light/Green light or maybe pounding on rolls of caps with rocks on the sidewalk and I'd veer off from him, joining whatever they were doing. And he'd continue on alone into the house, the forgotten beer nuts in his hand.

***

I am backed up against a counter in my mother's kitchen in Skokie in 1970, pinned there by my grandmother's best friend, Mrs. Botwinik, also a Krivich Holocaust survivor. The fact that she's a survivor is, of course, no big deal to me by that time. I'm flippant about this survivor thing, not understanding the true severity of what it means, only knowing that if I wander into the kitchen at a family party there will be some accented adult wandering about with a story to tell, looking for the ear of a child to tell it to. The various accents and Yiddish dialects ring out like a tower of Babel. But one of the hazards of entering the kitchen during any of our parties is that the one who will nab me will be Mrs. Botwinik.

Even though I'm just ten, I'm already taller than Mrs. Botwinik. Of course, she's 4'8", maybe 4'9", but a powerhouse of determination, packed with purpose. This height of mine is a good sign to all the old country visitors; I must be eating well to sprout up so; I must be healthy. I won't die so fast if the Nazis come again - and the Nazis *are* coming again, they assure me. Everyone around me is always anxious as they scan the newspaper and watch the TV for evidence of this. Sometimes in the middle of a conversation they'll grow silent, like they're listening for the sound of boots on the march.

When Mrs. Botwinik first corners me, she tells me I'm a pretty girl, but she says it in Yiddish. She beams, pinches my cheeks like I'm horseflesh and then says, with a heavy accent, "Oy, what a shayna maydala!" She punctuates these words with each of her hands grabbing at my cheeks and twisting, so that tears come to my eyes from the pain. I hate being cornered in the kitchen by Mrs. Botwinik.

Then she moves in a little closer and she says, "Tell me.

You know what your Bubbe and your mother went through in the old country? Your mother told you, yes?"

Now I may just be ten years old but I already know that this is a trick question. There's no good way to answer this question. There's not going to be any reward for telling the truth. And the truth is that, of course my mother has told me about it – just morning, noon, and night; just winter, spring, summer, and fall, just until I could scream with the Holocaust, that's all.

I answer honestly. I say, "Yes, she's told me the whole story."

Somehow this gets me into trouble with Mrs. Botwinik. Just hearing me say that in my squeaky, unaccented, ten-year-old, American voice makes the Holocaust sound flippant, like I'm talking about the Beatles.

She rolls her eyes at me, hisses, and moves in closer until she has me bent over the counter. Almost spitting at me, she says, "You! You little pisher! You don't know nothing! You think you know? Ha!" She says it like she's happy to find me lacking because I know she wants to talk about this and talk about this and talk about this, until time grinds to a halt.

She turns away then, giving me a disgusted cold shoulder and I think maybe I can still escape out of the kitchen and back downstairs to where my sisters are hiding, watching TV. But I don't get off so easily. She's back on me with no warning, like a cat.

"I'll tell you what you don't know – that's what I'll do!" And I have to paste my interested face on top of my exasperated face, start my head nodding in a "You don't say?" kind of agreement that I'll perfect by my teen years so she'll think that I'm listening, but I'm really a thousand miles away.

The next time, I'm ready for her. This time I answer the other way. I tell her that, no, no one has ever told me a thing about what my mother and my grandmother went through in the Holocaust - thinking my ignorance will buy me a quick exit.

Instead, it's even worse - she has to tell me the entire story of Krivich, of how they were all massacred, of all the wonderful things my grandfather did to save everyone's lives. She's friendlier; she warms to her topic; she takes me under her wing. She drags me off to the living room, pats the couch next to her saying, "Zezech, mameleh," and I'm sure I'll be stuck there all my livelong days. I will flunk out of grade school, I'll die of starvation; I'll never stand up again - not to go to the bathroom, not to go to college, not to get married. She'll release me only when one of us dies, and it will probably be me.

It would help if Mrs. Botwinik could remember that she's already asked me this before, in just the same way, backed up against the counter, her eyes steely on mine behind her bifocals. But she can't tell me apart from my sisters; there are seven of us, after all, and she can't even tell me from me. It's indiscriminate on her part and bad luck on mine, being cornered in the kitchen. She has a story to tell and she doesn't care which one of us does the hearing.

At ten, I've had enough of the Holocaust. When my parents start their stories, I can feel my brain click off. After all, I know the ending of every story, how everyone dies, the death that comes closer and closer no matter how funny the story may seem, no matter how amusing the anecdote. And I can't stand to hear that ending to every story.

With two survivor parents and about ten thousand survivor relatives and their friends milling around our house, I've definitely tested out of the Holocaust. At ten, I'm old.

***

Tante was short and boxy and pleated, somehow, like an accordion. She walked in to my grandmother's apartment wearing a printed rayon dress with darted breasts and a thousand pleats falling half way between her knees and her ankles. Her closet must have been filled with these dresses. She wore a thin belt wrapped around her waist like a tie around the middle of a sausage, nude-colored hose, and sensible low orthopedic shoes. Her legs were thick and she crossed them at the ankle probably because she could no longer cross them at the thigh.

She was known just by the name "Tante," which meant 'aunt' in Yiddish, but with no first name, just Tante. But since I had no idea what "Tante" meant, I had no idea who she was or why she was at all the family get-togethers for my mother's side of the family. She arrived with Uncle, who was also known by that one word name, but at least I knew what uncle meant. It was an English word, and, anyway, I knew he was my grandmother's brother, Uncle Izzy.

Tante was heavy like a rock and, the minute she and Uncle arrived, Uncle would sit her down somewhere - plant her - and leave her there, like maybe she was needed in that location to hold down that side of the room. She never left her position. She couldn't get up again anyway. Not only did her bulk prevent this, but the plastic covering the chair or the couch she sat on either formed a chemical reaction with the rayon of her print dresses, gluing her there, or she stayed very still to avoid sliding off and ending up in an undignified puddle on the ground.

Although Tante was old, she still had thick, inky black, Jewish hair; blunt cut, with creases in it, like it had been ironed.

She wore her hair pulled back from her face with a comb of some type, but there were little ringlet-type bangs allowed to curl on her forehead, like maybe this had been in style in Cuba in the 1920s, when she was young.

Uncle brought her morsels of food from the dining room, because she was trapped in that chair, trapped also in her Yiddish because she couldn't speak a word of English, so food appeared in her hands, coffee appeared on the table before her. She sat alone, smiling with a pretty good attempt at a Mona Lisa smile, though she wasn't young and wasn't pretty, even though her lips didn't quite meet over her teeth. She clasped her hands before her.

She reached for us as we ran past and we tried not to get caught because what could be worse than being caught by someone you didn't know at a party filled with people you did know? And what could be worse than being caught by the one person at that party who didn't know a word of English? And what could I say to her, sitting there in her printed rayon dress, just another icon from the old country even though, little did I know, she was really from Cuba, one of her first languages Spanish, not just Yiddish?

Who was she, I wondered? Every time the house would fill with relatives, she would come, following with Uncle Izzy, jabbing at everyone around her to translate all the conversations into Yiddish. Uncle Izzy seemed to enjoy her presence, seemed to like how she sat in one place, where he watched her, where she couldn't get too involved in conversations. Sometimes then he ignored her, or smiled benevolently, or condescendingly, or patronizingly.

One day I asked Mom about it.

"Who is Tante, Mom? How is she related to us? And

why does she always come with Uncle Izzy?"

And she gasped, and when she was done gasping she said, "She's Uncle's wife, don't you know that?"

When I figured out the family connection, I realized that somehow my Aunt Miriam was Uncle Izzy and Tante's daughter. And, of course, since nothing in our family made sense, this didn't either, and not just because Miriam was really Mom's cousin and so couldn't be my aunt. But the far more troubling issue was Miriam being related to Tante.

There was no way to conceive of a way that my aunt with the chic, ash blonde, Marlo Thomas-flipped hair, the impeccable Chanel-like suits, and the Psychology doctorate, had somehow emerged from Tante - from that tightly cinched waist, from somewhere underneath those printed rayon dresses, from inside the girdle, the garter belts, the stockings. How could my polished Aunt Miriam emerge from a woman who never learned one word of English, not even "Hello"? A woman who sat as placid as a side of beef at all those parties, year after year, until one day she was gone?

But Miriam was Uncle Izzy and Tante's child, and a child who married legendarily too. Unlike my Mom, who married Dad, a Polish immigrant who became a laundry man and stayed a laundryman, who never completed his education, and who retained his Polish accent, Miriam married an American. We never knew what Meyer did for a living before he was forty, but we did know what he did after that: he became a Cardiologist and then he became Better Than Us.

Dr. Meyer Goldman, Miriam's husband, did not come to family parties. Who would he talk to? My father? About what?

Running a laundry? To Uncle Barney? About what? Running a laundry? We were a laundry-running family. Owning a laundry was a stain not even our laundries could remove. It sullied all seven of us, not just my Dad, since we all were tainted by his low-status occupation and our presumed destinies as laundresses.

Miriam showed up at the family get-togethers, chic, flipped, suited, educated, grasping each of her sons by the hand. Meyer was never with her. There was always an excuse, from hospital rounds to seeing patients or attending medical conferences. But we knew the real reason: he was too good for us, at least that's what I heard Mom say after each and every one of these parties. She said, "What does he think? He's too good for us? He thinks he's such a hot shot because he's a doctor? He didn't even become a doctor till he was in his forties!" Like maybe she thought there was still hope for Dad, the laundryman, in his white, v-necked T-shirt and khaki work pants, listening to her while he chewed on a toothpick.

Miriam was a serious woman, much more serious than the adults I was used to. Because she knew that Mom thought I was brilliant, she spent a little too much time with me. There was none of that off-hand interest in the answers to questions that I usually got from grown ups about my favorite subjects in school or who my teachers were. No, Miriam was watching me, psychoanalyzing me, peering into the empty hole of my brain and finding out what even my own mother didn't know: I wasn't so extraordinary.

Miriam and her family lived in downtown Chicago in an old brownstone in what used to be a very Jewish part of town. Despite their family's escalating income, they couldn't leave the old brownstone because Miriam wouldn't leave her father and mother, Uncle and Tante, who lived above what had once been her father's tailor shop. Uncle Izzy had to be within walking distance of his shul, not to mention the kosher butcher and bakery. He wasn't leaving and Miriam wasn't leaving without him, so after a few years she and Meyer bought out the owner of the brownstone and lived there. Miriam, Meyer and the kids on the top floor, Uncle Izzy and Tante the floor below, and, when Uncle Izzy retired, a shoemaker in business on the ground floor.

Miriam had a different parenting theory going on than her two cousins, my Mom and Reva, who were raising the twelve of their communal children to get through high school but, if we didn't, to work; and to marry Jews, but, if we didn't, who wanted to be Jewish anyway with Nazis hidden everywhere ready to kill all of us?

Miriam was raising her boys Orthodox, or, at least, Uncle Izzy was raising them Orthodox, schlepping them off to shul with him each Saturday. And they were being raised to go to medical school, to meet or exceed the achievements of their father. They would not suffer a mid-life career change as their father had. They were being raised from scratch to be cardiologists.

Kenny and Ronnie looked different than the rest of us when they arrived at our family get-togethers. They wore dress clothes - slacks, neat dress shirts, and sometimes suit jackets and ties. They had slick Bryl Creamed hair. Ronnie had glasses that a forty-year-old physician would wear - myopic, black-framed glasses; Kenny had bucked teeth.

Kenny was one year older than me, and he'd lurk around me each time we were together because he knew we had a lot in common. We were both the pianists of our families. But even though I tried my best, I couldn't play like Kenny. I took piano lessons just like all the little Jewish girls in Skokie do, and I was considered quite a prodigy, always playing the harder version of all the songs being played by the other girls in my class. I had a little lined musical composition book in which I meticulously composed my own songs, and a little white plaster Beethoven who stared down at me from our upright Cable piano. But I couldn't play like Kenny and we both knew it.

Each time I saw him, I thought I had prepared enough; I was ready. I had perfected my *Love Story*, worked on the entire book of songs from *Fiddler on the Roof;* I had nailed down *Alley Cat*. But there was no time for me to show him anything. He walked in the door, spotted the piano and charged over. Then, while I stood with my mouth open gulping air, he began to play concertos and movements, throwing in some blues and then some jazz; he played with one hand, then two, then three or four hands. He played with his feet.

He said, "C'mon, Linda. Play something!"

But each time he did this, my hands turned into stumps at my side. When I sat down on the bench, I pulled out the best I had. I started the trill to *Fur Elise*. But even I could hear that it sounded trite. Immediately, he sensed my weakness, my faltering. So he pushed me off the piano bench, stealing the keys from me, and then played the whole piece better than I ever played it, and laughed at me while he was doing it, his bucked teeth gleaming.

Thirteen

Yiddish Illiterate

I'm sitting on a lawn chair in our backyard, my relatives all ringed around me, the sun beating down on our heads, mottled through the leaves of the trees overhead. There's a lot of boisterous conversation going on around me, but I sit there staring straight ahead, the idiot American granddaughter. They talk around me, over me, under me, like I'm a vegetable. I don't understand a word they're saying. They're speaking Yiddish.

I've made a concerted effort not to learn Yiddish. For some reason, from the moment I hear it as a small child, I cast it off, decide it's not for me, that it's a relic of the Old Country. I resist Yiddish, fight its penetration into my brain tooth and nail. I give my mother a blank look when she tries to speak to me in it. I make her translate.

I give myself several reasons for my antagonism. First of

all, I decide right off the bat that it's a dead language, so there's no reason to learn it. After all, only the grown ups around me speak Yiddish, none of the kids. I figure I can wait this thing out. I've also absorbed my parents' desire to be American in all things, to cast off the Old World and embrace the new, and so I cast off the Old World's Yiddish and embrace the New World's English. Of course, they don't mean to do that with language; they want to be able to speak to their children in their mother tongue. And, last of all, since Yiddish is used to hide everything interesting and tantalizing from me, I have a certain amount of hostility towards it.

My refusal to learn Yiddish causes some problems because one set of grandparents, my father's parents, never learns English. They resist English as well as I resist Yiddish, eventually dying without letting a syllable touch their lips. And why should they learn it anyway? Yiddish serves all their needs; they commission their sons and daughters to learn English for them, to handle all their transactions with non-Yiddish-speaking merchants, to handle their communications with the outside world. These two grandparents of mine seem to know that it just might not be worth the time and effort to learn such an elaborate, messy and confusing language like English before they die.

My Dad's parents are determined to spend their days in America relaxing and enjoying their new status as "senior citizens" in this new country, even if those days stack up together into years and even decades. They never get over the novelty of safety; never take it for granted. They never stop marveling at the amazing American innovations. The convenience of grocery stores - so much better than starving! The traffic signals on every street corner regulating the cars - so much better than cars and horses and wagons all insisting on going at the same time! The mild weather in Chicago compared to Poland and Siberia - a heat wave!

Just because I can't speak Yiddish doesn't mean that I can't understand some of it. I do understand adjectives and imperatives and direct commands and reprimands. If my mother is mad at someone and decides to hurl an insult under her breath, I can understand that too, the *goniffs*, the *schlimazels*, the *yachnehs*. But the regular conversational ebbs and flows, the make up of ordinary sentences with nouns and verbs, that escapes me.

My other grandparents, my mother's parents, learn English, my grandmother better than my grandfather. She understands every word I say; there's no escaping her, tricking her, or pulling a fast one on her. She's watching me all the days of my life with eyes magnified by her glasses and ears sharp with the nuances of five languages. All this while my grandfather sits nearby in a suit, his fedora always on his head, even inside the house, practicing the words he has just learned on me.

"Linda, *mameleh*, tell me again. Beetles are bugs, nu? Monkeys are animals. But now the Monkees and the Beatles sing songs on the radio? How can this be?"

I'm sitting in my Dad's mother's dim, shiny-tiled little kitchen eating ice cream. My grandmother loves getting me alone in her little apartment, tempting me up there with ice cream. She pulls out the tiniest carton of ice cream in the world, which has been made smaller still by being subdivided into three Neapolitan flavors, and then scoops some out for me. Even though I don't speak Yiddish, I'm somehow able to communicate to her what flavors I like because she gives me the vanilla and strawberry. And then I sit there, eating it in the silent room, the spoon clinking against the dish, echoing off the tile floor, the tile walls of her kitchen, while she watches me.

There's nothing fancy about this other grandmother of mine, Sosha Burstein. She's short and stout with a round head just like my Dad's, but wrinkled up, her face fallen. She has long, steel gray hair that she winds up into a bun and then wraps in a hairnet, and she has an army of cotton housecoats that hang in her bedroom closet and smell of mothballs. She wears a different one each day along with practical orthopedic shoes and stockings that sometimes sag. And when she sits down, she's all lap. Even her breasts are part of her lap. She wears no bra.

Her gray hair hangs long when out of the bun. I catch her like that once in her apartment by accident - all round and wrinkled, antique and male, and the incongruous hair, long down her back, and gray.

She reaches out nimble fingers, both wrinkled and chubby at the same time, for me, and I, the three-year-old, the four-year-old and the five - veer around those fingers, not wanting to be stopped in my mad dash. I am heading somewhere important, to the swing set, to the front yard, running from Mom, to trail one of my sisters around the house. I veer away from those hands and she, heavy in her housecoat, trapped in a nearly busted through lawn chair, flails her arms in the air for an extra moment before they flutter back down to her sides.

When she needs to dress up she puts on a black dress with a fake fur collar, but otherwise it's a cotton housecoat every day, striped or plaid, buttons running down the front. She's no fashion icon, she'll throw anything on, pairing her housecoats with my grandfather's socks and shoes, his glasses perched on her nose. She doesn't let herself go after he dies in the early sixties; she had let herself go the minute she got married under the chuppah in Poland. Vanity was for single girls.

She smiles at me; I smile back at her. To tell her the ice cream is delicious, I have to roll my eyes upward and say, "Mmmm!" Other things I have to say in pantomime. She offers me water by taking an imaginary drink with an imaginary cup. If I don't feel good I clutch my belly or my head, whichever one is hurting. If I'm tired, I rest my head sideways on two hands folded together. I'm in a foreign country here in her apartment, a tiny slice of Jewish Poland right here in Chicago. I never know what she's thinking.

Even though I have two grandmothers, silence weighs heavily in all directions. With my Mom's mother the silence is made up of the things I'm not allowed to ask about and the list grows longer each year. I can't ask about what happened to her during World War II and I can't ask what happened to her family, and soon there's my dead Aunt Reva to add to the list of dead, of erroneous dead, all pinned behind her pursed lips. I'm unsure if she believes that by not allowing the words out she believes none of it ever happened, or if she just can't live with the talking, the normalcy of talking, of transforming something so horrific into the ordinariness of words.

With my Dad's mother, there's the chasm of no common language. Even though she has so much to frown about, my Dad's mother always has a smile on her face. Despite five dead babies, despite the death of her beloved daughter Faige, the aunt I never met, she is cheery, rosy with contentment. She grabs me to her like I'm her buoy, her lifeline to the future, which of course I am, but I am forever wriggling free. She speaks to me in Yiddish and I shake my head, not understanding. We live in different countries, she and I. My mother intercedes; she tells her in Yiddish, "The little ones, they don't understand Yiddish." But that I understand.

My grandmother didn't know exactly when my father was born, or if she knew she wasn't telling. We knew he was born in April, the 8th or 9th; we weren't quite sure, he wasn't sure, and my grandmother was mum. And we didn't know what year. Was it 1925, 1926, or 1927? How could she not know when she gave birth to her first son? Of course, she had been told not to remember by a village Rabbi long ago, and so she held the secrets of my Dad and his siblings' infancies under lock and key.

First came my aunt Pearl, the oldest daughter. Then, and this started all the trouble, came those five dead babies, or babies who were born alive and then died in my grandmother's arms, born with no rectums.

Then my grandmother Sosha, stocky and plain, who had caught herself a husband, my grandfather, the one-eyed Gershon, went to ask for help from the Rabbi.

"The evil eye is watching you, Sosha," the Rabbi said. "Trick him. Give your children names to fool him; don't dress them as babies and don't coddle them. The Angel of Death will be fooled and he'll move onto the next house."

The next baby was born, Etta, and she lived. And then Faige was born, living eighteen years but dying of Typhus after the war in Tashkent. When my Dad was born, the third living child and the first boy, my grandmother was ready with an arsenal of tricks to fool the Angel of Death. Baby? What baby? She forgot his birth date, his birth weight; there was no coddling, no babyhood. He was erased from existence as soon as he existed.

And then came two more boys, my uncles Meyer and Sid. Before the war, my grandmother could count six living children and five dead ones, but after the war her numbers switched. Six dead, five living.

What does it mean to have no idea when your father was born? And even now with his temporary Arizona Driver's license as irrefutable evidence that he was born in 1927, it's not.

My mother says, "Oh, he always liked to use 1927 for a birth date, but it wasn't true. He didn't know. Even his mother didn't know."

If I don't know when he was born, then how do I know how old he was when he died? Birth certificates were casual things in the old country, maybe you had one, maybe you didn't, or maybe the synagogue burnt down with all of them. Who knew? In a religion where so much was specific, the dietary laws and the prayers, the rules for men and women, something that would seem to be very exact - one's birth - was instead, inexact. Lost in the war, lost in someone's memories.

Coupled with not knowing when Dad was born is the issue of not knowing where Dad was born. Russia kept gobbling up Poland but Poland kept resurging, reestablishing its independence, and then tiny provinces kept breaking away, and on top of that, Jews weren't citizens at all. The map of the world where my parents were from was a great unknown, with shifting boundaries, Russia teeming at the edges of Dad's native Poland and Mom's native Lithuania so that sometimes even Mom and Dad had no idea where they were from. Sometimes Dad was Polish, sometimes Russian; sometimes Mom was Russian, sometimes Lithuanian. They tugged over the city of Vilna between them, disagreeing over whether it was in Russian, Polish, or Lithuanian territory in a certain year, sure that as a place that once harbored one hundred thousand Jews they both wanted to claim it.

Besides the question of when he was born and where he was born, there is, of course, the issue of what Dad is called, because in a very real way he's like God - I don't even know his name. There's the garbled mess of his first name and the garbled mess of our last name; there's the way our name doesn't match the rest of the family's, and the way the spelling wouldn't match even if the sound did. He's incognito, anonymous, hidden; and because he is, so are we.

We called my grandfather on that side of the family Zayda Gershon. Since he died when I was two or three, I know him mostly as a photograph, an older man forever sitting in our sun and shade-dappled back yard on a broken lawn chair, a patch over one eye. My Mom now insists I'm wrong. She says he never had a patch, and anyway, I was too young to remember. Maybe I've gotten him mixed up with photos I've seen of Moshe Dayan, she says. I remember a patch.

How he lost his eye was a story always told in one sentence. He was trying to avoid the Tsar's draft and so shot out his eye. Later I realize it's impossible to shoot out an eye without shooting off a head, but at the time this answer seems reasonable enough and romantic, like a one-man duel.

It turned out it was a little less dramatic in execution. He was served with a draft notice, which would have meant twenty-five years in the Russian army and, as a Jew, certain death since Jews tended not to survive their army terms, ending up dead in mysterious ways. To get out of the compulsory service, some Jewish men faked respiratory illnesses, infections, limps; some lost weight, gained weight, or cut off fingers. My grandfather blinded himself in one eye.

Although he was well loved, my Dad had assumed his father's place in the family. My grandfather was placid, peaceful; he missed half the things other people saw. He lacked peripheral vision.

For her weekly visits to our house, my grandmother Sosha dressed up. She took off the housecoat she always wore and put on her dressy dress, the black, knee-length sack with buttons down the middle and an oversized fake fur collar. Her hair stayed in the bun. Then she picked up her purse and waited all Sunday morning by her window looking out on Sawyer.

She was looking for my Dad, looking for the blue roof of his station wagon driving down her street like a rectangular box, watching as he parked in front of her building, as my father's round head came out of the car and bobbed up the skinny sidewalk to the building. He rang the buzzer underneath her name down in the vestibule of the building, his thumb pressing on the one below *Burstein,* and she let him up.

Hobbling out of the door next to Dad, she rambled in Yiddish, telling him all the news she stored up all week, all the way down the muffled, carpeted steps, through the vestibule, in the car, and as Dad drove through the streets of Chicago, cut through a sliver of Evanston, and then headed into Skokie, to get to our house.

Once there, he escorted her in like a queen, and set her upon a sofa from which she wouldn't move the entire day. He settled her in with coffee, with pastries from the kosher bakery, a pillow for her back. I sat down beside her trying to talk with hand gestures, with charades; I tried to write out sentences, like maybe she was deaf to English but she could read it. But she sat there placidly; both of us mute across our great language divide. She was an observer watching her American descendants.

She watched my older sisters in their mini skirts, watched the HI-FI with its loud Beatles music, watched all of us with our matching Sassoon haircuts, watched Mom bustling around her non-kosher kitchen. My grandmother sat there, a benign smile on her face, happy just to sit there, her dress a black swathe across Mom's Amerikanish couch, smiling and shaking her head "no" to offers of Mom's non-kosher food, talking in one Yiddish dialect to Dad and in another to Mom, the Litvak.

She sat there, her steel gray hair parted in the middle, pulled back in its bun, her round head, plump arms, her veined legs encased in thick orthopedic shoes. She sat there the whole day, into the evening, as the sun set around her, shadows fell over her, Mom flicking the lamps on beside her.

She sat until Dad came and got her, escorting her out like royalty, like a queen. Out the door and into the car and back through Skokie, through just a sliver of Evanston, and then back into Chicago, to the apartment on Sawyer Avenue. Then he sat her back down on her couch by the window, and she looked out the window at his round head bobbing as he walked down the sidewalk to his car, watching as he backed the blue rectangle of his Oldsmobile out of his parking spot and drove away.

Aunt Etta sometimes came over to see Mom on weekends alone. Our house cleared out fast with her arrival, all seven of us disappearing out of the various doors. Etta's critical eye could notice the slightest evidence indicative of impending adolescence - when she asked our mother if we'd gotten our periods yet - or she noticed the slightest precursor to a pimple showing up on our faces, the need for the shaving of our legs before we noticed, when we thought we were still just children loping around the house like foals.

Aunt Etta always had an ulterior motive for coming over, something new to show off, or something about herself that was so new and improved that she just couldn't wait till the next time the couples got together to show Mom. No, it couldn't wait; Etta had to schlep all the way from downtown Skokie in her brand new Cadillac to show her. She had to risk parking the brand new Cadillac on the curb with all those dirty neighborhood kids playing in the street outside and next to Mom's dented and beat up 1965 Chevy Nova. Even parking next to such a *schmatta* of a car was a danger for her brand new Cadillac, but it was so important Mom had to see, so she had to run the risk and come.

Aunt Etta stood in the middle of our kitchen, Mom seated in a chair at the table, and showed off to Mom in all her glory. Sometimes it was just possessions she showed off, maybe a new fur coat, which she wore even if it was summer, maybe a new alligator bag, maybe a new wig. They wouldn't leave the kitchen, not even if Mom wanted to show something off, like her four chandeliers (one in the upstairs bath even!), our new HIFI system, or even the new cut velvet wallpaper she had put in the upstairs bathroom to go with the chandelier. There was some type of force field holding them in the kitchen. They couldn't leave.

Normally, however, Aunt Etta was there to show off her body. Aunt Etta was always on a diet and had always just transformed herself from her former dowdy, drab self of five pounds ago into a svelte teenager. It was the 1960s and everyone wanted to be a teenager - even Jewish ladies from Poland. She turned, pirouetted, pranced, and strutted all over our linoleum like a fashion model, showing off clothes that, she swore, she couldn't even pull up over one *foot* five pounds ago but now were hanging off her. She'd have to buy more.

Sometimes I walked in and found Aunt Etta stripping off her clothes because Mom just had to see the true glory of her weight loss to appreciate it. Maybe she just wanted to show how her stomach had gone in or how her hips were measuring smaller - she brought along her own tape measure - or how her breasts retained their cleavage - *kenehora!* - but were five pounds smaller. And there went her clothes. Orange mini-dress, lime dickie, white wet look boots, patterned tights, all on my forty-something aunt in 1960s Skokie. She kept on her plasticine wig, her fake eyelashes, and her 18-hour bra and girdle just in case someone came in. She was in the kitchen, after all, and Mom did have seven daughters zooming in and out of the screen door.

The five pounds that Aunt Etta lost had come off one molecule at a time from every crevice of her body, slimming down thighs and buttocks, smoothing jowls and cheeks and giving her the courage to dress like her sixteen-year-old daughter, and frightening half the kids in the neighborhood while doing so. This was not a pretty sight. Etta had spent much of her life frowning, so by her late forties her entire face pulled down towards the earth, the corners of her mouth like two arrowheads pointing due south. This wasn't the face you wanted to see on top of a mini-dress or emerging from a lime dickie.

My Mom, always polite, sat at the kitchen table nodding,

exclaiming with Etta over the vanished five pounds. She shook her head in wonder at Etta, *Where did the five pounds go?* - like maybe a thief had come and stolen them in the middle of the night from Etta's apartment.

"*Takeh!*" she said, exclaiming in unison with Etta over her dramatically slimmed down body. How young she looked! How svelte! How perfect in the young hippy clothes! Had Uncle Saul noticed?

And where *did* that five pounds go? Did it bounce around the world looking for another woman to land upon? Did it lurk in the dark corners of our house, waiting for one of us to eat another mouthful of kishka and then jump on our bellies, forming another roll? Did it join with other orphaned five-pound weight losses rolling out of Weight Watcher's and TOPS meetings and become a huge fifty-pound boulder careening through Skokie looking for a skinny woman to land on?

"Or maybe," Mom said once Aunt Etta climbed in her Cadillac and rumbled back down the street, "maybe it was all just water weight." And the five pounds were even now following Etta up the stairs to her apartment, to bounce back on her by sundown.

Etta could buy a lot of things, a lot more than Mom could with a laundry man for a husband. She and my Uncle Saul owned a gas station on a key corner of downtown Skokie, where two angled roads came together in a sharp point, right next to a car dealership where a new car always rotated on a platform fifty feet up in the air. They also lived near their gas station in an apartment on another street that met at a thirty-degree angle with all the other streets converging all across downtown Skokie. In there,

Etta's decorating scheme was very simple - everything was done in gold leaf, gold lame, and gold brocade.

Besides two sons, Etta had a daughter, my cousin Sharon, who was good friends with my sister Francine because Sharon, too, was lovely. She had blonde hair, angled eyes, and was, before her downfall, angelic. But in 1966, when she was sixteen, Sharon had a downfall. There was no hiding this downfall from her family, from our family, from downtown Skokie, where she lived, or the suburban neighborhoods, where we lived. She got pregnant and my Aunt Etta found out, her voice ringing out with the news through the open windows of their apartment one Saturday morning.

I never found out what Sharon had been doing to be found out. Had she been knitting baby booties? Looking up names in a baby name book? All I knew for sure was that my second cousin was nesting there in her flat teenage belly at the moment when Etta began yelling, throwing dishes, slamming doors, calling people, everyone she knew.

Sharon's teen years were over; cut short, a train wreck. Where before she used to huddle with Francine and gossip about boys, compare *Teen Beat* magazines, and talk about music bands, rock stars and which dreamy guy of their imaginations they hoped to marry, now Sharon was pregnant, laden, heavy. There was some temporary husband following her everywhere, looking on possessively, a guy my aunt and uncle are first eager for her to marry and then crazed for her to divorce. There was Sharon's blonde bouffant, now going brown, lifeless, hacked off, her makeup undone, her clothes unmatched; she wore pregnancy muumuus. She had grown up.

***

My Dad's oldest sister, Aunt Pearl, wore high heels too small for her feet, dresses that were too tight for her body, and a permanent worry crease between her eyebrows. When she and my Uncle Zalman came out to Skokie to visit us from their apartment in Chicago, they no more than pulled up to the curb than she was out of the car, teetering off on her high heels, rushing off into the house to spend the afternoon with Mom. There she sat down at the kitchen table, hauled her purse up beside her, fished out a pile of clean, folded, white cloth handkerchiefs and placed them in easy reach of her right hand. Then she started talking.

Sobbing, Aunt Pearl told Mom about her *meshuganah* son-in-law, her *zaftig* daughter and her son. She didn't lie or minimize her problems unlike other members of the family who could never admit anything was wrong with any of their children, circling their wagons around their children.

But not Aunt Pearl. She sat down at Mom's kitchen table, drank cup after cup of sugar-laden coffee, and poured out her *tsoris* to Mom in a never-ending flow of Yiddish punctuated by Mom's frequent "*takeh!*" which translated somewhere between "You don't say!" and "Oh my God!" Sympathy was what Aunt Pearl wanted and sympathy was what she got in our house. There were no solutions to these types of problems; after all, they weren't made up. Her son-in-law was a lunatic; her daughter was heavy. Her son? Who knew what he was? What could Mom say? So she soothed Aunt Pearl with fresh percolated coffee and rugalach from the kosher bakery.

Meanwhile, Uncle Zalman got stuck next to his car, a ramshackle 1954 Chevy Bel Air sedan, already fourteen-years-old by that time, since Dad would have come up to greet him. They stood there, kicking its tires, Dad comparing it to our 1964

Oldsmobile station wagon standing in the driveway. They were as different as their cars: Uncle Zalman formal in a shiny, aging suit; Dad casual, American, in a sleeveless undershirt and shorts, black socks and dress shoes. Dad never understood the concept of sandals.

Dad waved his head in the direction of Zalman's car and said, "It's still running?"

Zalman hung his head, shrugged, "A little knocking here and there; not so bad."

Then Dad gestured over to our car. "You should get one like this."

"Aah," Zalman shook his head like this was an impossibility that he just couldn't imagine. "Maybe some day."

As the afternoon wore on, they made their way around the house to stand outside on the patio. There Uncle Zalman admired our backyard, our lawnmower, the sprinklers, and the swing set, like our family lived in a foreign country where Jews were allowed to own these things. He shook his head wistfully. Somehow where he lived - in the terrain inside his head - none of this was allowed. So settled in; so hard to pack up and run when the Nazis come again. There was a sense of wonder about my Dad among my apartment-dwelling relatives: what an incredible optimist he was to buy a house.

Our cousin Gilda came along on the visit with her parents, but she disappeared with Francine, Lauren, and Brenda, their bedroom door slamming shut on Mindy and me, but we sat outside listening anyway. We were in awe of Gilda, with her over-developed body for sixteen, her busting tight hippie jeans and the halter-tops she wore that didn't quite cover her dangerously swinging breasts. She wore pasty makeup to cover acne scars and heavy black eyeliner around her tilted eyes, evidence, we thought, of some Cossack ancestor.

Through the door we heard her woeful tales of dating boys who asked her out and who then parked on dark side streets groping her, and how she let them up her bra or down her skirt, or maybe it was down her bra and up her skirt - I wasn't sure - and then she told how the boys never called the next day. We heard about her newest diet, since she was always on one, in a never-ending war against a body that thought it was still in Poland, meant to give birth to ten children and breastfeed them all while milking cows and plucking chickens. Then the door opened and Gilda reappeared from the gloom of my sisters' bedroom, her tilted eyes now teary, her black eyeliner now smudged, her black hair bedraggled.

Sometimes Neil, Gilda's brother, came along too, floating through each room, pale, smooth-faced and skinny, his inky black hair swept away from his face revealing a widow's peak, dressed in skinny, too-short, pants with white socks and tie up shoes. A teenaged Jewish Count Dracula. In a family where awkward was not unusual, where all my boy cousins seemed to be aging not so much into men but into giant overgrown boys, Neil seemed odd, even against that backdrop.

There were a few other daughters in this family too. The one married to the lunatic son-in-law showed up with her husband and he was just nutty enough to play with us little girls, but then sometimes he'd play a little too long, too hard, too fast. He'd swing me by one arm and one leg in a circle, spinning and spinning, and just when he'd picked up an alarming amount of speed, that's when he'd let go, and I'd go spiraling off into space. After a while, he didn't come anymore and then, after a longer while, he wasn't the son-in-law anymore.

In retrospect, it appeared that Pearl was right, she did have a lot to worry about those days that she sat at my mother's table, searching for clean handkerchiefs, sobbing about her children. More misery was on its way.

There was a family legend that she had fallen in love with Zalman and was determined to marry him even though it was a common belief in their village that his family had a curse on it. Pearl scoffed at this, saying she didn't believe in such nonsense. When she and Zalman got visas to leave Poland and then got into Panama before World War II broke out, and when she had her first three children with no problem, this curse business must have seemed like nonsense.

But in Panama her luck began changing.

One of the children had a birth defect. Later, a grandchild died of cancer at twenty-four. Even later, my cousin Gilda of the dangerously swinging breasts, committed suicide, jumping out of her bedroom window at their home in Florida when everyone else was in the other room and thought she was in her room safely lying down.

But right then, in 1968, Pearl was able to sit at my mother's kitchen table, innocent in her belief that things were as bad as they ever were going to be.

Fourteen

By Blood and By Marriage

Here's how my aunts and uncles walk in our house: my aunts herd my uncles along, out of their cars, down the sidewalk to our front door, out of their coats, scarves, and hats, and down through the foyer to the kitchen. They talk to them slowly, enunciating every word, like the uncles are their extra, fully-grown, but kind of dense, younger sons. Each of them gets their husband a plate of food and a drink because my uncles have never served themselves food. They stand befuddled before stoves and refrigerators, mystified by where the plates and silverware are located in their own kitchens. They are helpless.

I had a lot of aunts and uncles. Sometimes it seemed like I had more aunts than I had uncles, more aunts than I should have, since in my mind there should be one aunt for each uncle, like our family was Noah's Ark. And being in a female-centric family, I always believed that the aunts were my blood relatives and the uncles were just the men they married. It was quite a shock when I realized that wasn't true, that some of the uncles were my blood relatives and that some of the aunts had married in.

There were a lot of reasons for this. My aunts had a lot of presence; they had strong personalities with strong opinions. Aunt Ida could express a textbook-sized opinion with just pursed lips and a shake of her head. Also, when the aunts came over, they'd come in the door talking, a continuation of the endless phone calls that ran between our home and their homes. In contrast to this, the men didn't talk except to the other men. When left alone with a child, they were struck dumb, all they could ask us about was school, and they were never alone with another woman.

The uncles' needs were taken care of because they were to devote themselves one hundred percent to that thing that the women weren't going to handle - earning a living. So they cruised through their lives like blipless EKG screens, my aunts running their lives like army generals, smoothing over the rough spots, insulating them from bad news and bad report cards, from the real cost of everything they bought; making the uncles' lives smooth - ponds with no ripples.

My Mom wasn't good at any of this. She didn't insulate Dad from the vicissitudes of life - he was out there bumping around. He worked fourteen days a week because she forgot to tell him to work just seven or even six. He never relaxed. She had no chance to raise him because when she met him he was all grown up, badly grown up. My Mom was no match for Dad; he had a towering will. He knew everything; his word was the law. How he came to believe this started well before their marriage, it started with him being the man of the house in his parents' house.

Because my grandmother Sosha ran their household and treated Zayda Gershon like he couldn't do anything right - and maybe because of him being blind in one eye - my Dad was treated like the man of the house from the moment he was born. My grandmother deferred to him in all things, while ignoring my grandfather. Dad ended up with quite a view of his own capability, of his own immortality, of his infallibility in all things.

Dad needed his brothers around him; nothing made him happier than being around them. Because of this, Dad and his brothers end up living near each other with Uncle Sid and Aunt Ida right by our elementary school in a house that was different than all the other cubes lining the street. It was a right triangle; a house with a roof so slanted that it looked like half of it had been sheared off. In the living room, this angle formed huge windows, the light of which my Aunt Ida would combat by covering them with light-obscuring, heavy, beige, drawstring curtains that pulled from one side of the enormous living room clear across to the other side.

Uncle Meyer and Aunt Rose lived a couple blocks in the other direction and over into the Skokie school district. I was happy to have Aunt Rose so close by because she was my favorite aunt. At each family get together, once our seven sister line-up was over, my other aunts paid little attention to us. They preferred their own children, considering them more attractive, more interesting, smarter. But not Aunt Rose. Of course she loved her three sons. But Aunt Rose had wanted a girl and didn't get one, and so she'd look at us wistfully, admiring something unique about each one of us till we were hypnotized by her, listening to that praise, or overexcited, like puppies circling, wanting more attention.

Uncle Meyer and Aunt Rose lived in a box, like us, not a triangle. Their first house had one big picture window in front, no garage, a tiny kitchen, a living room, three small bedrooms, and one and a half baths. Both Dad's brothers' houses had basements down treacherous sets of stairs, about ten thousand of them; and half-finished basements, which had the cold dank smell of all the basements in Skokie, and which were filled with cast-off furniture. Furniture that wasn't allowed upstairs.

Mindy and I had spent some time in Rose's basement when Mom dumped us off there to play with our three cousins. Since Rose always wanted a daughter, she was excited to have us over for about the first five minutes, but then she got too busy scrubbing imaginary stains out of her linoleum floor and cooking a five-course dinner for Uncle Meyer to really pay any attention to us. So she sent us downstairs to play with the boys.

We descended the wooden steps, down into the bottomless pit of her basement, down stair after stair into the gloom, holding fearfully onto the railing, calling out the names of our cousins like we were Hansel and Gretel in the forest. Just as we were done inching out way through the blackness, around a final curve, thinking our next toehold would find nothing but air, a sheer drop to our deaths, the place was lit up to reveal a romper room, their downstairs recreation room, and our three cousins' faces.

We immediately looked for something to play with. We didn't have unrealistic expectations; we weren't expecting Barbies. But what we found was all testosterone. There was a big box of GI Joe action figures with their armored carriers; there were jeeps and guns; there was a foosball table; there were two games, Rock'em Sock'em Robots and Knock Your Block Off; and there were some miscellaneous toys, like boxing gloves, baseball mitts, bats, a set of bases, a catcher's mask and an umpire's vest. Mindy and I sat down on the couch, exasperated. Nothing had caught our fancy. The boys began to entertain us like anxious dates. Did we want to play baseball outside? Did we want to play touch football, wrestling, watch sports on TV, maybe play catch in a pickup game outside? How about handball against the side of the house?

Mindy and I drifted from toy to toy. Finally we wandered up the stairs, clomping steadily upwards, climbing this Mount Everest of stairways, barely seeing the peak of the light brown door at the top, the crack of light of Rose's warm, brown kitchen gleaming up ahead. Breathlessly, we broke through, gasping for air, the boys piling up behind us, almost knocking us down.

They invited us into their rooms. Mindy went off with the two younger ones and I went with Aaron since we were the oldest. After some perfunctory jumping on the beds, and some examining of the contents of his bookshelves, we sat down on his bed, and silence enveloped us.

Suddenly Aaron said, "Can I ask you a question?"

I nodded because I was ready to answer lots of questions. I was sure he wanted to know about the books I liked, my teachers, my friends, and my school. I also had somewhat of a crush on this cousin of mine since, despite being ten, I was obsessively concerned with whom I would marry. I looked at him expectantly.

But instead, he hemmed and hawed and finally burst out with, "Can I see your boobs?"

I remember the blood draining from my face and then looking down at the flat expanse of my chest, just to make sure that no breasts had actually grown there sometime in the last few hours; that I was still ten-years-old. I thought for a second that I must have heard him wrong but no, there he was, sitting politely on his side of the bed apparently waiting for me to lift my shirt. And then I ran.

***

Of all the people who married into our family, my Uncle Saul was the unlucky one; at least that's what Dad said. Marriage to Aunt Etta, whom he called the shrew of the family, was no easy job. In his marriage, Saul did the placating, the wheedling, the calming down, the avoidance of topics, the hiding. Since Saul had tried to leave Etta twice, once he stopped trying to leave her, she was forever suspicious, and then he was forever trying to make up for leaving her. She'd force him to pump gas in the snow so they wouldn't have to hire help at the gas station; she whined, she complained, she nagged; he nodded. When they came over for a Poker or kalooki night, Etta would walk up the path from the street complaining, in the front door complaining, complain all night, and leave complaining. Uncle Saul would nod.

During these parties, my sisters and I would hide in the basement watching TV, not wanting to stand at attention in the seven sisters line up. But sometimes we couldn't wait; we had to send someone upstairs to sneak in the kitchen to get food. Since I was the sneakiest, I normally went. We were starving down there.

Then, even though half the kitchen was bathed in light and cigarette smoke and the other half was dark and there was the dividing line of our counter and the overhead cabinets, every time I did this I got caught.

"Linda, mameleh, come kiss everyone goodnight!" my mother called out.

I sighed. Now I had done it. I'd have to circle the table saying goodnight to them all, the lone representative of the seven daughters. I approached my aunts' furry rouged faces and hard crunchy hair and kissed them as their hands rose to pinch my cheeks.

"Ah, this one's your prettiest, Helen. So smart! So thin! I think I'll take her home!" Aunt Rose teased, smiling.

"My Sharon's prettier, and not so skinny either," says Aunt Etta, pinching my arm as I kissed her cheek. Aunt Ida squeezed my hand as I kiss her goodnight. I swooped past my mother's pink lips smacking into the air.

I approached Uncle Sid's scratchy day-old bearded face as he lamented, "Harry, this one should have been a boy. Seven girls, oy vayesmere." I sigh.

As I approached Uncle Saul he quizzed me about the names of state capitols, not that he knew them. As long as I got Illinois right, he'd never know the difference.

"What's the capitol of Florida, maydala?"

"Um, Miami, Uncle Saul."

"New York?"

"New York City."

"Illinois?"

"Springfield."

He beamed. "Oy, so smart already! Kenehora!"

I rounded the bend, almost done. I kissed Dad, his face beet red from hitting the schnapps a little too hard; then I made it to Uncle Meyer who kissed me and said, "Goodnight, Lauren."

Across the table Aunt Rose hissed at him, "Meyer, that's

Linda!"

And he said, "Linda, Lauren, who can tell?" shrugging to Rose across the table.

I escaped with my food.

My mother's sister, Aunt Reva, was seldom at the poker parties because my Dad just preferred his side of the family. She could be invited in a pinch but not on purpose like his family was.

Aunt Reva was beautiful, like an overweight Snow White. She had glossy black hair, pale white skin, ruby lips and light eyes, all in a sweetheart-shaped face. She looked out on the world with sweet innocence, mainly because she didn't understand half of what was told her; she was not a bright woman.

She gave the impression of being tall both because of her weight and because she was so much taller than her husband, the diminutive Uncle Barney. Her hard helmet of black hair added additional height; her large bone structure even more. She had big feet, dimpled arms, exaggerated shapely calves, and a chest that was so large it arrived at the house a few minutes before her body came into view – the prow of the ship that was Aunt Reva.

Aunt Reva didn't dress to minimize her bulk or those breasts; most of the time her clothes exaggerated the flaws in her figure, making them more apparent. She wore a lot of cotton dresses with darts as big as tents for those breasts; there was always a v-neck showing a cavernous cleavage that things fell in: food, kids' toys, missing keys. The dresses had cinched-in waistlines that emphasized the in-and-out of her, the bust-to-hips of her, which was not a good thing. Many times the patterns of the dresses were also unfortunate, large prints or polka dots, with one large polka dot falling over each breast, beaming out like two giant, oversized nipples, search lights, so that it was impossible to look at anything else when you were looking at her.

There was one good thing about Aunt Reva having breasts as large as she did. When one of us got hurt playing - and we were always getting hurt if we were playing with her sons - we'd come into the kitchen crying and be faced with an immediate choice - Mom's flat, cold, hard chest, or Aunt Reva's voluminous, suffocating chest, for comfort. We always chose Aunt Reva's.

When Aunt Reva would sit at the kitchen table, she'd rest her huge chest on the tabletop, like she had just carted her breasts over there and laid them down, too exhausted to carry them around anymore that evening. Then our Uncle Herbie, a bra salesman and Reva and Mom's brother, would sit across the table eyeing it up with somewhat of a professional interest. Was he formulating mathematical equations in his mind, devising a set of ropes and pulleys, perhaps, that could be made to bring that chest upright, to make it stand at attention?

Adding pressure to Reva's existence as a larger woman was that she was married to Uncle Barney, small and bandy-legged like a rooster. He stood 5'3" on a good day, on a stand-on-his-tippy-toes kind of day, but, like all Jewish men, he insisted he was 5'8". His hair was one big graying, curly poof on his head, and he had the crazy charm of a short man, always diplomatic so he wouldn't get beat up, but as inflexible as a steel bar.

Uncle Barney was a self-made businessman, talked into the laundry business by Dad, but he had a different attitude about material goods. Unlike my parents who agreed that food and shelter deserved some outlay of money, Barney didn't believe in ever parting with one cent. My cousins lived in a rickety, broken down old Victorian on the South Side of Chicago; the children wore thrift store clothes.

Reva had three boys to Mom's oldest three girls, matching across the board. They were even all the same ages, like she was trying to keep up with Mom. Phil was Francine's age; Markey was Lauren's; Louie was Brenda's. Then something happened. My Mom was able to cover some distance by popping out the twins, which brought her to five children, and then messing up her birth control two more times, for me and Mindy.

Reva had no more children for eleven years, from 1955 to 1966, when she, too, had fraternal twin girls. One twin was even bigger than the other just like our twins. She also messed around a little with the naming thing just like Mom did, changing the smaller one's name after the girls were home.

Because of the mixed brainpower inherited from their parents, my five cousins became the lower achieving side of the family, which was always blamed on Aunt Reva. Not even Uncle Barney's wily, agile intelligence, his forbearers possibly including great talmudic minds, could resist the pull of Reva's empty head, her vacuous stare, her low I.Q. points. The brain waves pulsed like an EKG through the members of the family - careening highs and lows, and then finally flat-lining.

When I was little, all my crushes were mixed up in my head - the possible with the impossible, the likely with the unlikely. There was Davy Jones from the Monkees, who was pretty much a permanent mainstay. Since he was grown up and a big star, this may have appeared to have been an impossible crush, but I thought that I might be able to get around the grown up thing because I'd seen the movie *The Perils of Pauline* about ten times and I was aware that he could have himself frozen, wait for me to grow up, and then get thawed. But he wasn't Jewish. Now *that* was a problem.

Then there was my cousin Markey. Dark haired, six years older than me, and, at that time, when I was seven and he was thirteen, he was suspended in some primordial ooze during which his later flaws were not apparent. Later, out popped his bucked teeth - where could they have been hiding? Later he ended up lopsided, with a heavy bottom and a thinner top. Later he seemed mean-spirited, telling a lot of jokes all at the expense of his younger brother Louie, and then laughed at them himself, over and over again.

But at the time, I loved him. I was encouraged in this hopeless crush by Mom who gave me this interesting tidbit of Jewish Law: Jews were allowed to marry their first cousins. She failed to tell me that this law conflicted with United States law, which forbade it. When I found this out, Markey had to be downgraded to an improbable love interest, even lower than Davy Jones, even though Markey was Jewish. I realized I might just have to look beyond my family for my future husband.

After Reva arrived at family get-togethers, always at our house or our grandmother's since no one in their right mind would travel to her neighborhood; after her breasts arrived, then the rest of her, then Uncle Barney scampering in beside her, standing in her shadow; then my boy cousins came in.

They walked in and lined up - just like all of us lined up. In this case they formed a pattern – big, small, big, my cousins Phil and Louie forming a set of bookends for the smaller Markey. Aunt Reva dressed the boys in too-short pants and too tight shirts, and all three had shiny hair plastered to their heads with heavy, clearly defined side parts. Phil wore black, heavy-framed, square glasses and planted himself on the living room couch with a book - maybe something on Quantum Physics - to show his derision towards his brothers who were hopping up and down, ready to play.

Even though Markey and Louie were the same age as Lauren and Brenda, my sisters wouldn't go near them. They didn't need to go to the same school as these cousins of theirs to know where they fell on the social spectrum - below the bottom. And the twins had to reject anything the older girls rejected. So that left the boys to Mindy and me with small forays off with Sherry and Denise, just because if the twins knew we wanted something, they had to show us how easily they could take them away from us. But after a while they'd throw them back.

The boys spent a lot of time at each family party trying to get Mindy and me to go down to the basement to play strip blackjack. We were thrilled and scared by this proposal each and every time it happened. We found it thrilling that the boys thought we were so attractive that they kept badgering us about this. And we were scared for the obvious reason. Just the idea of sitting naked, having lost every hand of blackjack, was pretty terrifying. And we had no doubt we'd lose because there was never a game that we played with Markey that he didn't win, even dreidel, for which he made up his own rules, not able to read the Hebrew on the spinning top.

They spent a lot of time trying to convince us to play. They tried to talk us into it using all their powers of persuasion, like used car salesmen.

Cornering us in a dark hallway, Markey started the conversation with a sly look down the hall to make sure no one was eavesdropping.

"Hello ladies." We were eight and five.

He continued, giving us an assessing look. "How would you ladies like to go play a hand of blackjack?"

"In the kitchen?" I was the spokesperson.

"Well, maybe not the kitchen. We were thinking of something a little more private, like the laundry room."

"Um."

"And maybe different rules than usual."

"Different rules?"

"Like strip blackjack."

We wouldn't have to be naked, Markey and Louie said, because they'd let us wear our whole wardrobes if we wanted to, even throw hangers over our heads.

So we played one time, draping our bodies with coat hangers, extra shirts, shoes and sweaters, since everything would count as clothes in the game. And, of course, Mindy and I kept losing, hand after hand. Hangers were discarded, our ten pairs of socks thrown off, and soon we were down to just our regular clothes and an outside jacket and mittens.

For some reason, it seemed that Markey and Louie wanted to end up naked. They had no shame; they didn't pile on any extra clothes. It was like a day at the beach for them. They both end up sitting across from us with bare chests, both hairless preteens. I was becoming concerned that soon they would be down to their underpants, at which point Mindy and I would have to bolt.

Just as they were about to take off their belts, Mom happened to come downstairs. She seemed to have no idea what she was looking at, just that Mindy and I had strewn hangers all over the floor and the boys were sitting there topless.

"Boys! Get your clothes on! Linda, Mindy, clean up!" she

said, breaking up the game.

On May 29, 1969, Mom was on the telephone with Uncle Barney. It was early evening and she had been waiting for news about Aunt Reva, who'd had emergency surgery that day. The surgery, even though sudden, wasn't expected to be a big deal, just a suspected ectopic pregnancy, so no one was at the hospital; Barney had run his laundry all day, planning to go over after he closed.

The doctors opened up Reva's thirty-seven-year-old abdomen, expecting to find the ectopic pregnancy, perform a quick D+C, clean her out, and set her back upon her feet as good as new. But instead they found bleeding and a blood clot that stayed just ahead of their instruments until Reva lay dead on the operating table.

My Mom stood there next to the wall phone, talking to Uncle Barney who had gotten the news at his laundry and who had then called my grandmother and grandfather, my Uncle Herbie and my mother. My Dad sat at the kitchen table eating his solitary nighttime dinner. Things got quiet on her phone call. Right when I realized how quiet she was being and a second later that there were tears rolling down her face, Dad got impatient about the length of her phone call.

He said, "Chasia, get off the goddamned phone! Get me another beer!"

She turned to him and said, "Reva died."

Then, because Dad knew a little something about dead sisters, he didn't say anything else.

My Mom left the house that night with Dad, the seven of

us alone, parentless. Mindy and I were to be watched by our older sisters, who never checked to see if we were alive. They drove with Uncle Herbie down to my grandparents' apartment where they found my grandmother collapsed on the floor in her nightgown, wailing and crying, tearing at her hair, and banging her head against the wall. My grandfather sat immobile in a chair.

That evening I walked down our street with this mind-boggling news item - that my aunt had died - and I told everyone. I was the grief-stricken nine-year-old, the fragile, mourning, Shiva-sitter, the bearer of ill tidings. I milked it for all I could get. I became popular for a brief time that night, from six pm until nine pm, when the fading light and the calling mothers emptied the street, when my Dad's car pulled back in our garage and brought my parents home again.

Aunt Reva's family sat Shiva at our house for a lot of reasons. There was the list of problems with their house: the south side of Chicago problem, the bad neighborhood problem, the crumbling house problem, the fact that no one would travel that far no matter who had died, no matter how young. There was the fact that my mother was ready to assume this duty for her sister's widower and our house was ready, always sparkling clean.

Hundreds of people packed in during the week of Shiva, most of whom hadn't even known Reva. They knew my mother and my father, or my Uncle Herbie, or my grandparents, or they came from the Old Country and had heard that someone else from the Old Country had died. So they came. Although I didn't go to the funeral, the Shiva sitting taught me a lot about Jewish death rituals. There was the paradox of mourning amid mountains of food, of speaking of the dead in solemn tones while kvelling over the white fish. I felt right away that starving suited mourning a little more than all that eating. How do you express sincere condolences with your mouth full?

This was what everyone had to say about this premature death of my aunt, besides the miserable shaking of heads about my orphaned twin cousins, beyond the incomprehensible idea of Uncle Barney raising five children on his own. Every person said, "For *this* she survived the war?" And I wondered at this reasoning, the idea that there was no use in Reva surviving the war if she ending up dying anyway. I didn't understand. Wasn't it worth it to have come out alive from the forest for the twenty-four years she got? Would it have been better if she had died there if she was only going to get twenty-four years?

Or maybe it's just that every death in our family feels like a Holocaust death.

After her death, Reva's family exploded like a grenade had hit them. Louie gained weight; Markey became crueler, Phil seemed to distance himself from the family. My twin cousins were two and a half year old orphans, but the boys were taking care of things, raising them like a pair of footballs. They'd toss the girls to each other, swinging them so high in the air they'd almost fly away, and then they'd nearly miss catching them as they careened toward the ground. And they were in charge of the girls' wardrobes too. The girls were sent off to school each day like miniature bag ladies with mismatched shoes and socks; clothes that were too small, cheap, ripped; their hair unbrushed, unwashed.

Uncle Barney dated a lot after Reva died. He wasn't a Mr.

Mom type, trying to learn a new role, like being both mother and father to his five children. Rather, he told my mom, he wanted to get married again as soon as possible to have someone else take care of the children. And he knew precisely what he wanted. He wanted Reva back. But since she was gone forever, he seemed to be looking for a replacement Reva.

Since Uncle Barney was a Holocaust survivor who had spent the war years in concentration camps, his Jewish pedigree was strong. He started off dictating his own terms. He would date only Jewish women. He started off with match ups from people he knew, but those soon dried up. Then he signed up for a dating service, specifying that he wanted to be matched up just with Jewish women. The women would meet the package that was Barney - short, obstinate, frugal. He was wary of gold diggers, sure that all the women he met were after his money, which it wasn't apparent he had. He drove an old car, lived in a crumbling ruin of a house, broke his back working at his laundry day in and day out, like Dad. And if the women got past that, then they got to meet his children: three gigantic, teenage boys breaking the house to pieces, raising two scruffy little urchin twin girls, filthy in their diapers, hair matted on their heads. Uncle Barney was mystified that he didn't have women lining up to marry him once he began dating.

When Jewish women wouldn't have any part of him, Barney got a little looser with his requirements. In 1975, still unmarried, he showed up on our doorstep when my mother became available suddenly. He showed up because by then he was on red alert for any and all Jewish widows anywhere, even in Arizona, even with seven daughters, even his sister-in-law. After all, didn't Jewish Law say he was supposed to marry his dead wife's sister?

He showed up and said with no preamble, "What do you say, Chasia?" She said no.

He continued loosening up his requirements, looser and looser, to the point where even nuns leaving the convents in Chicago during the upheavals of the 1970s could apply. In 1976 he finally got married. To a Catholic ex-nun.

Fifteen

Separated At Birth

Before I ever start school, I am bursting at the seams for it to begin. I have sat home for years in some suspended babyhood waiting to join my sisters at College Hill Elementary School. How important they are in their dresses and knee socks with their library books, their piggy tails, and their penny loafers.

I'm an afternoon kindergartner and form the tail end of a four Burt girl cadre at our elementary school at that time, with Sherry and Denise are there in second grade and Brenda's in fifth. My first day is notable for my teacher calling attendance by reading my name as "Jane Burt" while I flush red then purple then white. Apparently, the school had been given evidence only of my father's legal name change but not of my mother changing my first name by crossing out one name and writing in another above it.

I stalk up to her desk afterwards and say, "My name is

Linda."

She looks at me and says, "Your name is Jane but you want to be called Linda?"

And I say, louder, "My name is Linda." And that's that. I never hear the name Jane again at school.

That first day I ride the bus home alone past thousands of streets with boxy brick Skokie houses, all with square fixed picture windows in front and rectangular bushes dotted here and there. We pass countless neighborhoods with white concrete streets and black tar lines like lightning, repairing the cracks. Nothing looks familiar from up inside the huge, yellow school bus, or it all looks familiar, but none like the top of my block, which is where our bus stop is.

I miss my bus stop and I miss all the bus stops before it and after it. And then I'm alone on the bus, a five-year-old sitting on a hard, green, vinyl seat, the bus driver looking back at me in her rear view mirror from time to time.

She stops the bus at the depot and asks me if I know where I live.

Even though by then I'm crying, I know the answer to this question. "8606 N. Drake," I say.

And she takes me there, the school bus winding down the streets of my neighborhood. The driver pulls up in front of my house and yanks open the bi-fold doors. I hop out with a "Thank you," and then I hop all the way into the house.

I spend Kindergarten singing "Over the Hills and Through the Woods," and the "ABC Song," and listening to my teacher read us stories on a big rug in between her suspicious runs to her desk drawer, and napping. The teacher rushed us from one activity to another in order to get to nap time, when she sat at her desk, not to be disturbed. What was in there? A gigantic candy bar? A romance novel?

When she wasn't distracted, or when the principal was visiting, she took a sudden bright-eyed interest in us, deciding to go around in a circle and let us tell her various snippets of information about ourselves. Like what we wanted to be when we grow up, or what our dads did for a living. Since the girls' choices were limited to Teacher, Nurse, Librarian or Mother, I picked Mother, even though it didn't seem to express the total of all my life's longings, but overall it went better than when I said that my father was a laundryman named Harry, and the whole class laughed.

With a curriculum that consisted of singing and playing, and a school day that lasted just three hours, it was still somehow necessary for the kindergartners to take a nap. But before anyone could take a nap, we had to have rugs to nap on, and in order for me to get a rug to bring to school, Mom was going to have to give one up from the house. This was a dilemma since she wanted to keep all her rugs. We hadn't covered our hard wood floors yet with wall-to-wall carpeting so Mom was still laying down all the rugs she had, end to end, pretending she had the panache of carpeting.

After some deliberation, she chose. It would be the clown rug from the room I shared with Denise, Sherry and Mindy. And this was bad because I hated clowns and I hated that clown rug. Despite Bozo's Circus, despite that smiling, happy, painted-on face, I hated clowns. I could always see the face underneath the paint, that unsmiling man-face and it made me concerned, that they paint on the smile over that poker face; that the clown wasn't happy at all.

The clown rug was just the round head of a clown, no body. A decapitated head; a rolling, guillotined, French-revolutioned kind of clown head, missing just the Xs for eyes and a basket to fall into to fully belong in eighteenth century France. There was fringe hair all the way around, not just where hair belonged, so that my clown rug had side burns that connected into an Amish kind of beard and then a spiky hair do, not a good look for a clown. And worst of all, this yarn hair wasn't all one color - it was splotchy - first red, then white, then blue - so the clown had some quasi-patriotic look to his C. Everett Koop hairstyle.

Dad drove me the day we brought the rug to school. He had to since someone had to carry the clown rug in and Mom had just learned to drive. At that point in Mom's driving career she wasn't very adventurous with the car, venturing out just for groceries or to go to my grandparents' apartment. She wasn't about to test her skills further, deal with the elementary school, the gaggle of kids, the crossing guards, and the introduction to the *goyische* American teacher. Also, carrying rugs was Dad's job just like it was his job to carry all those laundry bags.

I end up in Dad's station wagon and he is running late, the rug rolled up in back. After parking in a no parking zone in front of the school, he grabs the rug under one arm and stomps in, assuming I'm following. We walk into my kindergarten classroom and everyone sees him. I realize at that moment that my Dad looks remarkably unlike everyone else's dads. Is he older; is that it? Madder? Redder? He has an accent, he's wearing work clothes, he has huge white laundry bags in the car; this is all different. There's his impatience to be out of there, his lack of greeting for the teacher. Maybe they think he's the clown rug delivery person. Either way, he's clearly not savoring my childhood.

Then he's gone and naptime arrives and I pull out the clown rug. It grins eerily beneath me. Obviously, I won't be able to sleep on this rug, not when his staring eyes are wide awake. I'm not going to be able to sleep unless the clown head sleeps and those eyes aren't shutting. So I spend naptime arranging and rearranging the yarn hair, laying it flat color by color. Mark Sherman, the boy I love right then but abandon in first grade, edges his way across the floor, shimmying over on his rug, to help me. The clown is vigilant.

I spend first grade sitting on top of Larry Aronson's chest, holding his arms down with my own and smacking kisses all over his face. I do this several times a day, pretty much any time anyone in the classroom says, "Hey, Linda! Go kiss Larry!" And Larry can run but he can't hide because I get him every time.

He's not even safe from me outside of school in our neighborhood, which, somehow with first grade, has gotten smaller. Now I know where all the other first graders live. Now I know that I can ride my bike past Larry's house, spot him, jump off, tackle him, and kiss him, and then ride on my merry way. One time he even rode past my house and Sherry and Denise nabbed him while I stood by and performed a fake wedding ceremony marrying me to him. Somehow, that felt different.

Until first grade, I'm just a neighborhood kid, one of a roving band of children, moving as a mass, up and down the street. We're outside every day, all day and all night, till we can't see anymore. I'm always the odd girl out in the neighborhood, not the twins' age and not the little kids' age. Then, in first grade, when I meet Linda Winkler and Dina Fisher, my best friends, I discover that there's a world beyond Drake Avenue.

In September, 1966, I meet Linda Winkler when we both start first grade at College Hill, both of us unaware that our name is common or that there are any other Lindas anywhere else in the world. Little do we know that there were over twenty-two hundred other Lindas born in Illinois in 1960. At the end of that first school day, I go to what I believe to be my locker, which I recognize by the letters L-I-N-D-A written above it. I reach my hand in and, instead of pulling out my hand-me-down coat I pull out Linda's coat. She goes to what she believes to be her locker, also with the name L-I-N-D-A written above it, reaches her hand in and pulls out my hand-me-down coat.

We both burst into tears and run to our teacher, Mrs. Hart, crying out, "Mrs. Hart, someone took my coat!" and then see each other standing there, holding the missing coats. It's like love at first sight; best friends at first sight, right then and there. We're amazed at the coincidence of our identical first names.

We soon meet Dina Fisher, an irresistible force even at age six. Dina is the wild one, the one with nerve, with chutzpah. She's always willing to yell anything at any boy and then ride like hell away on her bike. If someone insults her for being bigger than Linda and I, Dina's right back at them calling them ugly, stupid, anything she can think up in that split second. And she'll defend Linda and me, too, when we get picked on, because she's loyal, the best of friends. You don't mess with Dina Fisher.

We play at school in the bark, on the heavy metal-poled playground equipment. And one day we figure out where we live in relation to one another. They both live in brownstone apartment buildings shaped like upright cigars on Trumbull, two streets over from me, so I know that all I have to do to find six year olds to play with is walk to the far end of my block, hang a right on Monticello, walk down two tiny blocks to Trumbull, and then pick if I'm going to turn right and go to Dina's or turn left, cross the street, and go to Linda's.

In fifth grade, we add a fourth to our group, Jill, the girl who moved into the Saltzman's house. Because no one ever moved away from Skokie, no one ever moves in, so we never get new girls at school. Galaxies could form and wither away in the time that elapsed between one new girl showing up and then another. But the Saltzmans move out one day and Jill Monette moves in the next. I wait as long as I can to go over and claim her for my own - so I go over while the moving van is still unloading. It's important to stake a preemptive claim in these matters, to show up at school with the deed done, the new girl mine already, no questions asked, before someone else steals her away.

Jill comes with some downsides that would have deterred someone less determined than me. First of all, her mother is an Aryan German who, I imagine, had probably spent the war as a member of the Hitler Maidens, her rosy cheeks shining as she imagined a Germany free of all Jews. And, of course, my parents are Holocaust survivors. A clear conflict. Why Jill's mother chose to plunk herself down in the middle of Holocaust survivor Jewish Skokie is hard to imagine.

Unusual for the time also is that Jill is from her mother's first marriage, to a Native American, whom she then divorced. Later she married an East Indian man with whom she had a second child. Her sister had also left their Aryan heritage behind, marrying an African American. Now when their children got together the family didn't look Aryan any longer.

So Jill isn't just a non-Jew; that's just the tip of the iceberg. She's half Aryan/German/Lutheran and half Native American - maybe some tribal religion. None of this, of course, prevents her from pretending she's Jewish later on and going to our synagogue youth group with the rest of us.

Despite these drawbacks, I plant myself on her doorstep and claim her. All that matters is that she's a new girl and Dina Fisher had gotten the last one, staking her out even though that one had moved in right across the street from Linda Winkler. It wouldn't have mattered if Jill had two noses or webbed feet; she was mine.

When Linda Winkler and I met, we were amazed by our similarities.

Here's how we were the same: we were both named Linda, which was just about the most amazing thing to us in the world. And we both ended up the same height so all through our childhoods we grew at the same pace, like we really were twins separated at birth. We were both thin and had brown hair and we were both born in March 1960 on dates with sevens - mine the seventh and hers the seventeenth.

We were Linda and Linda and we didn't care how stupid that sounded. We were a team, a partnership, a couple of Lindas, and we didn't mind sharing a name. We thought it was magical and mystical that we had the same name; after all, they barely sounded the same when we attached our last names: hers Jewish - Winkler - and mine a chopped off, changed travesty - Burt.

Here's how we were different.

She had one brother, named Mitchell. A painfully geeky brother two years older than us with thick black hair that stuck up in tufts, heavy horn-rimmed glasses, and an unquenchable zest for the minute. He'd sit down with Linda and I where we were playing Barbies in her living room, Barbie at the ice skating rink most often, since the plastic wrapped sofas lent themselves to a look of ice, and he'd start telling us about the properties of water - the solid, the liquid, and the vapor - about the polar ice cap, and about weather phenomena around the world. During this, Linda and I would provide our interjections, nodding when necessary, saying "Wow" when needed - everything that was required to be polite but send him on his way.

But he wouldn't read our cues just right because then he'd get kind of worked up and he'd say, "Do you want to play 'guess which state's missing'? Because I've hidden one of the states from the magnetic map on the refrigerator door."

Linda and I would then turn around a little more, hoping the interruption was temporary, thinking maybe we could play the state game from the living room. Our dolls were still in our hands, gliding along on the ice, each with one leg down, wobbling in her imaginary skate, the other leg flung back in an arc, but Mitchell kept on talking and talking and failed to heed Linda's exasperated sighs and rolled eyes, and then soon our Barbies were smashed flat against the ice and we were turned around, sitting down instead of kneeling, our game over, Barbie's dreams of Olympic gold forever dashed.

Before you knew it, we'd be trooping off to the kitchen to stare at the hole in the map of the U.S. while Mitchell chortled in glee, heeing and hawing, snorting and snuffling at our vain attempts to guess which state was missing. Since all we knew was Jewish geography, we could identify Florida and Illinois if they were missing from the map, but he'd have nabbed something square and in the center of the midland plains, like Iowa or Nebraska. And since Linda had been ordered by her parents to be nice to her brother, we were stuck guessing until he pulled the magnet out of his little carry-along lap desk with a flourish and stuck it back in place, but by that time it was too late. I had to go home.

At my house, of course, there were no boys, just five older sisters and one younger. The twins were the same age as Linda's brother Mitchell and Dina Fisher's older sisters were the same age as two of mine, but my sisters would rather have thrown themselves into a live volcano than spend a moment talking to any of the Winkler or Fisher siblings. After all, in our part of Skokie we considered ourselves near royalty. Francine was legendary, like Princess Grace of Monaco, and she was our popularity legacy so there was an expectation that I would also be popular. But to become popular, I needed to pick friends who would raise me up, not drag me down.

I'd show up at our house with Dina Fisher, the little sister of Lisa and Joyce Fisher, and Linda Winkler, the little sister of Mitchell "Weenie Weenie" Winkler, and I could just feel the waves of my sisters' disapproval. These were the friends I chose? I knew my sisters thought that with the siblings they had, Linda Winkler and Dina Fisher were disqualified from being friends with a Burt girl. But I liked my friends, most of the time better than I liked my sisters.

Linda and I were also different in that I had a house, not an apartment like the Winklers had. I didn't care what anyone said about owning an apartment building being different than just living in an apartment, the fact was that owning a house was better and that was that. After all, we had a front yard, a driveway, and a garage; we had a backyard with a swing set and trees and room to lope freely. But Linda had strangers living downstairs and upstairs, peering out their windows at her, watching us if we played in the building's backyard. The building cast a big shadow too, like a smokestack, and there was nothing to play with in the backyard, just dried up crabgrass and the stump of a tree.

We had other differences. If my sisters ever came by to say something to Linda and I while we were playing, it was in a series of decibels ranging from yelling to screaming to tearing our eardrums so that we would never hear again. They made fun of anything we played with, from Barbies to jump rope; if we were doing it, it was automatically categorized as babyish. And my sisters wouldn't have dreamed of playing "guess the missing state" even if we'd had a magnetic map.

On the playground, Linda and I would both climb up the monkey bar ladder, but I'd stand at the top, the eternal klutz, looking at the horizontal bars, knowing I couldn't even swing on them for a second without yelling, "Ow, my hands!" and jumping off. But Linda could leap into the air, cross the bars, and on the way back she could hang upside down in a bird's nest. And while I waded around the public pool swishing around the shallow end for years, Linda became a Junior Lifeguard, earning merit badges.

Linda dressed geekier than me but it wasn't her fault. Her mother bought everything on sale and was willing to fight her to the death to force her to wear it. Soon it all became Linda's taste, the Sears discount specials, the mismatched patterns, and fighting was no longer necessary. But I had five older sisters, all ready to critique the most minute details of my outfits, my face, and my body. I wasn't to become an embarrassment to our illustrious name. After all, we were the Burt Girls.

Inside our houses our situations were very different. I, of course, was crammed in with a shoehorn in a bedroom with three other sisters until Sherry and Denise kicked Mindy and me into the basement. But Linda, being one of two children, got coddled more than that. She, of course, had her own room, but she also had her own bedroom furniture set, all pink and frilly, from the bedspread to the scalloped edges on the mirror.

Later, when we were getting big, the furniture stopped fitting and Linda and I had to duck down a little to see ourselves in her vanity mirror, and crouch to sit on her pink tufted stool. Her mother bought her this furniture once and once was all – she was expected to keep it till she went away to college.

We both had preoccupied mothers but my mother could take care of an injury even when she was on the phone and sewing. She could treat any injured limb with one of her whiskey compresses. But Linda fell out of one of her bird's nests one day, falling out of the monkey bars upside down, face first into the bark with blood everywhere, and we ran home to her house, but her mother pushed her away, screamed at me to go home, and had a tantrum. Where was Sheila Winkler's whiskey compress?

There was also the problem of our parents' origin - her parents being American and mine being Eastern European. My parents had impeccable Jewish pedigree; I knew that. My parents were clearly more Jewish than Linda's, if hers were even Jewish at all. Linda and I would hover just out of sight of my mother, observing her, conducting our own scientific experiment, to test our theory.

My mother would sit at her antique Singer sewing machine, which had been amped up with a foot pedal and a motor, all in a utilitarian beige cabinet so it could flip down and out of the way, and she'd sew while she talked on the phone. In Yiddish. I'd nod at Linda and say, "See?"

My mother was easy to find. We'd start out in my kitchen, see the wall phone missing its receiver and follow the stretched out cord through the kitchen, across the foyer, down the steps to the basement, across the family room, and halfway across the laundry room. That's how we'd find her, attached to the phone like to a respirator, carrying on Yiddish conversations with a circle of family and friends that she could plot out on a map like a general.

She'd start each day with the people most important to her, her mother and her sister, my Aunt Reva, all speaking in the same dialect of Lithuanian Yiddish. Then she'd move on to the aunts, Dad's two sisters, Pearl and Etta, and his brother's wives, Ida and Rose. Mom would be able to continue speaking Yiddish but it got a little dicey, requiring a Polish dialect for Dad's sisters, a Russian dialect for Rose, and a Hungarian dialect for Ida.

In my favor was also the evidence of all those relatives with all those accents. Jews obviously came from somewhere else and spoke many languages; English was the latest among many, the last to be learned, learned through the necessity of immigration. My parents were the ones that everyone assumed were dead, assumed were concentration-camp-gone, Nazi-gun-gone, mass-grave-dead-and-buried-gone until they came stumbling out of hiding places, out of hollowed out tree trunks in the forest, stumbling out of Siberia, after the war.

Linda's parents, on the other hand, were dull Americans - no accents, no exciting foreign language, no insults to people right in front of their faces cloaked in another language.

Jews also bought a lot of stuff. In my family, everyone owned cars, and the women bought new furniture, it seemed like every week. They redid the curtains on the windows and, my Mom at least, seemed to feel better and more secure with more and bigger chandeliers around, nearly falling from ceilings.

I also knew from observing that the husbands worked very hard, almost always owned their own businesses, and were always self-made men. They paid for everything in cash. My Dad gloried in hard work and the amazing notion that with just a little more work tacked onto his mornings, nights, noons, and weekends, he could accumulate money that could work magic. Money that could change his geography, move him across the world, from a tiny hovel in Poland to a suburban home in Chicago. With money he could get a car, two cars, buy a business, an apartment building, and stack those things, one on top of the other like a wall, between the past and the present. Making money was serious business to Dad; he slammed out of our door each day with a frown on his face, ready for the grim task of making more of it.

But Mr. Winkler wasn't a self-made man; at least I didn't think he was. As far as I could tell, he worked at a company that manufactured magnets, charging out of their apartment building each morning in a suit, with a chipper smile on his face, a hat on his head, and took a series of buses to his downtown office. Taking buses, wearing suits! Two more pieces of evidence that Linda's parents could not be Jewish.

And Mrs. Winkler worked, unheard of in the '60s among Jewish women. This resulted in Linda going to camp each summer at the JCC, while I sat home like kids were supposed to, getting kicked out of the house each morning by Mom and playing listlessly outside under the white Chicago summer sky while I waited for Linda to get home each day. My Mom stayed home, like she was supposed to.

And Jews bought food. They ate a certain way, as evidenced by my parents and the way we ate; and this, more than anything else, led me to tell Linda one day that her parents could not be Jewish. My family ate food made out of fat, we ate a lot of meat, and we ate soup with unidentifiable contents floating among the round fat globules. Our Jewishness was impeccable - we were *Holocaust* Jewish, after all. My mother could peel anything, a potato, a carrot, an apple, all three at the same time, with a knife in one hand, the peel coming off in one strip, the telephone hugged between her neck and her shoulder, and all while her foot was tapping on the pedal of her sewing machine.

Like that time I ate over at Linda's house all that was missing. The vegetables - vegetables? - were from a can. My mother never bought cans. How would she have opened cans in the forest, she'd like to know? The forest was the litmus test for all our food.

Jews weren't quiet like Linda's family. Jews were noisy. Nothing was spoken that could be shouted; nothing left unsaid that could be said. But Linda's family sat there quietly eating dinner, sitting in their proper seats, placemats in front of each of them, Mitchell talking about his day at school with their father, and their father interested in both kids. What was with that? My father made sure he got home too late to have dinner with us each night, eating alone in the kitchen, insisting on quiet and multiple course meals served by my mother clad in an apron, like a French maid. Dad never showed any interest in my schoolwork like Mr. Winkler. As a matter of fact, sometimes he'd look at me with a blank stare, like he couldn't quite place my face, like maybe I was some child visiting from a neighbors' house and he was wondering why I'd gone and changed into pajamas.

When faced with this evidence and the unthinkable idea that she might not be Jewish, Linda was horrified. If she ended up being Christian then maybe she'd have to marry the most hated boy in our school - who happened to be a non-Jew - Joey Wilson, the skinniest, smallest bully alive. Faced with this possibility, Linda had to find out. So she approached her mother.

The shriek could be heard for miles. Sheila Winkler, nee Plotkin, yelled, "What do you mean, 'Am I Jewish?' How would you be Jewish if I wasn't, Missy?"

In the end, we had to go with circumstantial details. Her mother's kinky black hair; her maiden name of Plotkin, which it turned out was a very old Jewish name indeed, and her ability to shriek when called upon to do so.

Linda and I had our difficulties, of course. We had trouble brewing in the Larry Aronson situation since we both planned to marry him. It helped that we were realistic enough to know that we wouldn't be able to share - only one of us could marry him. Since I dominated Linda, treating her like the shadow Linda, he soon became mine alone and she got stuck with Larry Greenberg, the fake Larry Aronson substitute. So, even though the boys didn't know this, we were Linda/Linda loves Larry/Larry.

We played in different ways too. Since by the time the family toys got to me they had been through five older sisters, they were in pretty sorry shape. The Barbie collection was headless, legless, deformed. There were shrunken Skipper heads on big Barbie bodies, and, since we had one Ken doll for all the

Barbies, the other dolls had to date the little Remco Beatles dolls that were less than half their size. That was pretty humiliating for them.

I learned to improvise. Since our Monopoly game was missing so many of its pieces, I'd pull it out and tell Linda, "Let's play 'House for Sale.'" The board could form the neighborhoods, the hotels now mansions, the green houses bungalows at the beach. She could be the tycoon and I could be the impoverished rich lady trying not to sell her beachfront property.

Linda would just frown and put the houses back in the box in neat little piles, divide all the money up according to denomination and lay the properties out color by color awaiting purchase, even though so many were missing.

She'd say, "Let's just play the regular way, Linda. The way it's supposed to be played."

Then I would frown. How could we be twins at all? We were both named Linda, both the same height, both skinny, underdeveloped sticks. Maybe we were just identical on the outside.

Here's how else we were different. Linda apologized and I never did. I was her tyrant, her queen, her despot. Even when I was wrong, she apologized to me. So we were different in this: I had a huge, lumbering ego, and, as my ego grew, Linda's shrunk. I became bigger and she became smaller. I was the real Linda after all, and she was just an imposter wearing my name.

After a couple years of this, she had enough. We had a fight where I was wrong again, but this time she didn't come crawling back to me to apologize, although I waited at my front picture window, nursing my righteous anger, waiting to see her shuffling down the streets on her way back to me.

Instead, she gave me up. I apparently wasn't worth the trouble any longer. I was high maintenance, "No kind of friend anyway" - I could see her mother's hand in this. I was sure Linda never could have thought of this tactic on her own. I left my house, my head down, my feet shuffling and scraping the few blocks to her apartment, and I apologized.

Other than all that, we were twins.

By third grade I have been stalking Larry Aronson for three years. I am a master stalker by then. I just happen to ride my bike by his house every weekend on my way to the Skokie Pharmacy rather than making a left hand turn like I'm supposed to, or taking the short cut from my house like I'm supposed to. Sometimes I walk by his house with Linda Winkler and Dina Fisher and we fake injuries, falling over the giant elm roots in front, hoping he'll rescue us, pick us up in his heroic boy's arms and whisk us away into the house. I'm willing to leave Dina and Linda injured in heaps on the sidewalk, to go it alone, just so I can be taken into his Boy's Bedroom where I can be healed by the mysterious mother who gave birth to my future husband.

Everyone in my world, in the few blocks of Skokie where I live, at College Hill Elementary School here in the late 1960s, and, I think, even in Evanston, Illinois, knows that I love Larry Aronson. They know I'll kiss him on demand - all I have to do is catch him - and I'll marry him over and over in as many fake wedding ceremonies as my sisters can come up with. But there's a serious side to this. I love him so much that I can't wait any longer to know if he's going to marry me when we grow up.

Today will mark the end of my agony. I've proposed to him in writing and I'm waiting for his reply. I've sent Dina Fisher as my emissary across the entire bark-strewn playground to accost Larry where he's swinging back and forth on the monkey bars. Dina stands in front of him, her hands on her hips, and I hear her demand the note. After all, she slipped it to him a week ago for me, so he's already late in responding. Larry jumps off the monkey bars and lands on his feet in front of her. He reaches in his front pocket and hands her a small white slip of paper. She stomps back towards me.

"Read it already!" she yells at me when I hold it in my hand for a second to long, worried about what it says. But I'm nervous about opening it; my whole future depends upon his answer. Was I too abrupt? Did he not like the way I phrased it? I thought the "Will you marry me?" with a "Yes" box and a "No" box was pretty much standard form for a proposal. Should I have given more options, multiple-choice perhaps? What if I had and he chose "none of the above"? What if he penciled in an essay answer?

"Okay, already!" I glare at Dina. I unfold the slip of paper and look down. The boxes are both empty but he has written in the word "maybe" in between the "yes" box and the "no" box, emblematic of the attorney he will one day become. I show it to Dina. She gets very excited.

"Wow! He really likes you, Burt! He would've marked 'no' if it was 'no.' He marked 'no' on mine!"

Maybe Dina's already imagined herself in a junior bridesmaid's gown, lock-stepping her way down the aisle to my *chuppah.* There Larry and I would stand in front of a Rabbi who'd be eyeing up the two nine-year-olds standing before him.

The Rabbi would ask Larry, "Do you take this girl to be your lawful wedded wife?"

And Larry would answer, "Maybe."

By the time I get to seventh grade, that slip of paper is crushed inside my fake leather purse alongside a few quarters and a Primatene Mist asthma inhaler. Larry had inexplicably disappeared for the intervening years - fourth, fifth, and sixth grades - and left me with paltry Larry substitutes: my oldest sister's boyfriend, Larry Coffman, destined to be my brother-in-law, and Larry Greenberg, the dorkier Larry in our grade with reflective-lens eyeglasses and Tom Jones hair who I used to pair up with Linda Winkler. I had pondered over whether I could switch my allegiance to Larry Greenberg; force myself to fall in love with him just because of his first name. After all, my diaries were already filled with a multitude of "I love Larrys" and "Linda loves Larrys"; the idea of me loving Larry - any Larry - is like a well-worn groove. I try the idea of Larry Greenberg on for size but I ended up rejecting him. There is only one Larry for me.

When Larry Aronson returns to our school, I find that now that I'm a dignified thirteen-year-old, I can't have pratfalls in front of his house anymore, and I would die of shame if my sisters yanked him off his bike and forced him to marry me. And my goals are different too. I want to start off with dancing together at a Bar Mitzvah, move up to going steady, and then have him be the first boy I kiss. So I have to go undercover and become more ingenious when I stalk him now. I make phony phone calls to his house with Dina and Linda on weekends, hanging up after he says hello. I watch him closely at school until I have linked together each time he glances my way, irrefutable proof of his enduring love, all these sightings of Larry Aronson meticulously documented in my diary, like he's a UFO.

Since Larry's in the popular group and I'm somehow wanted by the popular girls because my sister Sherry is a popular girl two years ahead of me, I even consider abandoning Linda, Dina, and Jill and joining that group. I spend one weekend day with the most popular girls in the seventh grade, Carol and Edie. I watch them run through the various faces of their personalities throughout that day: petulant, bossy, domineering, tyrannical and sulky. I watch them have tantrums and hissy fits; I watch them pick on the other girls just because they can.

At 9:00 p.m. that day, the popular group huddles, leaving me alone, and then Carol and Edie offered me the honor of being in their group, of being one of their followers. I say yes, but I never show up again, despite their phone calls and entreaties, threats, and cold shoulders. It turns out that I'm too domineering to follow anyone, even for Larry Aronson. And anyway, I think I can get him on my own.

After all, our teacher, Mr. Greenfield, seated the entire class alphabetically, so I am seated right behind Larry for all of seventh grade. First the A's, then the B's. But that whole year I am unable to utter one syllable to him, the boy I married by stealth, my sisters sitting on him on our front lawn; the boy who wrote "maybe" on my marriage proposal. The entire year he sits in front of me, his brown wavy hair, his lumberjack shirt-clad shoulders, his jean-clad legs, just sitting in front of me.

It's not that I don't want to speak to him; I do. I want to talk to him so badly that the words team up inside my head and travel down from my brain to my tongue on a conveyer belt, where they bunch up, and get knocked out of the way by the other rapidly arriving words, until all the words I've ever known are just standing there, shuffling their feet and blushing. *Which one of you guys wants to go out first*, I say to them? My mouth, however, is clamped shut, my jaw locked. It will not be pried open until years later, tubes of Clearasil later, years of orthodontic tightening later; until I've learned to pretend my way through my awkwardness into a semblance of what I think confidence looks like.

Seventh grade passes and I never say a word. Larry spends the class periods talking to the "A" in front of him, Jerome Anderson, about sports. He never sees my mouth open to start a conversation, never sees the light glint off my silver braces, never look back at me to see the pimples dotting my face, my curled wings of hair. The bell rings on the final day of school and he shoots out of his seat like a rocket and is gone. And I realize that his "maybe" is an unenforceable contract and that I'm going to have to let him go.

Sixteen

Dumbing Down

I have other hobbies besides stalking Larry Aronson. Like all the other little Jewish girls in Skokie, I take piano lessons. Unlike them, I want to. Just like I'm desperate to get on that Kindergarten school bus, I'm desperate to try my hand at that Fur Elise trill. From the minute I'm born I'm hearing the tinkling keys of that song in my head. All five of my older sisters practice it day after day, with just the right finger order taught to them by Mrs. Nussbaum, piano teacher to all of Jewish Skokie.

First I'm two, then three, then four, and then five years old, lurking around our Cable piano in our living room with its piano seat of blue tufted brocade, and I'm watching my sisters play this song, which I am convinced is the most beautiful song ever written. My sisters think I'm a little bit like a pet monkey, so they demonstrate the trill for me until I have mastered it with my right hand, with my left hand, with my eyes shut. Mom, thinking that she's got a prodigy on her hands, hauls me off to Mrs. Nussbaum, who agrees to take me on as a student in Kindergarten, making sure she explains to me in ponderous detail during each and every lesson that first year what an exception she's made for me, taking me on a year earlier than usual.

She leans over the keys at my weekly lessons, marking out my mistakes in red pencil on my piano book, playing the pieces for me with her wrinkled, knobby, spotted hands.

Yeah, yeah. Sure I'm all excited about being able to play each piece of music all by myself. Sure. Most of all, I watch her right foot in its worn sling-back pump. I just want to know when I'll be allowed to stomp on that pedal and make that booming, echoing sound.

It's a big commitment, becoming a famous concert pianist; the whole family has to lend me their support. They have to understand the sacrifices that must be made for me to practice night and day, the shadows that will fall upon our house from the looming Beethoven busts I collect, the financial burden of lessons, of crisp new sheet music, of piano tunings.

"Stop playing that goddamn piano! I'm on the phone!" Sherry yells.

"Shut the hell up, Linda! I'm on the phone!" Lauren yells. Or Denise. Or Brenda. They all yell.

Boys are calling, the TV is on upstairs and downstairs, Mom's sitting at her sewing machine in the laundry room downstairs sewing miles and miles of draperies for some blank, staring picture window, and we have just one telephone, in the kitchen, on the other side of the wall from my piano. Since my sisters can't be expected to carry on their private conversations right there under everybody's nose, the phone has to be answered in there but then yanked right out of there to make it up the stairs. My sisters pull and tug this great jump rope into their rooms, talk with their heads under their pillows for privacy, but still, my playing annoys them. Perhaps if I played something more modern.

It's impossible to satisfy all of them, of course. Dad wants to hear anything Jewish, anything Russian, anything that is played at a wedding or Bar Mitzvah. *Fiddler on the Roof* is good; *Sunrise Sunset,* okay, now we're talking. If he's seen the movie, it's good, like *Midnight Cowboy*, like *Hello Dolly*. But my sisters just want the radio on or the HIFI. My hopeless versions of top 40 hits aren't going to cut it with them no matter what. And anyway, the piano is too loud. They can adjust the volume on the stereo.

For six years I trudge up the sidewalk squares from Drake Street to Crain, across Crain to St. Louis, down St. Louis to Mrs. Nussbaum's apartment building. Even though her apartment was identical to every other flat in Skokie, it was a place of great mystery, mainly because in her apartment, at the point where the living room connected to the rest of the apartment, there was a partition.

Her living room itself was all baby grand piano, some kind of Victorian horsehair sofa, and a few upright chairs that we sat on during recitals or waiting for our lessons to begin. But then there was that partition, beyond which I could hear the breathing, coughing, and twitching of men; maybe a husband, maybe even a grown up son lounging somewhere, an eternal bum, laying on a bed and letting his life pass by, wearing pants that Mrs. Nussbaum washes for him with her gnarled fingers, itching himself all day.

I never get beyond that partition. I was trapped at the

piano, trapped studying the music that Mrs. Nussbaum had chosen for me, trapped being trained as a classical pianist. In an era of *Soul Train*, of Marvin Gaye, of *Diana Ross and the Supremes*, of *The Beatles*, and *The Monkees*, I was playing Bach's *Minuet in G* and Beethoven's *Sonata No. 1 in C,* both of my hands thundering down the octaves, starting at one end of the piano and ending up at the other. When I tell Mrs. Nussbaum about my secret desire for pop music she tries to accommodate me. At my next lesson, with a flourish, she gives me the hippest piano book she can find: *Boogie Woogie Blues.*

By the time I started taking lessons, my three oldest sisters had already quit, so it was just Denise, Sherry and I marching off to Mrs. Nussbaum's each week. Then they rebelled on a Sunday afternoon at the end of the school year when the three of us were on our way to the annual recital. We were alone, of course. Mom had conjured up a reason not to go, or hadn't understood the exact reason she needed to be there; so it was just the three of us, with Denise and Sherry walking down the street like they were walking down death row.

That day, as I was envisioning another Beethoven bust in my hands, earned after the recital, Denise and Sherry were moaning and wailing about having to perform. Denise was concerned about messing up her piece but Sherry was just mad about the whole idea of it, of performing like a monkey anyway. And why did she have to wear her favorite powder blue sailor dress anyway? There she stood in the outfit I coveted but would never get because I'd grow taller than her before she ever outgrew it and miss the hand me down. It had a squared off neckline in the front and back and balloony sailor sleeves, all outlined with white piping, and Sherry had managed to get Mom to buy her matching white tights to go with it. And she didn't want to appear in that? I was incredulous.

Then Sherry just stopped walking.

"I'm not going. I mean it."

Denise and I just looked at her, then at each other, our mouths hanging open.

Then, since Denise wasn't saying anything, I said, "Sherry, you've got to go. Mrs. Nussbaum is expecting you. And you've been practicing *Sunrise Sunset* all year. And what about the duet with Elise?"

Sherry just looked at me, a sailor going AWOL, ready to walk the plank, mutiny on the bounty. She shook her head, said, "I mean it. I'm not going." And she turned around and headed back home, her sailor collar flapping behind her.

Besides piano, I'm also quite the swimmer. Each day in the summer I stand, swimsuit clad, my nose plugs around my neck like a necklace, my hair tucked under a white bathing cap, one of Mom's threadbare towels in my arms, a metal token sewn on my swimsuit, waiting for someone to ride their bike with me over to Devonshire, the public pool.

I'm not exactly an athlete. I spend each summer standing around in the shallow end of the pool, flailing my arms so it'll look like I'm swimming since I don't know how, and bumping into other kids in the water, and hairy men, and women in bathing suits with skirts and frilly bathing capped heads held carefully erect, dry like mine.

My role model in this swimmer's stance has been my mother, who glides through the shallow end of the pool in perpetuity, the blue and white buoys bobbing along next to her delineating her space. Her head is always visible, mouth pursed so no water will get in, makeup intact, her hair is stuffed under a tight, etched bathing cap even though she never dunks her head. She draws her hands out and then pulls them near in the water, like a modern dancer, making her way across the pool, sideways like a crab.

Because by fifth grade I'm still standing around in the shallow end of the pool pretending to swim even though I can't dunk my head, can't jump in, and can't tread water, Mom thinks that maybe I might need some swimming lessons. She wants more for me than this. More than my sunburned arms and shoulders sticking out of the water, more than me dipping my head backwards into the water to get my hair wet, my nose burned red.

She signs me up at my sisters' high school and I go on successive Saturdays, starting with the five-year-olds even though I'm eleven. I move rapidly through the levels, achieving the goals at each level, my name announced over and over on the microphone as I master the various techniques. Jumping in, check. Floating, check. Back float, check. Kicking, strokes, dog paddle. Check, check, check. But when it comes to jumping in without plugging my nose or opening my eyes under water, I'm blind, flailing through the water, sputtering and gasping. I flunk out.

In third grade I learned a lot at school. I finally learned how to tell time after bluffing my way through it for a few years. I learned to wear shorts under my dresses after having a few boys flip up my dress and see my underwear. I learned how to write cursive, swiftly becoming an expert at the capital letter L since my name began with one. And I learned about prejudice, and not against me.

I was conscious of several things at College Hill Elementary School in the mid-1960s: the white students were mostly Jewish and middle class from Skokie and the Black students were not Jewish and were poorer, and from Evanston; and all my teachers were white and old and definitely not Jewish.

The teachers appeared to favor the white students more than the black. Each day as we lined up to go into school the teachers implored us to stand "single file, single file," though I didn't know what that meant, but when we all stood in nice straight lines they'd stop saying it. One day the principal stopped the line as my grade was passing by and pulled Kimberly Johnson out. Picking up the hem of her dress, which had a tear in it, she questioned Kimberly about her torn clothing and then told her not to wear ripped clothing to school again. I looked down at my dress, which I knew also had a tear, relieved that the principal hadn't stopped me.

On the field at recess I could get away with anything. I could steal balls away from other kids, pretending I didn't know they were playing with them and the teacher would believe me, not them. I learned that I was a golden girl, always right.

Then one day as we were getting ready to take a composition test, I noticed that Larry Aronson, who sat behind me, had forgotten to write his name on his composition paper. I had to help him, to save his non-studious, sports-minded self from a failing grade. After all, he'd be my husband one day so this could matter. So I lifted my paper over my head, my skinny arms reaching high above the scarred and beaten wooden desks, high above the heads of all my classmates, and I whispered, "Larry!" I pointed to the left hand corner where our names went so he'd remember to write his own there.

Our regular teacher, Mrs. Petrie, had been off work already for a few months. She was renowned for sustaining an injury each year at a student's house, which seemed to serve two purposes. It gave her some paid time off from the grueling school year and it got her one year closer to retirement. Or maybe she was just a little clumsy. That year's injury had given her more than she bargained for, however, since she had slipped and fallen on an icy doorstep at Larry Aronson's house and broken her hip. So our student teacher, Miss Roberts, was forced to take over.

Miss Roberts was a throw back to a different era of teachers, back when teachers were all spinsters and had no choice about their occupation. She was about twenty-three but was as wide as she was tall, she already wore eyeglasses on a chain around her neck, already had a moustache and hair limp against her head. She didn't seem happy about being forced into this full-time job nor about us little girls, prancing around in our little dresses.

When I lifted my paper over my head for Larry to see that he'd forgotten to write his name then, it was Miss Roberts standing in front of me who caught me.

She said, "Linda Burt, why are you showing your paper to Larry? Put your paper down this instant! There will be no cheating on this composition exercise!"

My breath was knocked out of me. My breath was knocked out of me. I was supposed to be the golden girl - doing wrong always but always presumed right. Yet there she was, yelling at me in front of the whole class. And this time I actually *was* innocent. Humiliated, I not stopped speaking in school for the rest of third grade, I didn't speak again in a class for the rest of elementary school, junior high, and high school. I didn't speak during all my undergraduate years of college and during my first time in graduate school. Finally, when I returned to graduate school in my forties, I pried open my mouth and talked. Thirty-four years later.

And that was the final thing I learned in third grade.

I was lying on the rock hard, vinyl surface of the cot in the nurse's office at my school. It was dim in there, the curtain drawn around me, like I was sick, and I could hear the school nurse at her desk just outside scritching and scratching on some paperwork.

It was the fourth Wednesday of the month and, being the fourth Wednesday, I had come down with a whole list of psychosomatic complaints that earned me a trip right out of my classroom to the nurse's office.

By fourth grade, Mrs. Petrie was back plotting her new yearly injury, though she wasn't my teacher anymore; Miss Roberts was gone, having done her damage; and I had already been staying very quiet at school for an entire year. Larry Aronson was gone too, transferred by his parents to the Martin Luther King Jr. Laboratory School, and so no longer sat in front of me distracting my thoughts during each and every class period. So I'd had some time to concentrate on my class work. I end up getting moved from my fourth grade math class into the fifth grade math class and from my fourth grade Language Arts class into the fifth grade class.

It just so happened that on the fourth Wednesday of every month in the fifth grade math class I was in, along with a few other wan, miserable, fourth graders, it was game day. Free play day. There was no structure, everyone could do whatever he or she liked. And it turned out that what all the fifth graders liked to do was to play with the fifth graders.

Wendy Saltzman was in this class - the last year before she moved - and she'd strut about, a foot shorter than me already, carrying the extra seven months she had on me around like a trophy, her jaw jutting out, determined to snub me in front of her class, pretending she had never seen me before even though I had lived across the street from her my whole life. There was a hierarchy of age at College Hill and the fourth graders had fallen off the horizon by being the wrong age in the wrong class.

On those days the fifth graders would bunch off, their desks circled like stagecoaches, and the few fourth graders in the class, including me, would have to pretend that was okay, pick up books and read, or do crossword puzzles. The other fourth graders didn't seem to care that they were alone those days or they seemed to care enough about learning that it was worth it to them. But I wasn't like them; I was miserable at this social isolation, miserable at being pointedly ignored.

Since I had no choice, I got sick.

I pretty much settled on a vague stomachache as my sickness of choice. It required no medicine, no one could verify whether it existed or not, and it always earned me that coveted trip out of the math classroom and to the nurse's office. There I waited for Mom to pick me up. She took her time, taking so long to come get me that the class I was avoiding ended and I could have returned to my regular class with the fourth graders, but by then I was committed to being sick.

When she did come, pulling up in her car and beeping her horn, I dashed out, feeling odd at being in the wrong place at the wrong time. Then I rattled around in our empty house with her, disoriented, because our house was never empty. It was like a heart that had stopped beating without my sisters filling it up, on the phone, fighting, yelling, the TV on in the background.

My principal, in the meantime, had become very excited by my academic performance. He called home during a rare interlude when Mom had hung up the phone with one aunt and right before she picked up the phone to call another aunt, and he told her that they wanted me to skip fifth grade. They would like me to leap neatly over fifth grade when I finished fourth and careen into sixth; zoom into junior high a year ahead of all my friends, like a high speed train. Even though I was thrilled at the compliment ("They want to skip me!" I said to my friends, shrugging my shoulders) in another way it wasn't a good thing at all. Instead of social isolation two class periods per day, I'd get it all day long. And then I'd bound into Junior High an instant geek - not the right age for the class.

But Mom was thrilled she had answered that call. Now she could get back on the phone after she finished talking to the principal and call every person she knew and crow about her brilliant daughter Linda and how the principal wanted to skip her because she was burning up the curriculum at school. And, especially, *had this ever happened to them?*

Then, to further my trauma, Mom told Dad. Mom, as a rule, never told Dad anything about school because normally all she had was information to hide: our trips to the principal's office, our truancy, the fights we got in. But this she told him and it was so momentous to him - he might not have had a boy but at least now he had a girl who was acting like a boy! - that he had to announce to the whole family what a genius I was and that I'd probably grow up to be the President of the United States and also Miss America. This was not exactly thrilling news to my sisters.

Mom didn't just agree to this skipping a grade thing without discussing it with me. And, of course, I was appalled, sickened, and terrified by this news. I already stuck out of the fourth graders every time I left them to join the fifth graders. At least the other smart kids looked like geeks; at least they weren't trying to pass for normal. Unlike me, they were at school to learn, but I wasn't. I was at school for social reasons - to have friends, to laugh and play, and to have crushes. Learning happened by accident.

I said no and Mom turned down the offer on my behalf. I ended up learning a lesson I apply to my academic career for years - I dumb down. I learned that trying my best will, in the end, get me nothing but heartache and misery, stomach cramps, and a ride home in Mom's car, waving weakly at my friends playing on the playground. I create a new educational persona for myself. I continue to be silent in class because of Miss Roberts, but now I add the element of not working hard. For years and years I will never again read an entire assigned chapter or an assigned book. I will skim beginning paragraphs, ending paragraphs, summaries, *Cliff Notes*, and outlines. I will read first sentences of every paragraph in a chapter but I will never do all the work again for decades, until I can't be skipped, until I'm safely ensconced in adulthood and it doesn't matter anyway.

In our school, despite the prejudices of the teachers, it wasn't good to be white. I understood from all that I learned that whites had been privileged and blacks enslaved, but during civil rights things seemed to have shifted a little. In the Evanston schools I went to, it was very cool to be black, cool to have an Afro, cool to know about *Soul Train*, *Gladys Knight and the Pips*, and *Shaft*. Of the sibling groups of the late '60s, the black kids automatically got *The Jackson 5;* the white kids were relegated to the Mormon *Osmonds*.

There were a lot of rallying cries at the time. There was Black is Beautiful, Black Power, there was some pride in the Black Panthers. Everything was a political statement, even clothes: The black kids wouldn't wear white because everything white was scorned and despised, from the color of our skin to the color of cloth.

They also divided up the school for us according to black and white, proudly pointing to our principal and our fourth grade teacher; they even threw in our Hawaiian math teacher since she was of "color" to show proof that the school didn't have all white teachers and administrators any longer. Whitey was going down in flames and I, apparently, was Whitey.

The black kids at my school had no time or patience for nuances, for the distinctions between Jews and other whites, recent immigrants and older immigrants, and Southerners versus Northerners. These were just more attempts to evade responsibility for the enslavement of the black people. Our skin color was all the evidence they needed. We are all slave owners - present tense.

I went home one day and asked my mother, or at least I tried to, tugging on her phone cord. She lifted her chin from the receiver.

"What, Linda? I'm on the phone."

"Did we own slaves in the South, Ma?"

"The South?"

I nodded. "At school they say that all white people owned slaves on plantations in the south."

My Mom got so angry she almost spit.

"I was so poor, I grew up in a small wooden house without even a toilet! You tell them that! We were in the old country! Me in the forest, Dad in Siberia - we just got here not even twenty years ago, how would we own plantations? *We* were the slaves in the old country! You tell them the next time they say anything."

Then she put the handset back up to her ear and resumed her conversation without missing a beat. Oh yeah, I'd tell them all right, right before a fist crashed into my face.

My parents paid no attention to school districts when they bought our home in 1960. They were just happy to own a home and that we'd all get to attend school for free. They never asked for school district information. They were buying in Skokie, the Jewish suburb of Chicago, that's all they needed to know. How bad could a neighborhood school be, anyway? There would be no Nazis, after all.

We end up living two houses away from the dividing line between the Skokie School District and the Evanston School District. We're two houses away from those lily-white schools, from those schools frozen in time; we're two houses into the battle zone. On the Skokie school district side, the most dangerous rebel would be a boy who refused to learn his Bar Mitzvah portion. But on the Evanston side I'm caught in daily race riots with my classmates who, before 1970, were my friends.

Although there are more white kids than black kids at my school, we are definitely the minority. Getting our butts kicked each and every day is a distinct possibility and for any of a list of infractions, from looking at someone too long to talking back to someone who might be picking on us.

None of the Jewish kids fought back no matter what happens. Our family histories include the Holocaust, Cossacks, pogroms, and other assaults that had given us a genetic fear of confrontation. I froze up; my friends froze up. The ones that tried to fight back end up getting beaten up after school. So I clutched my books to my chest; I didn't look at anyone in the hallways.

What the black kids didn't realize was that I didn't exactly feel a kinship with white America either. I wasn't black; I knew that. But sometimes I didn't feel quite white either. Unless someone was Jewish I didn't feel a connection; but if they were Jewish, it wouldn't matter what color they were, they could be polka dotted, I would feel it.

Seventeen

Holocaust Vacation

Here's how my parents pick vacation spots: Mom and Dad look at a map of the country, Mom with one chipped and cracked, Holocaust-damaged fingernail poised over it. She touches down here, then there. Where do they know the most people, where can they visit the most people they used to know from his hometown in Poland, from hers in Lithuania? Where can they sit the longest on hard, plastic-covered couches, force us to sit the longest, while they speak in different Yiddish dialects to their hosts, laughing over their differences, then grow silent as they remember the dead? Where can they go to find the most tragedy?

Where can we drive - how many hours - to hook up Mom and Dad's tragedies to these other tragedies and form a human chain of tragedy to criss-cross the country?

In 1970 Dad buys a brand new Ford Country Squire and he's suddenly ready to hit the road, to take a vacation. This is a very big deal since he hasn't taken a vacation since arriving in the United States in 1951. He'd been busy in the nineteen years since then working at any job he could get his hands on, having daughters, buying a house in Skokie, then an apartment building in West Rogers Park, and a few cars along the way. But after nineteen years, he's earned a break. One week's vacation.

My teenage sisters refuse to go on our trip because, of course, they're teenagers and they aren't going to just disrupt their social lives so Dad can take a vacation. And where'd he get that idea anyway, *vacation?* The word sounds kind of foreign to all of us. Our family didn't take *vacations.*

The youngest four of us go on that first trip - the twins, Denise and Sherry, who are twelve, Mindy, six, and me, age ten. The twins are a little mad that they're forced to go, wanting to stay home in a parentless household. Mom mollifies them by describing the sons of her Toronto friend Bluma and how they just might end up married to these boys. You never know.

My parents pick Toronto for our first-ever vacation because Mom has an uncle by marriage, Sholem, who needs visiting, and who won't last forever, and who was from Krivich. There's also this friend from the old country, Bluma, who lives in the suburbs of Toronto. She and all of Mom's other Krivich girlfriends, all smiling with their gold teeth and floral dresses in all those photos from the Displaced Person camp in Germany after the war, end up scattered all over the world like marbles. Some are in Israel, some in the U.S., some in Canada, and one in Mexico. Bluma is close enough to visit.

Dad won't let Mom make any reservations for our stops along the route. How can he possibly commit to where we'll be on this day or that day?

"It's impossible," he says, shrugging. After all, he's running a permanent race against himself, mesmerized by the lines in the black top, the white dashed lines in the roadway telling him to *go faster, go faster.*

This is how Dad prepares for our trip: he pulls the car out of the garage, he fires up the engine, he points it towards Toronto, and then he steps on the gas.

We're officially on the road; we've just left our house, driving down Drake Avenue on our way to Main. The twins are in the center seat of the station wagon already feigning an air of teenaged boredom. That leaves Mindy and I in the way, way back, already fighting.

All of a sudden Mom says, "Herschel, stop! I don't have my purse! You have to go back." She still calls him Herschel.

This is typical; she always stops us on our way anywhere saying she's forgotten something. Sometimes Dad is able to convince her that she doesn't need whatever she's forgotten, but not this time. Even Dad can't argue that she might not need her purse for a week. He has to turn back. But Dad is too angry to turn. He is ready to be on his way, ready to make that left turn onto Main street, ready to head out onto McCormick past the Winston Towers and zoom off on the Dan Ryan Expressway on our way to Gary, Indiana, the first major city we'll pass through. So he slams the car into reverse and continues speeding, but this time backwards.

My Dad was a great backward driver; he had a lot of

practice because he drove backwards all the time, refusing to turn around for Mom. There were a certain number of things he did to show her that he was both going back and *not* going back at the same time. First he yells at Mom, rants and raves at Mom, and she yells back. Then he waves his hands in the air, up and down, and then, on one of those upward arcs of his arm, he hits the gearshift, thrusting the car into reverse and we take off. Past the textbook factory on Main and Drake, past the various neighbors and the staring children on the street. The car zooms backward staying perfectly in its lane, not hitting parked cars, and backwards we go. Past barking dogs, fire hydrants, street signs. With a final flourish, Dad swings backwards into the driveway and then slams on the brakes. Mom, impervious to his anger, hops out, runs in the house, grabs her purse and gets back in the car.

We leave the house again, starting again on the road to Toronto. This time we make it. Drake to Main Street; Main to McCormick; then McCormick swinging around past the Winston Towers, and then out to the Dan Ryan Expressway.

Dad is planning to stay a simmering kettle until we're out on the open road, past all the annoying tollbooths, which never end. He flies past them, his hairy laundryman's arm hanging out the window dangling one dollar bills, five dollar bills, quarters, throwing them all at the tollbooth operators in his haste to be gone.

Except for Mom, we're all quiet; we know not to utter a word. Mom, somehow, does not know this. She chatters away, bringing up all of Dad's least favorite subjects - who's running the laundry while he's gone and stealing him blind? Did he miss the exit for the freeway? To figure this out, she examines the roadmap upside down.

Then she says, "Does anybody have to go to the bathroom?"

Since we're on the largest expressway ever made, about twenty lanes of travel, a galaxy of cars zooming toward us, around us, in front of us, with our car in a bubble of diesel fumes and smog from all the other traffic, there doesn't seem to be a bathroom available. There are just cars and more cars, the biggest trucks I've ever seen, and concrete.

It doesn't matter anyway.

Dad glares at her and says, "No bathrooms!" And we're off, our hair flying in the air behind us, the wood trim of our station wagon a blur, as Dad peals down the Expressway.

Once Dad's calmed down, sure of no further interruptions, he's a friendly traveler. His sunburned left arm rests on the open window next to him, his right arms shoots out like a beam in front of him, resting on the steering wheel. He toots his horn as he passes other Ford Country Squires and as he passes other families; after we leave Illinois, he honks when he passes anyone from Illinois. We move ahead of all the cars that started with us on the day of our vacation, and soon we're traveling with those who started a day ahead of us, then a week, and soon we have moved ahead of them all and we're rounding the curve of the Planet Earth, heading into the horizon. Sometimes it seems like Dad thinks that once he passes that final semi truck, when he rounds that final bend, that he'll catch up with yesterday, and he'll start his life all over again.

We drive north and east, through industrial Gary, Indiana. Dad doesn't take the most logical way to get to Toronto, through Michigan, instead inching his way along Lake Erie for most of the trip, the longer route. After leaving Gary, we skim the rest of Indiana, Ohio, Pennsylvania, and New York. We drive past Niagara Falls, stop for a little souvenir shopping but not long enough to take a tour of the falls. I end up craning my neck trying to spot people going over the falls in barrels like they show in the movies, but I don't see any.

Instead, this is what we do. Dad drives like hell, all day and past sunset, past the time when he can see the road, and, since he won't get glasses, pretty soon we're sure he can't tell the difference between the road and the shoulder, and we hear Mom screeching at him in the front seat, "Herschel, enough driving already for one day! Let's stop before you get us all killed!"

At the next marquee sign flashing the word "Motel" and "Vacancy," the next billboard pointing towards a square, nondescript hotel flattened out like a donut on the edge of the highway, Dad gives up and pulls in.

We stay at a few of those flat motels and even a "motor court" on our way to and from Toronto. Mom insists on clean, Dad insists on a pool. He screeches the car to a stop, Mom goes off into the tiny offices to handle the paperwork while the rest of us stand with our luggage open, our swimsuits in hand, ready to jump in to any puddle they call a pool. We don't care if it's overcast, if it's Canada and just plain cold. We're from Chicago; we don't know any better.

In Toronto, my great Uncle Sholem lives in a high-rise apartment building with balconies, which is good enough for me. He's ancient and tiny, dressed up in a suit, and scrunched up in a corner of his enormous couch, his eyes hollow with the events of his life. He's a tragic figure, despite the new wife sitting next to him, dressed up and smiling politely because she doesn't understand Yiddish. And the conversation my mother has with Sholem must be in Yiddish; the tragedy that befell them can only be expressed in Yiddish. Since I'm uninterested in anyone over the age of thirteen at that point, Mindy and I turn to investigate the balcony.

Just the idea that we got to take an elevator in the first place and went up about a thousand stories to get to Uncle Sholem's apartment was almost a big enough thrill in itself; I could have gone home right then. But then we get to go out onto the balcony overlooking the entire city. Mindy and I stand out there, trying to decide what to drop on the people far below and wondering what damage various items would do. We are called in.

My parents have a satisfying visit with Sholem. My mother sits and cries as she finds out things she never knew before, how Sholem and my grandmother's sister, Tzipke, and her family, were all shot by Nazis at the border, Tzipke and her husband and daughter all dying there. The Russian soldiers found Sholem there, lying wounded in a swamp. They took him to Tashkent where it took him eight months to recuperate.

By the time we get to Toronto in 1970, Sholem, whom, my mom assures me, had not been an easy man for her aunt to live with, has been transformed by circumstances into a martyr. There were a lot of things that contributed to this: Baileh's prewar death of some undiagnosed and untreated cancer; the disappearance of his older daughter; the death of his younger children, shot by the Nazis and found by Sholem when he returned home one night. There was the banality of his escape during the first massacre of the Jews of Krivich: as the sole barber in town, the Nazis had jailed him to keep him safe from the massacre against all the other Jews in the town. There was his second escape and how he nearly died at the border with Tzipke and her family.

Uncle Sholem sits stiffly in his suit, narrating the events of his life, his new wife silent by his side. She doesn't understand a word of the conversation. She continues smiling, even though there's nothing to smile about.

At Mom's friend Bluma's house, Mom and Dad have a more social time, not there just to relive wartime memories. Or, at least, if they do, we don't have to listen the whole time. The four of us kids are supposed to be entertained by Bluma's sons but, of course, Denise and Sherry exclude us from every conversation they have with the boys, either trying to wrangle marriage proposals out of them or at least get close enough to refer to them as their "Canadian boyfriends" for when we return home. We watch for the rest of our vacation as they slouch in their too-long baggie jeans, as they flirt in an I'm-in-junior-high-but-I'm-very-mature-for-my-age kind of way, since the boys are in high school.

After a week of this, Mom and Dad have had enough; they've filled up their misery gas tanks. We head back - New York, Pennsylvania, Ohio, Indiana. We drive till nighttime, till the moon is shining on the Dan Ryan Expressway, till things start looking familiar again, until our street comes into view, and then our house. And even though I've learned the amazing fact that there are houses just like ours dotting all the places we drove through, that people live in other places besides Skokie, this is unmistakably my home, our house. Dad pulls the car in the garage and we're home.

Now we become a vacation-taking family. For one whole week, Dad declares his freedom, driving off wild and free. The trip to Canada the previous year was such a success that he can't wait to fire up the station wagon and hit the road.

In 1971 my parents pick Florida for our vacation. This time it's easy for my parents to pick a vacation spot. Florida, after all, is in the United States' Pale of Settlement after all. New York, Chicago, and Florida. Since my parents know Holocaust survivors in every port, they know of a few who came from Vilna and now live there. These acquaintances also happen to own a hotel on the ocean and Dad's always looking for ripe business opportunities, so they'll get to mix pleasure - talking about the war - with business, which will make it a perfect vacation.

This time Dad pulls the car out of the garage, points it towards Florida, presses on the gas and we take off. Once again, we do a quick jog over to Gary, Indiana - so far, Gary is the gateway to all of our vacations - but then we head due south, through all of Indiana, then Kentucky, through the red clay of Tennessee, and then Florida, which is much bigger than it appears on a map.

It turns out there are several different Floridas. The top of Florida is too close to the southern states, to Confederate territory, where I'm sure they still lynch Jews. The middle part is Everglade country, teeming with alligators and swamps. But the southern tip is Jew country, and in Miami, right before we drive into the ocean, we stop.

We weren't picky about where we stayed during that first trip to Canada; we pulled off the highway toward any flashing sign by the side of the road. This was okay for us at the time; any hole in the ground was okay to swim in. But by the time our other trips roll around, we've become motel snobs. There are now whole chains of hotels and motels that aren't good enough for us anymore - Travelodges, Best Westerns, and Motel 6s. Of course, there are also many that were too good for us, too, like the Sheratons and the Hiltons, hotels with prices that make Dad recoil in horror at the thought of the wasted money. We find our niche right in the middle, at the Holiday Inns.

The Holiday Inns have everything Dad wants in a hotel: a clean, nondescript room, a swimming pool, and a restaurant. Overall, Dad wants no surprises. He wants to know that when we pull up to our destination each night, the only thing different will be the city; it will be as if the hotel had traveled in the air above our zooming car all day, logging the highway miles with us, and then landed conveniently in front of us as we exited the freeway for the night.

Now that we are Holiday Inners, when my parents are done picking our destination, they check our intended travel plans in their Holiday Inn Passport, the chain's skinny travel guide. For the certainty of a Holiday Inn room, Dad will allow himself to be roped into reservations, into travel plans, into so many miles per day and an exact arrival in a specific city.

He walks in each lobby like a big man since he knows his way around a Holiday Inn or two. He knows the lay of the land, the lay of the lobby; he knows what to expect. He goes to the front desk, asks for our rooms, each with two double beds, an adjoining door between them. Somehow, Denise and Sherry always get the extra room; Mindy and I still get stuck in the other room with Mom and Dad. We can never quite get away from Mom and Dad and they can never quite get away from us.

Then he'd have the key in his hand and we'd walk down the corridor, locate the room, and we'd all pile in there, the freezing cold Holiday Inn air conditioning blasting us in the face.

Inside, the rooms are identical to the inside of a thousand other Holiday Inn rooms. The beds with their generic white bedspreads, a nightstand between them, their bolted-down lamps, a few nondescript scenery pictures on the wall. There is the toilet paper wrapped in Holiday Inn tissue, the Holiday Inn logo bath mat, the tiny Holiday Inn soaps. There is a slim desk in the corner with Holiday Inn stationary and postcards on top, all sitting in a tissue thin Holiday Inn bag, a matching pen nearby. I run my hand over it all, then take it for home.

We make a mad dash for the beds, claim our spots, our pillows, the least itchy blankets, the location farthest from Dad's snores, the premium location in the tiny bathroom; we test out the sunlamp in the bathroom. We settle in. Sleep. Get up. Do it again.

Dad only stops at the tiniest of gas stations he can find as we make our way across the country on our trips. Mindy and I prefer the big ones since they're always giving away collectible playing cards to get us to buy gas there, but Dad's suspicious of anything free, zooming past, calling them all thieves, saying that he just wants gas.

Since Dad doesn't just want to travel but wants to travel back in time, these tiny gas stations suit him perfectly. They have aisles barely big enough for our station wagon; the pumps are art deco relics from the 1930's - masters of industrial design.

Dad comes into his own here because he is diminished by big things and made larger by small ones, so he seems to get larger as he gets out of the car. To these country bumpkins, Dad's

Polish/Yiddish accent just may be French, his laundryman's clothes seem like fancy store-bought duds. Dad is an awe-inspiring city slicker.

Mindy and I discover that these stations are locked in time, the Sleepy Hollows of the Interstate highway. We get out, we hang around, we explore. We discover that the soda pop here, instead of being dispensed in cans or skinny-necked bottles like the rest of the country, is also archaic. The pop machine is old, the bottles are short and stubby, but the pop is fresh. We start collecting them.

We clunk west through the country, Dad charging off the interstate to get gas at these forlorn stations, our bottle collection crashing against each other at every stop. By Tennessee we have so many we can't muffle the crashing sound any longer. Dad isn't amused by our collection of garbage. When we pull up to the next rickety filling station, even before the sleepy attendant makes his way over to us, Dad is at the rear tailgate like a flash, demanding the bottles. We hand them over, he gets gas, and we drive on.

In Florida we find the people my parents know through mutual friends, the ones from Vilna, and find their hotel. It perches, pension-like, cracking in its Art Deco architecture, on the edge of its piece of ocean. The interior is dim, crumbling, condemned; there are no guests.

My parents' Yiddish is their calling card with these people who they've never met before. Their mother tongue forms a thread to link them together. My parents are eager to settle down as we enter their resident suite, but Denise, Sherry, Mindy, and I drag our feet as we go in there; we know what's coming. We're forced to sit like mummies for hours while Mom and Dad visit with this couple, listening while they laugh over dialectical differences, while they share gossip about the people they know in common - all living - and then as the conversation to falls into a lull as they lament the dead.

Though I don't understand the particulars of the conversation, I understand the cadence. First the joy of meeting, of speaking their first language, of discovering people they once knew in common, and isn't the world a small place after all? Then the conversation moves backward, to where they are from and how close that was to the other person's village or how far. Then back a little farther and each person's story gets tangled up in the knot of the Nazis and their villages that no longer exist, and how they spent the war, how they survived. And then there's the gradual slowing, the silences. The halt.

Who are your dead, they start off asking, and then, did you know my dead, what do you know of my dead, and have you seen my dead?

We sit immobile for days on that couch, watching our youth fade away, watching the clock tick as our lives pass by. We sit silent, perched on the couch, smiling at the hosts. With the room dark now, twilight descended, they search for an escape hatch and notice us - the children - sitting in the dark, stuck to the couch in our shorts.

"Oy, the kinder, sitting so long! You want I should get you some cream soda, some ice cream?" the man says, "Maybe a quarter to go down to the boardwalk?"

I look at Dad, not sure what I'm allowed to accept, but he and Mom have jumped up too.

Dad says, "How about a tour?" and we all walk through the hotel, Dad and the man oohing and aahing over how he got it for a steal, ignoring the cast off, ocean-sogged furnishings in all the guest rooms and the dilapidated musty carpeting.

We perk up a little when we get to the elevator and they say we can play on it. We get on, shut the cage, and press the number for the floor we want, the top one. We watch as the door shuts vertically in front of us, and jerk as it lifts off, hurtling through the air. We leave our parents floors and floors below us and take off into the sky. And we're gone, into the air and the fading light.

Eighteen
Panoramic Ambulance

Right after the trip to Florida, in the summer of 1971, I get sick. I am cast into our basement along with the dog and the cat and the dust mites, to languish all summer. Gone for me are Chicago's white summer skies, the rainstorms where I'm forced to play in our garage, all those interminable summer days waiting for Linda Winkler to come home from camp. Gone is watching the parade of our neighbors march by our front windows.

I'm ill but undiagnosed – sick with something mysterious, maybe something infectious. I sit in my basement bedroom hunched over a pillow listening to each breath wheeze in and out of my chest.

Mom begins to drag me off to the local doctors. First, of course, she takes me to her obstetrician, Dr. Wacker, who delivered six of the seven of us, and because she thinks he's God and can cure any medical problem. He sends us packing. My problem is not obstetrical.

She continues her search for a doctor, for a diagnosis, for a way to get me out of that basement. In the beige office of a doctor located in a medical building at Old Orchard Shopping Center, a doctor says the word asthma, and mentions that he runs an allergy clinic too, that I need allergy tests and, he's guessing, allergy shots. So Mom signs me up.

By the time I'm twelve I get worse. Mom finds a new doctor up in Gurnee, Illinois, and we drive up there once a week. This is not as simple as it seems. Mom's first car, her 1965 Nova, had died by then, abandoned under the tree in front of our house, eventually turning into a square, rusty, red tin can. She and Dad replace it with her new car, a swoop back 1969 Impala, which she not only learns how to drive, but learns how to drive on freeways, interstates, and expressways; she learns how to drive it on off ramps, on ramps, on toll ways - anywhere at all, to save my life. She refuses to accept that my suffering will be permanent. She seems sure that the cure lies somewhere at the end of one of the lines on the map of Illinois that she traces with her finger. She will not let me burn in the barn.

Mom takes me up to Gurnee once a week for breathing treatments on the ancestor of all nebulizers, the Lucy of the Neanderthal nebulizers, so primitive that the machine takes up an entire room in the doctor's office. I miss a lot of school. I miss kissing and flirting and going steady. I miss out on developing, on bra sizes that should have progressed from my double A to an A cup and beyond, on beige L'eggs pantyhose and high heels for all the Bar Mitzvahs I'm invited to that I miss.

Later I turn my parents' bedroom into my sickroom. I make my way up there every morning when I miss a half-year of school. It takes me one painstaking hour to get up there from my fold-out couch in the basement. There I just loll around in the t-shirt I sleep in; I can't even breathe well enough to get dressed each day.

Dad comes to my bedside one day. I am unwashed, unbrushed, bent over, my ribs showing as I struggle for air. He sits down heavily on the edge of his bed, where I lay watching TV and doing the schoolwork my teachers send home. He looks at me and shakes his head in frustration.

He says, "I don't know how you can live like this. Me, I wouldn't want to live like this."

I just look at him. What does he want me to do? Agree, and fling myself out the window to my death? Agree, and let him suffocate me with the pillow I'm holding? Agree, and shuffle out of the house dressed in my dirty t-shirt and underwear, drifting into traffic, there to get run over by a driver who can't see an asthmatic twelve-year old approaching?

I can tell I've become more trouble than I'm worth. I'm costing them a lot of money. First there was just the run of the mill childhood immunizations, then the expensive braces, now the asthma, the out of pocket expenses for my medications, the constant running account balance over at the Skokie Pharmacy. When I'm well, for a day or two here and there, I'm no great prize either, just budding into adolescence, arguing with Mom, fighting with my older sisters, and pummeling Mindy. I live an adolescent life of navel gazing, having petty fights with my best friends that I then lament in great, exacting detail in my paisley diary.

Dad doesn't seem to be honestly contemplating putting

me out of my misery. He sighs, like he doesn't expect a response, shakes his head like maybe the answer will fall out onto the bed, then gets up and walks out.

One day soon after that, Dad is working late at our laundry when he feels a sharp pain in his chest and a shooting pain down his left arm, bad enough that he falls to the ground. He drives himself to Weiss Memorial hospital, though he parks in a regular parking space because he doesn't like people to coddle him, and checks himself into the emergency room.

Besides immediately getting admitted to the hospital, he also gets diagnosed with a heart attack, which he downgrades on his own to "mild." But once his pain is gone, once the primitive 1972 version of heart treatment has taken place, he puts it out of his mind. He thinks the doctors have exaggerated his illness; he forgets how bad the pain was. He can't acknowledge this weakness in himself, this mortal heart.

When he eventually gets out of the hospital and has to follow-up with the doctors, he's a reluctant, stubborn patient, refusing to consider himself chronically ill. He goes to the doctors but never memorizes the names of his medicines and never remembers dosages. He just says, "I take a round red pill in the morning. A square blue one at night." He begins to pop Nitroglycerine tablets when he feels pain.

I can't go visit Dad at the hospital; really I can't even go visit Mom in the kitchen. I've gotten even sicker, now trapped in the basement, not even able to get up the two staircases to Mom's room, to rot all day watching TV and doing word search puzzles. So I rot downstairs instead on my fold out couch where Mom wouldn't hear me even if I called and would just find my cold, dead body at the end of the day by accident, maybe while she was dusting down there or resetting the mousetraps behind the bar with new pieces of cheese. Then she'd realize she forgot to bring me food, forgot to bring me my medicine, didn't hear my wheeze-racked voice calling for help.

Dad gets released from the hospital and a couple things are immediately apparent - he hasn't liked his brush with death nor is he happy to find me now trapped in the basement, the subterranean feel of it. I never know if it's my illness or his, but he's determined to move from Chicago, maybe to California but to somewhere out west for sure. He seems sure that Chicago holds death for the two of us in the old dark streets, in the dirty brick houses and in our crummy laundry. I become Faige to him; Chicago becomes Tashkent and Asthma becomes Typhus. He can't let me die.

He announces that we're moving, blaming it on me when he tells my sisters, telling them that otherwise I may die. They're not thrilled with this information; they seem to be considering whether it'd be better to move or let me die. Or maybe if they drag their feet a little on this move stuff, I just might die of natural causes before any of this comes to pass.

But soon I'm gone, temporarily anyway. Mindy and me and Mom and Dad take off on Dad's most ambitious road trip yet, all the way to California with a stop in Arizona to see where we should end up, to see where I get healthy again.

Francine's out of the house by then, but the rest of my older sisters can't wait for us to leave, for the taillights of the station wagon to disappear down the street. Francine's supposed to watch the house, make sure they don't go wild, but they do anyway and there's nothing she can do about it. The neighbors line up to report it all when we return: the boys over at all hours, day and night, the strange cars parked in the driveway, the loud music, all the goings on.

But right then, eager, they help us pack, push Mom and Dad out the door, pick me up in my hunched over position and load me like cargo into the rear of the station wagon through my own personal swing-out door. Mindy comes barreling into the center seat clutching crayons, coloring books, her Etch-A-Sketch. Dad inspects Mom, checks for her purse, her upside down map, her supply of quarters for tollbooths.

Then Dad looks at the three of us and says, "You have to go to the bathroom, you go now! I'm driving straight through. No stopping."

"Herschel! We can't make it all the way to Arizona without going to the bathroom!" my Mom says.

Dad shakes his head. "We're going to make good time this trip. I'm driving straight through - 20 hours at one hundred miles per hour. That's 2,000 miles in one day."

He wants there to be no fighting between Mindy and me, nothing to disturb his concentration on the road. This is fine because I can't even breathe well enough to talk.

And then we're off, and this time there's no detour through Gary, Indiana.

We make our way due west - Missouri, Oklahoma, the Texas Panhandle. I am bent over, my pills and sprays clutched in my old lady hands. The rear of the station wagon spits me out each time we stop, the tailgate flips down, it swings out, it flips up, it does a *do-si-do*. The rear is my rolling hospital room, my panoramic ambulance, rushing me off to an emergency ward as wide as the southwestern United States.

As we drive west, inch-by-inch I unbend. I cast off my inhalers, my pills, I find my voice when the dry air fills up not just my mouth and my windpipe, but careens down both of my lungs and all the way down to my toes for the first time in two years. My parents are first alerted to the miracle taking place by Mindy yelling out, "Mom!" plaintively and repeatedly. She begins fighting for her life as I come alive in the back of the car, reaching one pasty white arm over the seat to snatch away her Etch-A-Sketch, stealing her crayons one by one, plucking them out of her fingers as she's drawing, as I rip the pages out of her coloring book.

My parents don't interfere. They seem to be enjoying the sound of my voice again, even if I'm fighting with Mindy. As we pass through Gallup, New Mexico on our way towards Flagstaff, Dad's relaxed, enjoying the wide-open spaces and that particular feeling of Manifest Destiny that he gets infected with right then, and Mom's applying lipstick in the rear view mirror, the map now crumpled up in her lap.

By Arizona, I am up and healthy. I have changed into my bikini and Mindy into her one piece with its fringed skirt, and we're barreling toward the Holiday Inn pool, white bathing caps on our heads and beige nose plugs on our faces. We spend the day wet, somersaulting and hand standing until our lips are blue and our eyes are red, our colors seeping out of us like a watercolor painting.

***

The reason why Francine is out of the house by that time is because of some things that happened a few years before that. She finally fell in love.

It isn't enough that boys fall in love with her the minute

she turns fourteen, fifteen, the boys lining up in front of the house, camping on our doorstep, ready to date her, or marry her right off the bat with no dating at all. Francine never falls in love with any of the Skokie school district boys camping on our doorstep; she never falls in love with the Rabbi she dates, or the non-Jewish boy from Naperville. She won't just marry anyone; she needs to fall in love. And, in order to get married at eighteen, she has to fall in love at sixteen. Even I, a clueless eight-year-old, understand the math of spinsterhood.

Opportunity - or fate - comes knocking in the form of Francine's friend Talia Coffman. Talia's family plans to take a trip to California to visit family in the summer of 1969; they ask Francine to come along. Mom and Dad say yes. After all, Talia's Dad is the Cantor at the synagogue on Dempster; her mother is the President of the Temple Sisterhood, and Talia's brother is a typical fourteen-year-old, pre-growth spurt, post-bar mitzvah, Jewish nebbish. Francine will be well guarded. Also, my parents have heard about the eighteen-year-old boy cousin in California. Might he just be looking for a nice Jewish girl?

So Francine's trousseau is packed: some maxi dresses, a worn copy of *Catcher in the Rye*; her Menthol cigarettes - since smoking is the one activity she and Talia still have in common - and the Cantor's ancient station wagon takes off to the west.

When Francine returns to Chicago at the end of the trip, she has a boyfriend. She and the cousin, Larry Coffman, have fallen in love. After that there are several months of non-stop phone calling between Skokie and Van Nuys, Van Nuys and Skokie. Francine has become mom, wound up like a mummy in the phone cord, barely coming up for air.

One Saturday morning after that Francine is like a maniac,

waking up early, making sure one of our TV sets works, nearly muzzling us all to make sure we stay quiet, all to watch *American Bandstand.* It turns out that Larry is going to be on it that day and she wants to catch a glimpse of him.

She does. Not only does he get on the show when Paul Revere and the Raiders are on, he dances within camera range and the pictures beam to my sister in Chicago, of Larry in his late-60s era suit, his side-parted hair flopping over one eye.

This, then, is how I know that my sister has arrived at some pinnacle of teenhood that is well beyond my reach, light years beyond. First of all, she's dating someone who lives in California – near Hollywood - which is amazing to me. And now he's been on *American Bandstand.* I'm agog. Is this all going to happen to me one day?

Then she is suddenly engaged and Larry comes out from California to meet his new immigrant in-law family which consists of six future sisters-in-law; a father-in-law; and a mother-in-law who greets him, then picks up her phone one second later to call everyone to tell them about her handsome future son-in-law who's going to be a lawyer. Larry does not become a lawyer.

Larry's visit is nerve-wracking for several reasons. First of all, there's a male in the house who's not Dad and that's strange. Second of all, there's someone in the house who's interested in getting to know us and that's strange because before this time we have just spent all of our time screaming and fighting with each other. Now we have to go beyond that, pretend there's a real family here with family relationships, not just a constant battle for the best chair in the family room.

It's also strange in this: we have a family belief that any boy who likes one of us and then meets Lauren will fall in love with her instead. I'm barely aware of this when I'm younger, but I'm very aware of it right then, as Larry is introduced to the household. But Larry is unmoved by Lauren, unperturbed; he has no idea what anyone is talking about. Francine is the only girl for him. He passes the Lauren test.

Of course, most of Larry's future sisters-in-law are children. Mindy is six, I'm nine, the twins are eleven. He's nineteen, which seems like a grown man to us.

One night during his stay Mom makes an elaborate meal and we sit down for a formal family dinner like we do that all the time, not like we're the animals we are, always grabbing food on the go. Conversation runs dry midway through dinner so Dad looks to me, always a source of amusement.

He says, "So, Linda. Who do you love this week?"

I answer my usual way, which everyone but Larry Coffman expects. They all know I love Larry Aronson. Right then I happen to be in the middle of a mentally exhausting Larry Aronson/Larry Greenberg comparison: which one should I marry, which one should I cast off and leave to Linda Winkler? Should I marry both so she can't have either?

So I say, "I love Larry and Larry."

I realize my mistake immediately. The Larry at the table flushes, thinking I mean him. Everyone at the table knows that all the objects of my grade school crushes are named Larry. There's a deafening silence.

I try for a quick correction so I add another Larry to my sentence.

"… and Larry," I say. And then I cringe, which makes it worse. Also the lie shows on my face. I would never have a crush on a grown man unless it was Davy Jones or David Cassidy, who look immature. I'm the childish-boy type of girl; I don't even have a crush on a Beatle.

Larry's visit is also exciting because I know this is the first of six brothers-in-law I'll have in order, like a row of dominoes. I imagine our family then, like a 1970s version of "Seven Brides for Seven Brothers" but with a twist - Seven Grooms for Seven Sisters. Because I'm sure that in seven years I, too, will be eighteen years old and planning to get married to a twenty-year-old Jewish boy under a chuppah. I know that this will happen for the four sisters in between Francine and me, in order, and I know it will happen for Mindy. I can't wait to be a bridesmaid so many times.

Francine graduates from high school in June 1970 and her wedding is planned for June 1971. The opal high school graduation ring Mom and Dad bought her is on her right hand and her engagement ring is on her left. Since I want to be Francine-ish in all things, I make a note of this. Graduate high school, get an opal graduation ring, get married.

The wedding preparations begin. It's to be a pink wedding. All six of us will be Francine's bridesmaids; the photo opportunity of all seven of us standing there for the camera like a ripple of descending bookends is too tempting. Of course, the fact that we don't form a row of descending bookends never comes up. This is the event at which we became the seven sisters, as separate thing, an entity. We get our first formal seven sister picture taken, even one with the doctor who delivered all of us except Francine.

This is what I remember: learning to walk in a lock-step pattern with Mindy down a long white aisle because it looks better to walk that way, like we're taking a leisurely stroll instead of running down the aisle like lunatics. I remember six bridesmaid-sisters dressed in pink standing next to Francine dressed in white. I remember the guests arriving, jovial men pressing hundreds of check-laden envelopes into Larry's hands, the women smearing lipstick imprints on Mom's and Francine's cheeks. I remember hours of photos with all of Mom's friends, the wedding a Holocaust survivor's convention, all of them arriving from the four corners of the earth - from Mexico, from Israel, from New York, from Toronto; their stiff taffeta dresses pressed into my face as they squeezed me.

I remember standing and standing in an arc of six sisters during the ceremony itself, waiting for Francine to get married, wondering why the floor was shifting and the lights are changing from pink to yellow and back again. I remember the swift kick delivered down the line of my sisters, the hiss going from Lauren to Brenda and then down the line, to Denise, to Sherry and then to me, through gritted, smiling teeth, saying, "Tell Linda to stop kicking Mindy!" when I started falling over. And I remember my Uncle Saul grabbing me at that last second as I began to weave on my feet among the bridesmaids, making me sit down in the audience. It was easy for him to tell I was fainting; my Aunt Etta had perfected fainting during the course of their marriage. He recognized the stagger, the perspiration, the sudden cha cha cha of the feet right before the knees buckled.

Besides me falling down fainting, Dad was falling down drunk, although he managed to stay on his feet till the end, having a backslapping, wife-twirling, drink-spilling time. I recovered, eventually getting my legs back enough to play on the hotel elevators all night with my cousins.

We already knew that this wedding thing was hooked up

to the Bat Mitzvah thing in Dad's mind. He had already told us many times why he never sent any of us to Hebrew School. He'd throw his hands up in the air, get an irate look in his eyes and say, "What? Do I look like I'm made out of money? You want I should pay for seven Bas Mitzvahs and seven weddings?"

They went all out. Only the best: china place cards, calligraphied invitations, flowers everywhere, the largest ballroom at the Pick Congress Hotel, a live band, tuxedos, a sit-down steak dinner, and an open bar. They've certainly come a long way since the war, since Siberia, since the forest.

After the wedding, Francine is out of the house living in a tiny apartment with Larry that my parents provide for free in the apartment building we own in West Rogers Park. Dad somehow carves this apartment out of the tippy top floor, so high up that the final flight of stairs is more like a ladder than a staircase.

I go to this newlywed apartment and am awed by the wonders of Francine having her own home. She's surrounded by the miscellaneous gifts of her many wedding showers and of her pink wedding. There's a standing moose candle, place settings of fancy dishes, His and Hers matched towels, and crystal candy dishes. They're the youngest residents in the building, the only ones who don't leave the building each day pulling a wire grocery basket on their way to Devon to go shopping.

With her marriage, Francine becomes a grown up instantly instead of a teenager. She not only skips over the hippie era, she skips over her late teens right into married monogamy. One day she's wearing jeans and mini dresses and the next she has her hair set in a pert wedding cake atop her head with a fall on top fluffing it up further. She has nude hose on her legs, low-heeled pilgrim shoes on her feet, and a sensible dress with a built-in belt around her hips. She drives off each day in her Opel Cadet on her way to her job as a secretary while Larry continues college.

For some reason, in our family we're not raised to go to college even though I've got sisters who are brilliant and talented and sometimes both. We don't go to college mainly because we're not raised to go to college. Well, I am, because Dad decides early on that since I'm good in school I'm going to be his boy and have the boy achievements, but not the others, not right off the bat.

We're being raised to work hard, to get hard-working jobs. If we have to go to college, we can go to vocational technical schools where at least there's practical training - no dilly-dallying around for my sisters getting fancy college degrees they'll never use, they need to work or go to technical college, or both. Dad has some preconceived notions that will never change, of exactly what he's willing to pay for, and it doesn't include college, or camp, or Bat Mitzvahs. It includes weddings.

So Francine goes off to Business College, which, in 1970, really just teaches females how to be secretaries and gets to regular college much later. Eventually, we burn up the vocational technical curriculum: Beauty College, Dog Grooming Institute, Medical Assistant Training, Title Clerk Licensing. Almost everyone gets a real estate license.

We're also different than the typical Jewish family in Skokie in that when my older sisters show up at the house with non-Jewish boyfriends, nothing happens. This should sent Dad into a mushroom cloud of temper but it doesn't. I know I've heard somewhere that I need to marry a Jewish boy but apparently I haven't heard this at home. Maybe I heard it from my aunts and uncles, or from our neighbors, or at my friends' houses. But Francine dates a boy in Naperville and, even though he's not Jewish, his mysterious last name of Rosen is good enough for my father. Lauren dates the Jeep-driving boyfriend and there's no objection. Denise has the boyfriends with the hotrods and the only complaint is about the noise of the engines.

Instead of objections, there's a lull, a quiet hum; we get, instead, the quiet of our parents' tangled up thoughts. Of course we should stay Jewish but boy, do they hate being Jewish, hate the burden of being born Jewish, and wouldn't it maybe be better if we weren't, all the way down the line, to the fourth generation where that future Hitler couldn't hurt us any longer?

Nineteen

Late Bloomer

Unlike Francine's, right from the beginning, my adolescence starts off faltering. I never have her popularity, her panache, or her crowd of male admirers following me everywhere. From my first pursuit of Larry Aronson and his running, riding, and constant escaping from me - despite that "maybe" he wrote on my marriage proposal - I never hit my stride. There's nothing smooth about my love life.

Linda Winkler gets me my first entrée into a potential love life - her synagogue has a youth group and I join it with her. Each week after the organized activities of the youth group, our counselor says, "Go outside and play for a while." And so we go, starting with an innocuous game of dodge ball, boys against the girls. Over time, however, this game evolves into one in which the boys tackle the girls and try to "get the ball," which is our breasts. Most of the girls, including me, are excited by this game. We think the boys like us, that maybe we'll get our first boyfriends from all this dodge ball playing. Of course, most of the girls fight off the boys.

But not Linda Winkler. Her breast gets captured after a series of forays, of military maneuvers. When I talk to her afterwards I try to offer sympathy like she's a rape victim, despite the enormity of what happened (I mean her *breast* got grabbed by a *boy* and we hadn't even had our first kisses yet!), but it's like a different girl lives inside of her now.

She gives me a jaded laugh, a little like Bette Davis, and then says, "Oh come on, Linda! It's just a game! Big deal!" And I realize she did it on purpose.

I understand that one day my breasts will be touched but not by some scruffy boy trying to cop a feel. I've seen *Love Story* after all. I'm planning on being Jenny Cavalleri but not die. I'm saving my breasts for going steady, for a boyfriend, for maybe the legitimacy of an ID bracelet. My breasts are being kept on a pedestal, safe and sound for the right boy. I've also picked my true love, Larry Aronson, at age six and I don't ever plan to waver. I'm untrainable, I can't be debriefed or reeducated; I can't convince myself that the creepy little guys at the youth group are okay.

But Linda Winkler has an innate instinct, even at thirteen, for how to be popular. Does she spend time assessing her various assets at home in the mirror, deciding that her breasts would have to make things happen for her? Because her breasts end up blazing a trail, they serve as her entrée into a whole different society than my breasts, which lie flat and untouched on my chest. Her breasts knock on doors, slip coyly into boys' hands; her breasts go steady. My breasts stay home at night tucked safely into my training bra, the ten-clawed nails I use to fight off the boys curled up like sleeping sentries.

What's more, this entire experience of Linda Winkler's breast as the ball in Dodge Ball meant that whether or not she had ever gone to first base, without question she had gone to second base. So whoever had grabbed her breast was now her boyfriend. Linda was excited about having a boyfriend, but which boy was it?

The guys at the youth group get creepier and creepier week by week. The regular youth group boys tell other boys at their junior high and they tell other boys, all of them magnifying the allure of the grabable breast until it sounds like in our youth group all the girls play bare-chested, our breasts just swinging away on our chests; party synagogue youth group, party orgy. So they show up - gangs of scruffy, hostile, breast-seeking boys - and our counselor is beside himself with excitement. Jewish youth just pouring in the synagogue basement door! But they aren't there for the regular activities, the icebreakers and the games of Hebrew letter Bingo we play. The boys call us sluts behind our backs and only want to play dodge ball, from the second they get there to the second they leave. When they launch themselves at me, boy after boy after boy, I fight for my life, scratching until I'm alone.

When we're finally back down to our original group, all the interlopers gone, the boys backtrack, perhaps thinking they'll get farther if they start with first base. So one night we leave the preschool playground, circling around the synagogue until we're hidden from our counselor's sight, though we're in full view of all the cars zooming by on Skokie Boulevard.

I know I need to get my first kiss; I have an obvious hole

in my resume. I had planned on Larry Aronson being the first boy I kissed but I wasn't sure that I could wait that long. Also, there was some evidence that he hadn't been waiting for me, a hint here and there that maybe I was the only one who knew that we were in love.

We line up, the girls on one side, the boys on the other. We press our mouths against each other's. We even try it for longer periods, like in the movies, slanted heads, closed eyes, breath puffing in and out, our noses striking. But something's missing. Passion? Tongues? Our arms are at our sides; our mouths are closed.

We troop back inside and wait for our parents to pick us up.

Linda and I were also different in this too - once we got our first kisses out of the way, Linda always had to have a boyfriend. And - this was a surprise - she was unselective. She had bad taste in boys or aimed low, or she didn't care about things like looks and personality but cared about things a thirteen-year-old wouldn't be expected to care about, like money. After she went to second base, Linda began to have a lot of boyfriends, boyfriends from other schools, boyfriends we never meet, boyfriends she gets from Bar Mitzvahs she's invited to but not the rest of us. Her Hebrew School friends.

Linda Winkler had been reshuffled in the deck of cards in which she stood socially at Skiles Junior High - which was a no one, condemned by being related to a dangerously nerdy brother and having no fashion sense - into being an anonymous youth group girl with no past and no known history. She was the top card in this group, the big Ace.

I didn't know how to make sense out of this side of Linda; I thought I knew everything about her, but this was something new. I thought a probable explanation might lie in all those years she spent nodding at her brother, feigning interest while he blathered on and on about the fifty state flowers. Maybe that was what made her mind snap when it came to boys.

One time her mother was driving us home from the youth group where I had just met one of her boyfriends, David. He had stared at us without talking the entire evening, his eyes barely visible behind long bangs. He had worn a fringed vest.

Since we were such good friends, I thought I'd say something.

"Um, Linda, doesn't he dress kind of … funny?"

Linda whipped her head towards me like she was just waiting for me to criticize. She said, "You had a fringed poncho."

"That was a long time ago."

"Well, you're just jealous because you don't have a boyfriend."

Then her Mom piped up from the front seat, adding her two cents, "Well, I don't know if Linda Burt's jealous, exactly. Maybe she doesn't know what a nice boy David is like you do. Remember, Linda Burt hasn't been to Hebrew School like you so she hasn't had the opportunity to meet all the different people you meet, Linda."

That shut me up. If it wasn't the insult about being raised like a wolf by my parents with no Jewish education, then it was her calling me by my whole name again, like I wouldn't be able to keep track of which Linda I was unless she used my last name.

I also never understood what came so easily to Linda, that sometimes you've got to let a boy cop a feel - that sometimes the lid had to come off the cookie jar just a little to entice the boys. I never could quite understand that. Instead, when the youth group boys came towards me, their hands flexed towards my developing breasts, I reached up, unsheathed my claws, and left them bleeding.

No one at the youth group ever touched my breasts.

Linda spends a lot more time around the youth group boys than I do because, unlike my sisters and I, she's attending Hebrew School. And not only is she attending Hebrew School, but she's attending three times a week.

Although the three main branches of Judaism exist in Skokie - Reform, Conservative, and Orthodox - my parents find it necessary to create one of their own: Holocaust Judaism, which consists of the joyous celebration of the food that's been handed down to us by generations of Jews who believe in the God my parents no longer believe in. There are a few other tenets, like both a fear of being Jewish and a longing for the lost Judaism of their childhoods, when my parents had been sure that God was out there somewhere, up there somewhere; that if they looked up they'd find Him, but most of it is centered around food, especially since they'd had none during the war.

But when called upon to attend synagogue, my parents put all of us in dresses and we walk down to the Conservative synagogue on Dempster. There the old men pray any way they want, standing in the aisle, standing at their seats, on their seats, sitting at their seats, murmuring louder sometimes than even the Rabbi and Cantor.

We stand there silently. There are no excited prayers from my parents. They observe Judaism, and I mean observe. They watch other people being Jews, other people exhibit belief, like it's some interesting episode playing this week on Wild Kingdom and we get to watch.

Holocaust Judaism also means that my parents are in a permanent state of bewilderment about where God had been during the war. There are dangling sentences in all my parents' stories, questions with no answers, like why hadn't God bombed the railroad tracks? Why had God allowed all those people to die? What use did they have for Judaism with such a God at its center?

Although I never come up with answers to these fathomless questions, although I never understand exactly how God was supposed to fly an airplane, I have a question of my own: why does God get the blame for something done by the Nazis? And this thought, the ultimate irony: that Jews a generation later, learning of the Holocaust, which was created by the Nazis, stop believing in Judaism because of it. The Nazis, their war lost and over, are still destroying the Jewish people.

Even though I know my parents feel like that and even though I know they have ample cause, I don't. Atheism, agnosticism - none of that is an option for me. For me there's never any struggle with faith, never a problem with God's invisibility, unreachability, unnameability. He walks beside me, attached to me, conjoined to me, all the days of my young life.

We go to synagogue once or twice a year. That's all we need because, luckily, my family has tested out of Judaism. We are exempt. We've placed high enough on the entrance exams that we never have to join a synagogue, get a Rabbi, get a Jewish education, or do any of the other ritual or life cycle nonsense that our neighbors do. While Linda Winkler goes marching off to Hebrew School her three times a week, I sit smugly by knowing that I don't have to go, that I'll never have to stand in front of the congregation and read Hebrew.

We don't have to do any of these things because we're a Holocaust survivor family, both superior and inferior to the American-born Jews. We despise them for being safe in their cocoons here while we were dying over there. We're suspicious of them, wondering what they were doing while the whole Jewish world was being murdered in Europe. How hard were they working to save us? We're Jewish anti-Semites; both hating ourselves and hating them; walking the earth with a pall of gloom hanging over our heads, a gray cloud of misery floating in the air above us.

A few hours of shuffling feet, of whispering, "When is it going to be over?" in the middle of Mom's running Yiddish language critique of other women's outfits and whether their shoes match their purses, and then we're done. We burst out of the synagogue: renewed, rejuvenated, recycled. Rejewed.

There's a whole new set of rules in junior high. Three elementary schools have poured into Skiles Junior High - College Hill, which is mine, Walker, and Timber Ridge. And for some reason we are all sorted out into three categories right away: Most Popular girls, Kind Of Popular Girls, and Least Popular Girls in reverse order - Timber Ridge, Walker Elementary, and College Hill. I'm at the bottom of the heap.

We're expected to pay attention to this hierarchy - we need to notice Carol and Edie, the two girls from Timber Ridge who now sit at the pinnacle of the sixth graders. I have to ride over to their houses, through streets with Indian names (Pottawattami, Samoset, White Cloud) to familiarize myself with them like paying homage to a King and Queen. Of course, as I find out later, the most I can hope for is to be a follower of these girls.

Another rule that I have to get used to is that my business is now everybody's business and that things I may have thought of as private no longer are - they're the business of every other sixth grade girl too. Like whether I've gotten my period yet, or what size bra I wear, or if I've kissed a boy yet and, if so, have I French kissed one? Have I gone to any other bases? I'm accosted for this information day by day; I'm harassed when I develop before I get my period. Every girl in the sixth grade has an opinion on whether I'm lying and have gotten my period already. Right before I'm about to get beaten up by the Black girls who have taken offense at my developing first and getting my period later, I get it. In a family where I'm largely ignored, it's hard to be watched so closely.

Of course, this causes no fanfare at home. My mother searches each bathroom for an antique and dusty box of sanitary pads, since somehow all my sisters have moved beyond this product, and that's it. No exciting and distressing Ashkenazic face-slapping ritual as I had heard I was supposed to get. Welcome to womanhood.

The boys in sixth grade don't get the kind of attention the girls get. Of course, unlike the girls, they're all pre-adolescent, standing 4 feet 2 inches tall, so they attract no special attention and are impervious to criticism. There are no hallway discussions going on to mirror those of the girls' - about jock straps and whether their voices are changing. No one cares about them at all. They become important for one weekend each during seventh grade, when each has his Bar Mitzvah.

My career as a Bar and Bat Mitzvah attendee starts off

good, with my cousin Aaron's Bar Mitzvah party in December of 1972. As a girl from a different school I must have looked more alluring than usual because the minute I leave the protection of my parents and walk away from their table, I'm surrounded by boys, something that has never happened to me before. Even my cousins, Aaron and Barry, were pursuing me. They must have heard about that first cousin marrying thing too.

I fall for Aaron's friend Robby Feldman. He sits me down in a booth and starts flirting with me, and then, as his Shirley Temples start taking effect, he proceeds to make inappropriate propositions to me all night. The ones I remember have to do with what bases I have gone to and if I have any questions about how sex works. I'm unsure how Robby, a thirteen-year-old, knows how sex works, but, by the end of the evening, I do too.

He starts off with what I think is an innocuous question.

"Do you guys have bases at Skiles?"

"You mean like baseball?"

"Oh sure, I'm sitting here with a lovely young lady and I want to talk about baseball! The other bases."

"Oh. Yeah. There are bases."

"Well, they're probably different than ours at Middleton."

"I don't know."

"Well, let's compare. Our first base is kissing; what's yours?"

He comes on strong, strong enough that he becomes my imaginary boyfriend for at least six months. He gets my number but never called - the first in a long line of phone number-getters but not phone number-callers.

This is what the Bar Mitzvah services are like: I sit there

enveloped in my Jewish illiteracy, a complete Jewish dunce, for however long the service is those Saturday mornings - ten, maybe twelve hours. The Bar Mitzvah boy stands up there, so short that only his silk yarmulke is visible above the bimah, his voice squeaking through his Haftorah portion. He is wearing the usual outfit consisting of a miniature fitted suit, shiny lace-up men's shoes, a little mini dangling tie, a skinny little boy's belt around a pre-adolescent waist.

Other than my cousin Aaron's Bar Mitzvah party, which can never be matched again, all the other ones I go to are divided into the good and the bad. The good ones are any party where there is any boy/girl contact, even if I don't get asked to dance. Anything counts as good. Running around the room is good, gossiping about the boys is good, seeing someone walk toward me to ask me to dance and then chicken out is good because at least then I can talk about that all night.

A bad party is one where the girls are plastered against one wall and the boys against the other. The dance floor is filled with adults having a great time, slow dancing and foxtrotting, thinking the Bar Mitzvah party is for their enjoyment, not the kids'. The boys, as a paralyzed massive iceberg, never move toward the girls and, since it's 1973 and we're thirteen, the girls can't ask first. The girls stand by the girls and the boys stand by the boys, all waiting for it to end.

At a good party I get to dance but since all the boys are shorter than me, I always find myself dancing across from thin air. If I look down towards the dance floor I can find my dance partner there, gesticulating wildly in some bizarre mating dance and wearing a powder blue three-piece suit - not his Bar Mitzvah service suit but his Bar Mitzvah party suit - a boy who had the audacity to ask a girl a foot taller than him to dance. After all, didn't I know that adolescence can take all the way till girls are eighteen and boys are twenty-one? Did I have to shoot all the way up to the giantess heights of 5'3 already? Did I have to develop before I got my period? What's my rush?

In lieu of Hebrew School, in lieu of any formal training, my Judaism ends up being locked lips on the hidden side of a synagogue building. It ends up being a thousand cold nights at youth group playing Dodge Ball, of fighting off a thousand cold hands. My Judaism ends up being motionless slow dancing at a thousand Bar Mitzvahs that will never end.

Adolescence also coincides with starting Junior High, and with meeting my sixth grade teacher, Yvette Johnson.

Ms. Johnson, the first woman I have ever been instructed to call "Ms.," is not my first black teacher. I've had many by that time. In elementary school our teachers were divided between dried up old white spinsters with gray, mannish haircuts, and the more traditional black teachers, their hair straightened, their dresses prim and even. But Ms. Johnson is a Black is Beautiful, Black Panthers kind of woman. She's angry and it shows. And what she's angry about is Angela Davis. Each day, in every lecture, no matter what's being taught, Angela Davis and the charges that have been wrongfully made against her, are brought up.

When we conjugate sentences, we use "Angela Davis is not guilty of a crime" as our sentence. History is the South's shameful history of slavery, of segregation, of Jim Crow laws, of the trumped up charges against Angela Davis, how the FBI was trying to stop the Black Power movement or the Black Panthers. For math, we add up all the possibilities of Angela Davis' life sentences minus parole, plus time for possible attempts at escape, minus time off for successful appeals. We multiply, divide, figure out square roots, fractions, solve for the x - but somehow Angela Davis is still not free.

I am inflamed by these stories of Angela Davis, ready to march on Washington, grow out my Afro, embrace my ethnicity - until I realize I'm the enemy. I'm white. By proxy, by group guilt, I have falsely imprisoned Angela Davis.

All the days of sixth grade - until Angela Davis is acquitted in the spring of 1972 - Yvette Johnson stands before us, lecturing in a fury. She wears platform sandals, her toes visible, unpainted, and pants - always pants - that emphasize her youth, pants that break her off from the other teachers with their dresses, their sweater sets, their hosiery and pumps. She wears flimsy t-shirts with no bra right there in front of a classroom of girls who have spent the summer begging and pleading with their mothers to buy them training bras; in front of girls who walk out of her class into the hallway where all the other girls are judging each other's bustlines and whether we're stacked or flat, whether we've gotten our period yet or haven't.

She wears these t-shirts with no bra in front of a whole classroom of twelve-year-old boys who watch the rise and fall of her chest. Her angry expulsions of air, her gulping of air to begin another tirade, are just more excuses for the boys to watch the changing landscape on Ms. Johnson's chest. After class each day the boys don't talk about her lectures. They certainly don't talk about Angela Davis. They weren't even listening. They talk about who saw the outline of Ms. Johnson's nipples and just how mad did she have to be to get seismic activity going on there? And what would any of them do if once, just once, she just grabbed the edge of her shirt with both of those clenched fists and lifted that flimsy shirt in the air so they could see what lay beneath, higher even than her angry mouth, higher than her full Afro, higher than her chandelier earrings?

One of the more embarrassing things about my life at twelve and thirteen is that I don't seem to be growing up; I'm getting older but I'm not maturing. While other girls are getting boyfriends and are moving along into their teen years, I have a slack-jawed, dumb cow look on my face and one syllable emerging from my mouth, "Wha --?"

Of course, it's worse for me since I have five older sisters who are all experts at growing up. They graduate from elementary school, cast off their Barbies to the next younger sister in line, and head into junior high and their teen years without looking back. Then it's boys and more boys, clothes and more clothes, and on the phone night and day.

But not me. I go through the motions. I graduate from elementary school, I pack up the Barbies in an obligatory gesture, I get ready for the rest of my life to begin. And then Jill and I sit on the curb running along Drake with nothing to do, our chins resting in our hands.

"Well, we can still jump rope, right?" she says.

"Sure, I think jumping rope is okay." I answer.

"But no tag."

"Right. Tag is for babies."

"And no Cops and Robbers or dodge ball?"

"Right."

We both stop talking and then I say, "Jill, lets just do it anyway. Let's play with whatever we want. What do we care what they say?"

Then we're both off the curb and dashing in my house. We take the Barbies back out, though we have to be very, very careful with them, like they were contraband or drugs. If my sisters see us with them there will be hell to pay. The teasing, the razzing, the humiliation. We have to play with them at Jill's house where her mother would never think to look over at us, never wonder for one second what Jill's doing. And because she's German, she has European sensibilities, so she has no conception of adolescence being some arbitrary time period when girls have to stop playing with toys and start playing for real.

I feel a little sorry for Jill. At least with me there's hope. I am already a whopping AA cup bra; my figure's coming along. Boys are always looking at me, rolling their eyes and imitating my figure like this: they put their hands on their chest then go way, way out, then circle way back in like that's how big my chest is. I'm pretty sure that's a good thing. But Jill is, we've determined, a late bloomer. She's as flat as a board and not just her chest but her butt too and she's straight up and down in between, no hips and no waist, so that she looks like a plank of wood with feet. The idea of her sprouting cushy, shmushy, breasts, like in the copy of *Coffee, Tea or Me*_that we keep poring over, is beyond impossible. The most she can hope for is just some protruding nipples one day.

More than my refusal to give up toys, the thing that makes my sisters fear for my sanity and wonder if I'll ever grow up was my obsession with pens and paper and all sorts of markers and diaries. When they learn how to drive, they're always rushing off somewhere at a moment's notice. There's be a jingle of keys, a rustling of coats, a slamming of doors, one brief warning, "Who wants to go to the grocery store?" and, whoosh, they're gone.

I live in a panic at the thought of being left behind, left at home. I wonder what I'll miss if I don't go each time. They get sick of taking me places, of me wandering off to the school supply aisle. They start creeping out of the house to avoid me. No jangling keys, no rustling coats, no shouted warnings. I hear the click of the door and then the engine. I run out of the house and stand crying in the middle of the street, watching the car disappear down Drake.

Brenda's the main key jangler because she's the main driver in our house once Francine gets married. She's defined by these two main things she does - driving and smoking. There was the driving to get the smokes and then there was the smoking while driving. I can never be a part of that world, no matter how cool I look with an unlit cigarette held up to my mouth in front of a mirror, no matter how much I try to smoke without inhaling. I have mom's biology, which consists of weak, pneumatic Jewish lungs.

Mom had moved on from crocheting and knitting and had already sewn a new wardrobe, so she had taken on a new hobby, antiquing furniture, and when she was finished with her first project, she had turned a desk into a streaky brown mish-mash brownish color that could never have been mistaken for an antique. To hide it, she put it downstairs at an angle in the corner of the family room.

I adopted it as my own because it appeared without warning in the family room, which was my bedroom. I was thrilled to finally have a place to store my feather pens, my paisley diary, my Flair markers, my stencils and stickers, and my sketchbook. But mom didn't want me to put all my stuff on the desk, saying it would mess up the room. So, fine, I went behind the desk, into the right-angled hidey-hole made by the placement of it in the corner. Then when anyone came down the stairs there was an empty room, the desk in its corner, and my legs sticking out the wrong way. I finally had a room of my own.

Another way in which I didn't seem to be growing up is that I didn't quite understand the bathing suit/tanning thing. Since whiteness was associated with illness and tanned skin with health, my pale skin was supposed to be a problem I was working on, a problem I needed to solve with long weekends laying in the sun. When I hit adolescence I was supposed to want to do this, to get in a bathing suit and lay out for endless hours while mosquitoes buzzed around my head, while I felt my skin crisp.

But I refused to lie in the sun. Despite Dad's obsession with the lawn chair and tin foil-wrapped record albums, despite Lauren and Sherry's obsession with baby oil and the black roof of our house, I just couldn't seem to understand this as a matter of some urgency. I considered the misery I got from everyone around me a matter of urgency but ultimately not worth the price of laying out.

I had a long history of burning. When we were younger, Mom, Aunt Rose, and Aunt Ida would take all the cousins to the beach during the summer. They'd sit there on the sand in their skirted bathing suits "getting some color," as they called it. Aaron, Barry, and I weren't allowed to swim because this was when Lake Michigan was murky with oil slicks and dead ducks. If we waded in, cut glass from old bottles would swirl around our ankles. So we sat there broiling in the sun and playing with Aaron's tinny transistor radio. I'd burn and peel off huge swathes of skin afterwards.

I learned then that I just wasn't built for hours of boredom on lawn chairs, for the marathon tanning that my sisters engaged in. I didn't understand why I couldn't be allowed the natural color of my skin, or what was so wrong with it anyway. Without being a white supremacist about it, why couldn't I just be okay being the shade of beige I was born?

Maybe all the negative attention wasn't just about my skin color. Maybe it was my overall package: silver braces, a jutting out chin, flat brown hair curled in stiff wings on the sides of my head, eyebrows like large, black caterpillars placed above blue eye-shadowed eyes, a training bra, and white hot pants. And then there was my pale skin. Something there just wasn't right. When my sisters or my father looked at me, the first thing they'd blurt out was the first thing they came to - the glare.

Twenty
Real Estate

No one pays serious attention to Dad when we return from our trip, his decision now made, that we're moving to Arizona. My uncles listen to him, they nod, and then they change the subject. My sisters first scoff at Dad, then argue, and then they glare at me. They all go on their way doing their regular business. No one expects this to happen, for Dad to actually leave Chicago.

But Dad lists our house with a real estate agent and then there's a "for sale" sign stuck in the middle of our front yard like it's a tree that grew there overnight. And Mom gets a project; she gets to rush through the house dusting and mopping, wiping and washing, twirling through each room to pick up stray paperclips and shoes, and long pieces of brown hair fallen from seven brown heads. The house must be kept cleaner than before, with no evidence of that the seven of us live there or that we ever lived there. The house will be shown that day and the next and the next until it's sold.

We've left our mark. In the oldest girls' bedroom, there are Lauren's hand-drawn six-foot Craypa flowers smiling down from the wall. In the twins' room, a cupboard built into the wall contains hand-drawn windows with rolling hills, flowers and bulbous trees in the distance. The laundry room has a rickety, penciled measurement chart tracking all seven of us as we've grown. I'm mystified. Wouldn't the person who buys the house want to keep this stuff?

The house is bought by an East Indian couple, the wife wrapped in a sari, a black dot on her forehead, the husband in a tight green suit and black shiny shoes, both of them thumping on our couches as if they come with the place.

We take another trip to Arizona then, Dad, Mom, me and Mindy, piling once again in the station wagon, zooming out like a blur across the highways, Dad rocketing to Arizona, this time to buy a house, identical to our home in Skokie, a tri-level with three bedrooms, a bar, a wood-paneled family room, with a nice basement for Mindy and I to live in; and to find a laundry to buy so that we can duplicate our Chicago, just without the snow.

In Arizona we have to work fast. We need a real estate agent who can understand our unique needs. We're running from a lot of things, from Skokie, from family, and from being Jewish. And we're always running from the Holocaust.

My parents rule out certain parts of town right away as too *goyische* - we're too paranoid for that - and other areas as too Jewish, where we might not measure up. It's a fine balancing act for any professional. We go through a few real estate agents who don't suit Dad. They talk synagogues; we look away. They talk JCC; we yawn. We need just the right fit. We need Jews who don't act too Jewish among Christians who don't act too Christian.

We were looking at a house on a golf course, my parents inspecting the golf course view, the sunken living room, and the walk-in closet in the master, while Mindy and I were picking which would be our bedrooms, as if we'd ever get bedrooms of our own. Since we were coming from sharing a fold out couch in our basement in Skokie, any room with a door that shut would be a good thing.

We could hear the real estate agents talking in the kitchen.

"What's the asking price for this house?" The male agent said to the female agent.

"Let me see." There was some rustling as the female agent consulted a flyer, frowning.

"$58,500. A little high, don't you think?"

Then the man said, "Hmm. I wonder if we could Jew them down to $55,000.00?"

I remember freezing; my first thought was whether Dad had heard what the agent had said. I wasn't even positive of what I heard him say; how had the word "Jew" fit in that sentence?

It turned out there was no need for me to react at all. My father had heard and exploded, grabbing my mother's arm, yelling to my little sister and me, "We're leaving," and stormed out of the house, slamming the door as we went. When we got outside, he pounded his hand down on the hood of our car and said, "Goddamn pigs. Just like the Poles. I'll give them a 'Jew 'em down!'"

We stood there in the brown dusty dirt of North Scottsdale waiting to see what Dad would do. I wondered if we'd even buy a house; maybe Dad would just jump in our car and hightail it back to Chicago, forget the move, forget everything, forget that we were supposed to move to save my life.

Then Mom noticed a billboard right across the street. She pointed to it and said in Yiddish to Dad, "Herschel! *Kook*!"

Dad looked up and saw the sign, which was advertising a subdivision going in right across the street, like a mirage in the desert. The sign said, "Mitch Simon's Hacienda del Sol." A builder with a Jewish name. That was all Dad needed to see. We jumped in the car and Dad screeched over there.

We signed up that day for a house identical to the one we had been looking at across the street. Flat like a brick, fake windows in front of the sideways garage, a sunken living room, a pool we almost fall into the minute we walk out the back door, five bedrooms, and two and a half baths. Both it and the model were angled on their corner lots like gigantic pinball paddles; when a car came by, together they could flip that car all the way back to the end of the block and wait for it to roll back down again. They could do that because our street dead-ended down there; it went nowhere.

This neighborhood was just the right amount of Jewish for us. Sixteen houses on a desolate, desert street out in the middle of nowhere, being built by Mitch Simon, a Jewish builder married to a woman who converted but who still slipped up here and there, like by calling synagogues churches.

There were more Jewish expatriates from other eastern cities buying houses on the street, so we thought we'd fit in well. Mitch Simon regaled us with brief biographies of them since the neighborhood so far consisted of just the paved street, the one model, and dirt. It sounded like a Who's Who of Jewish America: the Rogoffs would be moving in the 3rd house down on the north side of the street; the Shapiros, with four, maybe five, sons, - maybe enough to marry off the rest of us girls - would be moving into the model; the Kaplans next door to us; the Fagans a few houses down. Mitch was building a house for himself too, even. Then there'd be a few Christians sprinkled here and there. The neighborhood was perfect - Jewish enough but not too Jewish.

Dad likes the idea of being the one to leave, of leaving everyone behind, of driving away. He loves to drive away. My uncles Meyer and Sid come over a lot in those last days in Skokie. They come over, bewildered, shaking their heads, wondering how far Dad is going to take this thing. I mean a joke is only funny so far. They scoff at our packing boxes, at our garage sale that goes on and on all summer. They're anchorless. They gesture, they argue in Yiddish, they strike their heads with the open flat palm of their hands.

They say, "Herschel. Enough already with this *fakockteh* Arizona. Florida we could understand. California - maybe even that we could get used to. A lot of people live in California - there are even Jews there. But Arizona?" Their hands flail in the air trying to find one reason why a Jew would move there. Nothing.

"And where are you going to live? A dude ranch? And who's going to marry the girls? Cowboys?"

Yet they know they'll be forced to come take a look at Arizona once we move. Dad is an irresistible force. First he'll call in a jovial mood, promising business opportunities just waiting to be plucked off the cacti. Then he'll call from poolside in the middle of winter when a blizzard has hit Chicago - he has an outside phone jack installed for just this purpose. When everything's easier and slower, when the tax bill's lower, he'll call. He won't rest till they come see, until he sees in their eyes that he was right.

Twenty-One
Last Summer

Now that it's my final Skokie summer, I set out to have my final hurrah, the kind that I'll always remember. I have to live all my teenage years right there, right then, even though I'm just thirteen. I have a lot to live up to. I have to live all of Francine's teen years in this one summer, get a boyfriend from across the school district line. I have to make it all happen fast.

Luckily, my developing body is coming along, especially since it had started developing before puberty officially hit. I imagine myself all breasts and curvy hips and so I wear my white hot pants and tight, horizontal-striped top to show my figure off. I wear this everyday. I can't give it up for a day for Dad to take it to the laundry to wash it.

Jill, Linda, Dina, and I spot our quarry on the next street, some fifteen-year-old boys who also happen to be the younger brothers of all the boys my older sisters dated. We plot out how we can gather up these boyfriends, who will get each one, and how to get our summer off to a roaring start. Of course, I'm most concerned about myself and whether I'll ever get a boyfriend; Dina, Linda, and Jill will be here forever. Since we're somewhat on the other side of popularity at our junior high, we only have that one hope, to nab some guys from a different school.

We have limited time in which to attract the boys. Not only am I moving on the dot, on August 1st, 1973, we also have limited time each day that summer. Unlike my mother who has no rules, Linda and Jill live in lock down jail cells.

Linda has a tight curfew of 8 p.m. The minute it's dark she has to be home. Just as things get going, she's like Cinderella. Her bike turns into a pumpkin, her shorts into rags, and she drags herself home to await our calls later that night with the news of what happened. And Jill is her mother's built-in au pair for her much younger half-brother. When her mother wants her home there's no avoiding her; her German-accented voice rings out across our neighborhood like a Kommandant in a concentration camp. We hand Jill over like a hostage.

Before dusk each day, Jill, Linda, Dina, and I park ourselves in the intersection of Drake and Greenleaf, right on the school district line, and play games designed by us to show off our budding breasts and our developing bodies. We've decided that some generic bouncing ball-type games will work well. We laugh loud and we miss balls that are bounced straight at us until the boys, peeking from behind homes and hedges and cars, are just itching to show us how it's done - simple games like catch. And when we laugh, we make sure we fling our heads down so that our mane of adolescent, unwashed hair will ripple over our heads, gleaming in the sun - mine with dandruff spraying around my shoulders - and then we whip our heads back quickly, our hair following.

The boys are no match for this level of subterfuge. And that's how I get my first boyfriend: through deception, sneaking, and plotting.

Philip Siegel wasn't an attractive boy. He looked a lot like Jim Croce: big nose, curly medium brown hair, and an undistinguished body with sloping shoulders, a pudgy middle, and short legs. He was probably very unpopular at his school, but that was the funny thing about getting a boyfriend from another school - I had no way to know where he fell in the social spectrum and Philip certainly wasn't going to tell me. I also could benefit from this, being able to tell all my friends that I had a boyfriend but that he goes to a different school. Linda Winkler knew her way around this idea.

Pretty soon, after days and days of ball bouncing and hair flipping, the boys - Philip, Mitch, Mark, and Joel - come out from their hiding places. First they yell things out at us and we have to stop Dina Fisher from yelling back since she can't stand to leave a yell unanswered. We have bigger stakes, after all. Then they come closer, start talking, and get in our game. Then Philip chooses me. He plucks me out of the Linda-Linda-Jill-Dina gaggle of thirteen-year-olds partially because of the white hot pants and partially because he knows that his older brother had been my older sister's boyfriend. Like sororities and fraternities, we are legacies; we can't avoid each other whether we like it or not.

It turned out that I wasn't the only one using subterfuge and deception in Philip and my relationship. There was a definite pattern to Philip's plans for me. First he singled me out from my friends, separating me from the others, removing me from my support system by getting me out of the game of keep away or catch or whatever we were playing, and moving me out of the intersection to sit on the corner near the game. I would have been happy just sitting there all summer, enjoying the novel thought that at last I had a boyfriend, thinking that this is what having a boyfriend felt like - sitting and watching him with a frozen smile on my face. I would've liked to be kissed, but each time I looked at his chubby, dry lips, I couldn't imagine it. I needed a movie kiss, a slanted mouth, swooping kiss, and Philip didn't appear up to it.

But Philip wasn't content with just removing me from the game and away from my friends. Pretty soon he inches us over to my front lawn where we remained for a few days, with him talking and me nodding. Then he moves us over to our side lawn by an apple tree my Dad had planted. Day by day after that, Philip moves us, inexorably pulling me towards the dark side of the house. He gets me into my backyard where we remain for a few more days, like I'm a wild horse he's taming and he doesn't want me to shy away. And never, during this time period, does he make a move. No kissing, no wetting of the large, dry lips, no lunging for my young chest, my waistline, no hand on my leg. He seems to have a bigger goal in mind.

Finally, we've circled the whole house and have ended up in no man's land. We're on the side of the house where nothing grows, not even grass; the side that's surrounded by tall bushes; the side where there aren't any real windows, just the fixed, foggy glass windows used in bathrooms to let in light, not air. Philip must have cased our house in the daylight hours, must have had a diagram hung up above his adolescent bed at home, with pins in it, like a junior General Patton, because when he gets me there, he finally makes his move.

Of course, since it took him about three weeks to do so, I plan to be magnanimous – I'm going to let him kiss me. No French kissing of course, but Linda, Jill, Dina and I have decided that a kiss will not be out of place. And he'd bought me a gift one day, for no reason at all, taking a bus with transfers into Evanston armed with twelve dollars in lawn mowing money. He came back and presented me with a necklace - a huge gold tone pendant, both shiny and matte, with dangly faux pearls hanging from it, about three inches in a triangle. It wasn't exactly the gift so much as the idea of a gift that made us decide that Philip deserved to be kissed.

Philip also proved his mettle by living through the test of the Burt family. One night when I didn't come out soon enough for our tryst, he had to come in my house, and there he was, confronted with my angry, suspicious-eyed, Polish father, his pajama bottoms hanging open to the world, and face to face with my mother, wrapped up in her telephone cord, jabbering away on the telephone in Yiddish to one of my aunts while cooking two dinners. He ran into my five older sisters, none of them stopping to glance his way, and my little sister, who sat on Mom's purple brocade couch, staring at him without blinking.

Then he met our Shetland Sheep dog, Rusty, who had just finished chewing up a Kotex pad stolen out of a bathroom garbage can, leaving it strewn in pieces throughout the living room. When my parents saw this, they both began yelling at me, right in front of Philip, in alternating heavy Lithuanian and Polish accents.

"Linda - look! Rusty pulled your thing from the garbage! All over the house!" My mother was incapable of saying the word

"Kotex," so she just glared at the torn up sanitary pad and pointed with her pointy nose at her own below-the-waist regions.

Then my father, looking up from behind his newspaper, added his perspective.

"Clean up this goddamned mess or no going outside!"

And so down I went on my hands and knees, picking up pieces of shredded Kotex pad and hiding it from Philip.

After Philip lived through this trial, I had more respect for him. He'd earned first base.

On the dark side of my house, so dark that I can barely make out his face, Philip moves closer to me and then he makes his move.

He says, "What would you do if I just started stripping you right now?"

I'm expecting a kiss, not a question. I frown.

"What?"

He repeats himself. Unfortunately, I'd heard him correctly the first time.

Well, I'd had plenty of experience with this kind of situation at the youth group, spending what seemed like a lifetime already scratching anyone who had gotten near me, so I tell him.

"Well, girls have this one protection – nails."

"It wouldn't be like I'd hurt you or anything. I'd just sort of pull your clothes up and down and around."

"Oh." What exactly am I supposed to say in this conversation?

Then he says, "If you started stripping me right now, I wouldn't mind."

"Well I doubt very much I would." There.

"Until you try it, you don't know how you feel about it."

An amazing thing is happening to my feelings for Philip each time he says the word "strip." I can feel my infatuation for him ebbing, my lips shriveling up, until there's nothing left, until it's folded up like a suitcase and put away in a closet somewhere.

I make one last feeble response.

"I'm pretty sure I'm not going to do that."

There are a few things that occur to me during this conversation. First there's the sheer disbelief that Philip thinks it's possible that a virginal thirteen-year-old would strip off her clothes and show him her naked body. The second is that he actually thinks that same virginal thirteen-year-old would strip him. This is all so phenomenally impossible that I don't remember what happened next; I just remember sitting there with my mouth open in a circle.

The last thing that goes through my mind is that I realize all at once that I'm not Francine and that my life isn't going to be like Francine's. The evidence is right there in front of me - a sham of a first boyfriend.

Somehow I'm pretty sure that Philip's older brother never asked Francine to strip.

The relationship with Philip Siegel is over as far as I was concerned. Of course, I don't bother to tell him that, and I don't run away yelling and screaming that night; rather, I pretend to hear my parents in the bathroom nearby and say that I have to go in, but I make sure I'm never alone with him again.

In my mind I lump Philip with cousin Aaron of the "can I see your boobs?" and with Aaron's friend Robby Feldman, the Bar Mitzvah seducer. Somehow the boys across the Skokie school district line are all the same: they want their sneak peak but aren't willing to pay the price, to get in a romantic clutch, to have a make out session and earn their way through the bases properly. They don't even want to touch, they just want to treat girls like Playboy centerfolds, look all they want, and then walk away.

Late in the month of July, 1973, the Allied Van Lines moving truck pulls up to our house, two huge doors slide open, two ramps slide down, and over the course of sun up to sundown, our house is emptied into that truck until we walk rattling through the rooms. Mom's chandelier hangs from the dining room ceiling, forlorn with no dining table beneath; Lauren's drawings of daisies and tulips now float in the air of the wall over no beds, no dressers, dangling in the now-empty bedroom.

The truck engine starts up and pulls away on its laborious way west. We stay on a few more days since Dad has everything meticulously timed - how we're going to leave on August 1st, 1973, and then overtake the moving truck in the Texas Panhandle, maybe honk and wave at our stuff as we zoom by. Then we'll cool our heels for a day in New Mexico before winding down the mountains of Arizona from Flagstaff, then pull up in front of our new house exactly when the truck does, which he estimates will occur on August 3rd, 1973.

Since our house is first emptied and then it's instantly someone else's house and this is before Dad's targeted departure date, we spend our two last days in Skokie at our Aunt Rose and Uncle Meyer's house while they're on vacation, two blocks farther down Drake Avenue. We stay two anticlimactic days beyond our welcome, running into friends and neighbors who see us as if we're apparitions.

They say, "We heard you moved. What, you came back

already?"

Then we have to explain Dad's trick plans with the moving truck; how we're going to beat it out in the Texas Panhandle, slide past it on the downhill mountain slopes of northern Arizona, how we're going to zoom up to our new house in a great cloud of dry Arizona dust, park, and then dive neatly into our brand new, sparkling blue, swimming pool, just waiting for us in the backyard.

I get those two days to ruminate, to evaluate, to complete a few more pages in my journal. And I'm staying in my cousin Aaron's bedroom; the same cousin Aaron who had asked me if he could see my breasts when I was ten; that cousin Aaron of my first Bar Mitzvah that past December; the cousin Aaron who I think would marry me in a second if he could, first cousins or not. And whom I might marry right back.

I snoop through his room each of my two nights there, searching through sock and underwear drawers, through his closet and under his bed. I slither through the bookshelves and cabinets, the closet and the nooks and crannies of his room. By doing this I find Aaron's yearbooks and, then, by poring through them, I find a picture of Robby Feldman, from Aaron's Bar Mitzvah party. I snip his tiny photograph out of the yearbook, planning to tell everyone in Scottsdale that this, this tiny little brown-haired head, this tiny, little-shirted, pale-faced, swoop-banged boy, *this* is my boyfriend, even if I've only seen him once in my life.

So I sleep in Aaron's bed and I dream not of him and the marriage we could have had in the old country, instead I dream of the inappropriate Robby Feldman, of the double entendres and the sexual innuendos he made the cold December night of Aaron's Bar Mitzvah party when he leaned far, far towards me on the vinyl banquette, breathed in my face with his breath the flavor of the Shirley Temple he was drinking, and asked me, "Do you have any questions about sex?"

For those two days I wander up and down Drake Street like a wraith, continuing my last summer there, the summer that now won't end. My friends are loyal; they trek two more blocks to see me than they're used to even though we've said our final goodbyes, over and over again. Dina, Linda, and Jill, my three best friends in the world, mill around me like mourners at a funeral. We've all cried. They've despaired of what their future lives will be like; they've rent their clothes, covered their mirrors, recited the Mourner's Kaddish. But still, there I am.

"We're all coming out to Arizona to see you really soon!" Linda assures me, and they all nod their heads.

"Let's write letters every day!" This is Jill's great idea and for a few hours we address and stamp envelopes, stuff them with blank sheets of paper awaiting the great events that will happen to us to be written there so that we can stuff the sheets back inside and mail them off.

We pose for final pictures. Our silvery braces gleam in the sun, our lanky, limp hair lays flat against our faces. Jill can't resist the parting shot of devil's horns above my head.

Although I know I've broken up with Philip Siegel, and Linda, Jill, and Dina know I've broken up with Philip Siegel, Philip apparently doesn't know this. On my last day he comes circling around the streets on his ten-speed bike, leaning over it like a vulture out looking for carrion, and I'm it - I'm the dead meat. We see him and all four of us go running into Jill's backyard but that doesn't stop him. He sees us, stops, parks his bike, puts up the kickstand, and marches over and stands there, hovering in front of Jill's house.

Jill pushes at me. "Go out there! You have to go! He's just standing there!"

"No! What if he asks to strip me again?" I look at her, then at him. He just stands there, apparently willing to wait forever.

Then I say, "Fine, I'll go, but you guys have to come with me." So we all lock step out to the front yard, a gaggle of thirteen-year-old quadruplet conjoined twins.

Philip says, "Aren't you leaving tomorrow?"

"Yeah," I nod. "Early in the morning."

"Well, I wanted to say 'bye and that I had a nice summer."

And I say, "Well, bye," and I glare at Jill as she starts giggling.

Then he comes over to me, wanting that kiss he never got on the dark side of the house, after he never got to strip me, after he never got to strip himself, to show me whatever horrible thing he wanted to show me.

He comes up to me, right in front of Dina and Linda and Jill, and he presses those thick, dry lips that I had spent the whole summer watching, to my closed mouth. He hugs me tight against his developing man's body, then lets me go and says, "Well, goodbye."

Then he turns around, walks over to his bike, gets on it and rides away down the blacktopped street while Dina and Linda and Jill are hooting and hollering in amazement at his nerve, and my lips are still tingling and I'm looking at him riding away down the block. I can still feel him against my body and now the absence of him against my body; the empty air there now whistling through.

On August 1st, 1973, Dad loads our two cars with his belongings: one wife, six of his seven daughters, our dog, quarters for toll booths, Mom's purse, and her Holiday Inn maps, heavily highlighted from our repeated trips out west. A final check of Uncle Meyer and Aunt Rose's house shows all is well, so Dad locks it up and we all pile into the two cars of our convoy. Mindy and I are, as usual, stuck with him and mom in the station wagon, while Brenda drives the Impala behind us with Lauren, Denise, and Sherry inside, cigarette smoke already pouring out of the windows along with the sounds of them fighting.

We slowly roll down Drake Avenue. I sit in the way back of the station wagon drawing pictures of the street on a clipboard I had made out of a broken picture book cover and a spring clip. I'm trying to etch everything on my memory every - curb, every brick, every barking dog. I stare out the windows of the station wagon as we drive, implanting these images of Skokie permanently in my brain.

The windows of the car offer a panoramic view of everything we're leaving behind as we head down the street. We drive past our house, already repainted like something had been wrong with the royal blue of the old paint, the bushes trimmed down like something had been wrong with the raggedy hedge along the front picture windows. We see our neighbors emerging from their homes for their day and Dad beeps the horn as we head down the street on our way to the expressway. He is ebullient. His left arm rests on the open driver's side window and his right on the steering wheel. He looks back like he can see all of

Chicago just stretched out there behind him, though really there's only Michelle and I.

We move in slow motion down Drake, so slow that from that point forward I always believe that the wheels of our car stood still while Skokie instead zoomed away into the distance, perfectly intact, and that someday - on my death bed perhaps - it will zoom back into view like some crazy taxi, idle there in front of my hospital room, and wait to pick me up again where I left off. Then I'll hop out of my hospital bed and back into my thirteen-year-old body, back into 1973 Skokie frozen there in front of me, and resume bouncing that ball at the intersection of Greenleaf and Drake, waiting for my life to start, waiting for Philip Siegel to notice me.

Of course, we keep moving. And I'm left with the pictures I draw on my clipboard: the houses on our street and the names of our neighbors and the names of all my teachers from kindergarten to seventh grade. And anything else I'm able to grab out of the window and onto my paper, as we drive away.

Acknowledgements

This book might never have been written were it not for the encouragement, support and patience of my husband Howard, as well as my children, Daniel and Rachel, and their ability to make their mother's writing a priority, as well as providing some very fine proofreading.

I was extremely lucky that one day in 2001 I happened to walk into my first Creative Writing class and that the class was taught by Dr. Lois Roma-Deeley who immediately assured me that despite my lack of writing experience it wasn't strange that I felt there was a book inside of me. With her firm, yet kind, instruction and Dr. Gabrielle Lawrence's guidance, enthusiasm and belief, that book now exists.

I've been surrounded, even enveloped, by people who have believed in my story even when I've faltered, and I'd like to thank them: my best friend, Lori Dreyer; my one sister who read the manuscript and served as a one-person cheerleading squad; my many friends and acquaintances, both virtual and not; and my fellow writers in all of the writing workshops I've attended. Their input and enthusiasm for my work has been invaluable.

This book would have been impossible to write without my mother's graciousness in providing me with the details of her Holocaust story as well as that of my father. It has been an honor to tell this story. I am also grateful for the experience of growing up in a family of seven sisters surrounded by myriad aunts, uncles, cousins, neighbors and friends, all of who made my childhood memorable and magical.

From the moment I started writing I knew that it was the people who were gone and who could no longer speak for themselves for whom I was impelled to write. This being so, I'd like to acknowledge them as well: my father, Harry Burt, from whose death I am somehow still reeling thirty-six years later; my grandparents, Jack and Goldie Kay and Gershon and Sosha Burstein; my Aunt Reva; and Linda Weinstein.

I'd like to acknowledge the Jews who died in the Holocaust and the ones like my parents who survived as well as they could. And I'd like to say that no matter how much I ran from it, it ran after me.

Sources

I consulted the following sources and others in the writing of this book:

Shoah Foundation - University of Southern California Testimony Catalogue. Search Screen: Interview number 43618, Helene Burt, month and year of birth June, 1930.
http://tc.usc.edu/vhitc/(a5qv3ljm0eadavnyww5wnlfw)/frameresults.htm
http://tc.usc.edu/vhitc/(a5qv3ljm0eadavnyww5wnlfw)/menu.aspx

Interviews conducted with Helene Burt in 2006 and 2007 regarding her war year memories, pre-war life, post-war time period, details of family life in Skokie, and my father's life.

Krivichi Web Site:
http://www.eilatgordinlevitan.com/krivichi/krivichi.html
Holocaust information about my mother's town in Lithuania, Krivich.

Jewish Gen Krivichi Yizkor Site
http://www.jewishgen.org/yizkor/Krzywicze/kry327.html -- this also contains other survivors' stories from my mother's town.

Includes reference to my great-Uncle Sholem (Shalom Ziskind - also spelled Sitzkin - the barber). Mrs. Botwinik's story, written in Yiddish, can be found here as well.

Jewish Gen includes the list of the Krivich Holocaust dead, which includes the following of my mother's family members: her grandfather Mordechai Katzovitz (referred to as Mordechai Ha Cohen), her uncle Itzche Velvel Alperovitz (listed under his Hebrew name of Yitzhak-Wolf Alperovitz), his wife and my grandfather's sister, Chaya, and my mother's aunt, Tzipke Katzovitz (listed under her Hebrew name of Tzipora.) The family of the tailor, Binyomin Gitlitz, who lived in the forest along with my mother's family, is listed here as well. http://www.jewishgen.org/yizkor/Krzywicze/kry158.html

History of Lithuania, the Jews of Lithuania, and the Lithuanian region during WWII.
http://www.historyofnations.net/europe/lithuania.html and
http://www.omnitel.net/ramunas/Lietuva/lt_history.shtml

Pale of Settlement history:
http://www.jewishvirtuallibrary.org/jsource/History/pale.html
http://home.earthlink.net/~chervinfamily/Ref/Maps/maps.html

Maps of the DP camps in Germany, Austria and Italy after the war including those of my father and mother, located in the American zone of the divided Germany, in the state of Hesse, northern portion. Hofgeismar (father) and Hesse-Lichtenau (mother). http://fccorn.people.wm.edu/HIST112-DisplacedPersonsCamps-Map.html

More information on Hofgeismar:
http://dpcamps.ort.org/camps/germany/us-zone/us-zone-ii/hofgeismar/

Maps of the Vilna region of Poland utilized to locate the towns of Krivich and Wyshkow. Hand-drawn map from the Kryvitsh Yzkor Book consulted.

Baby name Data, Social Security Administration Data http://www.ssa.gov/oact/babynames/top5names.html

Maps of Skokie, including http://www.mapquest.com/maps/8606+Drake+Ave+Skokie+IL+60076-2310/?

Krivich Yizkor Book produced by the survivors from Krivich, Yiddish hardbound copy, *Kryvitsh Yzkor-Book: Ner Tamid for Jewish Community. Always to Remember and Nothing to Forget.*

Various web archival sites for information on TV sitcoms, American Bandstand, cars of the era, Holiday Inns and maps to track our vacation travel.

Beyond Sarah & Sam by Linda Rosenkrantz and Pamela Redmond Satran, *A Dictionary of Jewish Names and Their History* by Benzion C. Kaganoff and *Drek: the Real Yiddish Your Bubbe Never Taught You* by Yetta Emmes.

Family memorabilia including photographs, immigration paperwork, letters, and birth certificates, as well as personal diaries.

Immigrant ship history, including information on father's ship, the USNS General R.M. Blatchford.

Yiddish Terminology

Balabusta – resourceful Jewish housewife

Bimah –podium in synagogue

Bubala – darling or dear; endearment

Chuppah – wedding canopy

Dumbkopf – dummy, stupid

Farkakte – screwed up, crappy

Flanken – flank or skirt steak

Fleagle – chicken wing

Goniffs – thieves or crooks

Goyische - Christian, non-Jewish

Haftorah – A reading from the Prophets that follows the reading from the Law in a synagogue

Hora – A circle dance found at Jewish celebrations such as weddings and B'nai Mitzvahs

Kaddish – Mourner's prayer

Kapushnikas – stuffed cabbage

Kenehora – an exclamation said when something good happens in order to ward off the evil eye

Kishke – a mixture of flour or matzoh meal, sugar and fat and stuffed in an animal intestine, or derma

Kvell – to be extraordinarily proud; to gush or rejoice

Latkes – potato pancakes

Litvak – a Jew from Lithuania

Loch in kopp – a hole in the head allowing the brains to seep out

Macher – a big shot

Mameleh – little mother or mother's little one

Maydele – beautiful girl

Meshuganah – nuts, crazy

Minyan – prayer quorum

Nu – Conversational prompt, similar to the English "So?"

Oy – An expression of dismay

Pisher – little big shot

Pulka – chicken leg

Shayna - pretty

Shayna maydele – pretty girl

Schlimazel – an extremely unlucky person; a habitual failure

Schmatta – rag, worn out or ragged cloth

Schvitzing - sweating

Shabbos - Sabbath

Shiksa – non-Jewish female

Shul – Jewish house of worship, synagogue

Takeh – Exclamation expressing surprise, similar to the English "Really!" or "You don't say!"

Tante - Aunt

Tchotchkes – knickknacks, trinkets or kitsch

Tsoris – worries, trouble, woes

Vayesmere – a melodramatic expression of suffering, "woe is me."

Yachneh - busybody

Zaftig – overweight, plump

Zezech - sit

Zimlanka – underground dug out shelter